NURSING QUALITY ASSURANCE
in Long-Term Care

Joan LeSage, Ph.D., R.N.
Chairperson
Geriatric/Gerontological Nursing Department
Rush-Presbyterian-St. Luke's Medical Center
Chicago, Illinois
and
Associate Professor
Rush University College of Nursing
Chicago, Illinois

Diana Young Barhyte, Ph.D., R.N.
Project Director
Graduate Database Project
American Association of Colleges of Nursing
Washington, D.C.

AN ASPEN PUBLICATION®
Aspen Publishers, Inc.
Rockville, Maryland
1989

Library of Congress Cataloging-in-Publication Data

LeSage, Joan.
Nursing quality assurance in long-term care/Joan LeSage
Diane Young Barhyte.
p. cm.
"An Aspen publication."
Includes bibliographies and index.
ISBN: 0-8342-0066-X
1. Nursing home care--Quality control.
2. Long-term care of the sick--Quality control.
I. Barhyte, Diane Young. II. Title.
[DNLM: 1. Long Term Care--standards. 2. Nursing Care--standards.
Nursing Homes. 4. Quality Assurance, Health Care. WY 152 L622n]
RT120.L64L47   1989   362.1'6'0218--dc20   DNLM/DLC
for Library of Congress
89-6653

This book was co-written by Dr. Barhyte in her private capacity.
No official support or endorsement by the American Association of
Colleges of Nursing is intended or should be inferred.

Editorial Services: Marsha Davies

Library of Congress Catalog Card Number: 89-6653
ISBN: 0-8342-0066-X

Printed in the United States of America

1 2 3 4 5

Table of Contents

Preface

This book supports the authors' belief that evaluation of care is an integral part of the care process. Health care professionals have a responsibility to identify opportunities to improve care and correct the deficiencies of the individuals, departments, and organizations providing care or services in nursing homes. The nursing department plays a major role in long-term care facilities. It is important that the nursing staff be active participants in a nursing home's quality assurance activities as well as in their own area's distinct quality assurance effort.

Information concerning quality assurance activities for nursing homes is not well disseminated throughout the nursing home industry. At a September 1987 conference for gerontological nurses held in Chicago, Illinois, the best-attended workshop session focused on promoting quality in long-term care. Nursing managers are responding to the pressures being exerted by a wide variety of societal forces influencing quality assurance: purchasers, patients, professional groups, technology, and government agencies.

The quality of care provided for nursing home residents is a critical issue. The Robert Wood Johnson Foundation and the American Academy of Nursing recognized the need for improving the quality of care in nursing homes when they cosponsored the Teaching Nursing Home Program. Both of the authors participated in the Rush University College of Nursing–Edward Hines Jr. Veterans Administration Hospital Extended Care Center linkage for a Robert Wood Johnson funded teaching nursing home project. One of us was the project director (Joan LeSage), and the other (Diane Young Barhyte) served as a consultant to the TNHP quality assurance effort. Between 1983 and 1987 we had the unique opportunity of adapting a hospital nursing quality monitoring tool along with its data collection process for a nursing home setting.

Nursing Quality Assurance in Long-Term Care was written for nursing home managers: directors of nursing, administrators, and directors of staff development and quality assurance programs. Ideas for monitoring both nursing and non-nursing departments are included. Additionally, the book can be used as a resource text for educational programs preparing individuals for nursing home administration positions. Researchers involved in the development of valid and reliable quality monitoring tools and long-term care consultants might use the book as a reference. The major objectives of the book are

- to introduce evaluation as an integral part of the care process
- to identify the major role nursing plays in providing leadership for nursing home quality assurance activities
- to discuss means of satisfying the various external groups applying pressure for assessment and evaluation of quality in nursing homes
- to present monitoring options for quality assurance programs
- to describe the development of a quality assurance program
- to identify steps in the implementation of a quality monitoring system
- to discuss ethical considerations associated with quality assurance activities
- to note factors affecting future quality of care in nursing homes

Quality assurance activities are best implemented throughout all departments and services, a facility-wide, team effort. Quality monitoring results can be utilized to reinforce positive staff performance, identify problem areas, determine educational needs of the staff, and heighten staff and consumer awareness of factors influencing quality care. Improvement of care and commitment to quality are significant sources of pride for staff. A formal quality assurance program enhances a nursing home's ability to meet its responsibilities to society.

Joan LeSage, Ph.D., R.N.
Diana Young Barhyte, Ph.D., R.N.

Acknowledgments

We wish to acknowledge the assistance of others who made this book possible. The Robert Wood Johnson Foundation funded the Rush-Hines VA Teaching Nursing Home Program, which gave us time and money to explore quality assurance initiatives in nursing home settings. Luther Christman, the former Dean of Rush University College of Nursing, and Janet Moore, Associate Dean, provided encouragement to develop leadership roles for professional nurses in long-term care facilities. Sue T. Hegyvary is acknowledged for her cogent comments and suggestions during tool adaptation. We thank the nursing staff on every unit that worked with the tools and others who gave us suggestions. Kathryn Roberts, Janice Neubauer, and Susan Hewitt contributed through data collection and development of the role of quality assurance coordinator in the Hines VA Extended Care Center. Janet Ellor, Margaret Kraft, and Patricia Linnerud, nursing leadership at Hines VA Extended Care Center, are recognized for their commitment to quality monitoring and evaluation. Positive feedback was received from many nursing home residents. Pamela Duchene, Kathleen Potempa, and unit leaders at the Johnston R. Bowman Health Center for the Elderly, Chicago, developed summary reporting forms for nursing units that are presented in Chapter 4. Valuable secretarial support was provided by Carole Carpenter, Paula Fenza, Katherine Conrad Mueller, and Asilee Mitchell. A special thanks is given by Diana Young Barhyte to Sarah E. Tew and David J. Barhyte, Sr., for their gracious geriatric role modeling.

Chapter 1

Introduction

Joan LeSage

Key Points

- The quality of nursing home care can be improved by involving staff in the definition and evaluation of care standards.
- Evaluation is an integral component of resident care. Managers and staff observe care on a daily basis. Organizations continually receive feedback concerning their staff and programs, whether or not they engage in quality assurance activities.
- Quality assurance activities can provide a means for interdisciplinary collaboration.
- Quality-monitoring results can be utilized to reinforce positive staff performance, identify problem areas, determine the educational needs of staff, and heighten staff and consumer awareness of factors influencing quality of care.
- There must be an overall plan for program structure and information flow related to quality assurance activities. An interdisciplinary quality assurance committee can play a major role in defining a self-monitoring plan.
- Standards recommended by professional organizations and consumers as well as government regulations should be taken into consideration by staff in delineating self-monitoring activities.
- Department heads' delegation of quality monitoring and evaluation functions does not mean they are delegating ultimate accountability for standards of care.
- The authority, responsibilities, and scope of activities must be defined for all groups involved in quality assurance activities: the board of directors, the chief administrative officer, department heads, staff, the interdisciplinary quality assurance committee, and department quality assurance committees.

1

1

EVALUATION AND CARE

The care provided for nursing home residents should be evaluated by a facility's staff. Hospitals already have a commitment to measure quality, although there is not agreement as to by whom and how care will be judged. Unfortunately, many long-term care facilities have not initiated self-monitoring activities. Yet the talents and problem-solving abilities of nursing home staff are needed to improve care through the definition and evaluation of care standards.

When Rush-Hines Veterans Administration (VA) Teaching Nursing Home Program's plans to develop a tool for monitoring the quality of nursing care were shared with non-nurses, there were many questions about the need for internal quality monitoring. Weren't there already enough licensing and certification surveys from regulatory agencies? One administrator noted quite seriously that a "good" director of nursing should be able to "just look around and tell if the care is good." A physician specializing in geriatrics shared that he could rate the adequacy of nursing care on a single factor: a check to see if confused residents were wearing clean eyeglasses. When people who suggested that a nursing home quality-monitoring tool for nursing services was not needed were asked how they judged good care, almost everyone's response was related to the provision of a neat and clean environment or the absence of odors. (One would expect environmental cleanliness to be an indicator of the quality of housekeeping services rather than of nursing services; odor, however, can relate to adequacy of intervention for incontinence.)

All nursing home departments have a need for quality monitoring, but nursing's efforts are especially important since this group has a 24-hour presence in the care facility. The Professional Practice for Nurse Administrators/Directors of Nursing in Long-Term Care Facilities project, jointly sponsored by the American Nurses' Foundation and the Foundation of the American College of Health Care Administrators, has developed a statement of roles and responsibilities for directors of nursing (Lodge, 1985), which is reprinted in Appendix A. It emphasizes that the director of nursing is ultimately responsible for the quality of nursing care. The nurse administrator needs an objective means for evaluating the care provided by the nursing staff. It is also important for nurses to have a quality assurance program that generates data that can be communicated easily and meaningfully to the nursing staff and to colleagues in other disciplines. Quality assurance depends upon readily accessible information that is considered relevant by care providers for use in decision making.

Assessment and measurement of care quality provide information that influences the way care is delivered, producing efficiencies or cost savings and improving the overall quality of resident care. Quality monitoring results can be utilized to

- recognize staff strengths so that positive performance can be communicated and reinforced
- identify problem areas that should be improved
- detect trends or patterns of care in reported data that signal potential problems or risks
- determine the educational needs of staff
- improve documentation, thereby reducing staff exposure to liability
- evaluate the effectiveness of past actions taken to remedy deficiencies found by quality monitoring
- provide managers with objective information to guide decision making
- document the quality of a facility's care for review by surveying regulatory agencies
- heighten staff and consumer awareness of factors influencing quality care
- evaluate the impact of changes in leadership, staff, or resident population on quality scores
- involve staff in the development of action plans related to monitoring results, thereby enhancing staff commitment to and involvement in measures to promote the health and well-being of residents

SYSTEM INFORMATION

Feedback concerning nursing home services is inherently present in the system. Managers and staff observe care on a daily basis. Furthermore, they receive comments, notes, and letters about people and things where they work. One does not necessarily have to engage in quality assurance activities to obtain such information. A letter commending staff or complimenting the efforts of an organization makes the receiver proud and is usually shared with others. It provides an emotional lift; everyone seems to bask in the success of a co-worker. Positive words from managers, residents on care units, and family members give good feelings to workers. Alert managers have been known to add their own congratulations to staff who have received praise from other sources. Complimentary letters may be posted, incorporated into employee-of-the-month programs, used in staff development activities, or even read in new employee orientation. Good news is definitely shared and well received.

Other, less desirable information concerning staff and programs is also present in the form of complaints, angry remarks, or posted memos reminding people not to do certain things. Newly admitted people might complain about the frequency of physician visits, desiring services similar to a hospital environment in which they previously received care. Criticism from physicians who expect hospital-type services may communicate an opinion that the staff merits only second-class status. For example, one nurse reported a physician asking, "What's a fine nurse like you doing in a place like this?" Receiving a complaint, whether in verbal or written form, can hurt feelings and can produce comments like "that really ruined my day." The bad news may be based on fact and truly deserved, or it may be based on false, subjective impressions. Unfortunately, it seems that there is more discussion of negatives than positives, and this information gets around a nursing home as fast as good news. Although comments may be merely careless remarks or based on limited information concerning care practices, the validity and reliability of the information may nevertheless go unchallenged if there is not available data to the contrary.

Even without quality assurance commitments, managers are engaging in quality monitoring when they investigate complaints. After someone tells an administrator that meals rarely match the posted menus, a check on food served could take place over the next two weeks. Reviewing staff performance or facility programs causes the manager to compare performance with an expected standard, possibly in the form of a policy or procedure, or a position description, that has been set by the facility. Negative feedback about operations can cause needed reforms in staff performance, laundry services, or facility meals. But are these changes sustained? Did the staff play an active role in developing performance standards or the plan to remedy the situation? Furthermore, was the original complaint an accurate representation of performance?

In addition to informal feedback concerning operations, a nursing home already may be collecting data about resident care, which could be incorporated into a quality assurance program and receive additional analysis concerning quality implications. It is likely that managers have information on injuries associated with falls, medication errors, hospitalizations, and staffing levels. The incidence of pressure sores and catheter use might be obtained quickly from treatment lists. Unusual-occurrence reports often highlight problem areas. The realization that data concerning operations are already being collected, a desire to give staff positive feedback, and the will to devote attention to the validity of negative comments concerning care delivery could provide the impetus for an organization to give serious consideration to developing a comprehensive, coordinated, and ongoing quality assurance program.

NURSING HOME STAFF AS REVIEWERS OF RESIDENT CARE

The development of a quality assurance program requires three ingredients: acceptance of a philosophy that self-monitoring by providers is a good thing, an organization that promotes quality assurance activities, and knowledge of quality-monitoring techniques (Chambers, 1985). Staff who implement a quality assurance program demonstrate accountability for practice. Their involvement increases the likelihood that the criteria and the monitoring process will produce data considered meaningful and useful by staff. Quality assurance activities also can provide a means to encourage collaboration among departments in a nursing home setting, which is necessary to build excellent care programs.

Often, more than one discipline contributes to a specific aspect of care programs. Where care responsibilities are shared, there can be joint definition of standards and monitoring criteria. Because all nursing home personnel are not equally responsible for different aspects of resident care, departments should not define monitoring criteria for areas over which they do not have either control or expert knowledge of performance standards. Quality-monitoring criteria reflecting unique discipline contributions, such as those of the nursing department, and criteria with an interdisciplinary focus (where appropriate) are both useful. Organizational commitment and funding for quality assurance activities can be important factors in both the initiation of quality-monitoring activities and the ongoing commitment of staff to the process.

It has already been suggested that there may not be agreement among people, among different professional groups, or even among organizations as to what is being assured when there is an attempt to define quality care. In its most basic form, quality can constitute promoting the health and well-being of residents in nursing homes, or there could be a commitment to strive for excellence in care programs. Value systems definitely play a role in defining quality. Care providers may not agree with consumers, and the staff in one nursing home may not necessarily agree with standards of care defined in another setting. Although the standards of regulatory agencies and professional groups have held top priority for defining quality in hospital monitoring efforts, in long-term care facilities the residents' viewpoints concerning adequacy of care are increasingly being recognized as a very important measure of quality, since the institution is likely to be "home" for its residents. Inclusion of the resident (consumer) viewpoint in data collection for quality monitoring expands the variety of data sources, enriching information obtained about care provided. Mixing information from interviews, records review, and observations allows for measurement of quality from more than one perspective. However, if the viewpoint of a single group, such as family members or nursing home residents, is desired, the monitoring results should clearly identify the group whose values are being reflected.

Consumers have high interest in avoiding negative outcomes, the "bad news" of care, such as death, hospitalization, infection, and fractures associated with falls. To balance this focus on communicating what can go wrong, it would be useful for nursing home staff reviewing resident care to make sure quality assurance reporting also notes "good news." This might be best achieved by monitoring staff activities and behaviors that are considered important for good care and that promote residents' well-being on a daily basis. Monitoring the care process can heighten awareness of what a department is actually doing to enhance resident care, rather than only emphasizing what has gone wrong. Quality-monitoring results should provide a natural link to staff development activities.

Evaluation of Nursing Care

Although outside agencies survey nursing home care, persons within the organization need to play a primary role in reviewing resident care. Analysis of quality-monitoring data can provide the nurse administrator with a database concerning her department's functioning. This allows performance analysis to be based on fact rather than conjecture. When the director of nursing hears a comment such as "You nurses always try to put catheters in everyone to make your job easier," she can express willingness to share objective information concerning catheter use that has been collected as a part of quality assurance activities, rather than only responding defensively to this criticism.

The documentation of nursing staff performance assists nursing in meeting its responsibility to the consumers of nursing care. Even in the absence of research linking many aspects of nursing care to the outcomes of care, nursing staff can identify pertinent aspects of resident assessment, nursing intervention, and care evaluation activities that enhance residents' well-being.

Audit results may provide the impetus for defining new standards, redefining audit criteria, changing the care delivered, or even modifying the organizational environment of the nursing home.

Unsuccessful efforts to remedy problem areas noted in nursing quality assurance reports may lead the director of nursing to consider whether the solution is within the control of the nursing department (Brown, 1983). This is likely to occur when nursing monitors care outcomes that depend on more than one discipline or that are affected by characteristics of the resident population. For instance, hospitalization rates and emergency room use could relate more to physician practice patterns than to nursing care. Other staff, such as, in this case, the medical director, might need to be involved in problem resolution. In some instances, increased dependency of residents requires additional budgeted positions for nursing staff, but facility consent may be withheld. Quality data can help document increased staffing requirements.

Evaluation of Non-Nursing Departments

Departments and services other than nursing can benefit from collecting objective information concerning their functioning. Activity therapy, food service, housekeeping, maintenance, laundry, social services, rehabilitative therapies, and pharmacy services have high visibility in long-term care facilities. They often receive evaluative comments concerning their performance from a variety of sources. Special committees, such as those with an infection control or safety focus, as well as consultants also might complete quality reports. Departments' self-appraisal activities should be relevant to practitioners, consumers, and facility interests.

Monitoring results and the associated action plans of the various departments must be submitted to a central interdisciplinary quality assurance committee. The quality action plans of one department often have implications for the functioning of other areas. It is important for departments submitting quality action plans to an interdisciplinary committee to have discussed problems and solutions with other affected departments and to seek these departments' involvement in developing the necessary action plan to correct problems.

If quality reports describe deficiencies or policies of one department that are adversely affecting another department, and if dialogue between departments is absent, resolution of the problem will be delayed, since it is obvious that joint planning is required for problem resolution. Physical therapy personnel might be concerned about missed appointments and need nursing staff cooperation to rectify the problem. Nursing may be reporting missed or late medication doses that are related more to scheduled times for pharmacy drug delivery or to the drug reorder process rather than just to staff actions. At times, other departments' roles are overlooked in developing action plans. An interdisciplinary quality assurance committee with representation from all areas of a nursing home provides a forum for the discussion of identified problem areas that require the action of multiple disciplines for resolution, especially when collaboration among involved departments previously has proved unsuccessful.

It may be cost effective to combine several departments' resident or staff interview items in a single interview survey, so that one person can conduct the interviews. This instrument could have scores for the different departments' subsections, if it focuses on a single standard of care. Another alternative would be for departments to incorporate their own raw interview data into individual quality-monitoring reports, linking data from monitoring criteria to appropriate standards. Planning could take place directly among departments or between care evaluation committees to which departments, committees, and consultants with closely related functions might report and receive assistance in quality-monitoring efforts.

Interdisciplinary Quality Assurance Committee

There has to be an overall plan for program structure and information flow related to quality assurance activities. Leadership can be provided by an interdisciplinary quality assurance committee responsible for developing an overall plan for a quality assurance program. That group can be charged with implementing facility-wide education concerning quality monitoring, developing interdisciplinary standards in collaboration with department heads, and coordinating interdisciplinary activity for institutional problem resolution. In small nursing homes, the committee also may serve as the focal point for the implementation of quality monitoring. Additional responsibilities of an interdisciplinary quality assurance committee can include designing program reporting forms; reviewing reports and making recommendations; investigating long-standing, unresolved department/service problems; writing a facility's resident- and family-satisfaction questionnaires; updating a facility's quality assurance plan; providing leadership in preparing for external regulatory surveys; and serving as a forum for the discussion of regulatory survey reports and facility action plans.

Figure 1-1 describes the information flow for a nursing home quality assurance program. Care evaluation committees have been placed on the chart between the departments and the interdisciplinary quality assurance committee. Small nursing homes might prefer departments to report directly to the interdisciplinary quality assurance committee. Larger organizations should recognize the benefit of related services becoming more actively involved with one another at a level below the interdisciplinary quality assurance committee. Communication among the individual departments and the care evaluation committees, if present, promotes quality and problem resolution. It is a mistake to have only the interdisciplinary quality assurance committee involved in quality appraisal. If a facility's self-monitoring activities do not involve unit/department staff in planning, monitoring, and action plans to improve quality, then staff are likely to have a "shoot the messenger" response when quality assurance committee members bring reports of quality monitoring to department meetings (Beyerman, 1987). Each facility might designate different departments and services reporting to nursing, medicine, and administration (or different groupings more pertinent to an individual nursing home's operations) for coordination of area-specific quality assurance activities.

Program participants must include the board of directors, managers from the various disciplines, representatives of different staff groups or departments, and facility consultants. For success, both managers and actual service providers should be included. The interdisciplinary quality assurance committee's membership might be appointed or elected by staff organizations, or might represent designated staff positions within the home. The Joint Commission on Accreditation of Healthcare Organizations (Joint Commission) requires that nursing home quality assurance programs have a written plan describing the program's scope, objectives, organization, and mechanisms for overseeing the effectiveness of monitoring, evaluation, and problem-solving activities (Joint Commission on Accreditation of Hospitals, 1985). The interdisciplinary quality assurance committee can play a major role in defining a self-monitoring plan.

EXTERNAL PRESSURES TO MONITOR CARE

The increasing number of older adults in American society is likely to create a high demand for nursing home services through the first half of the twenty-first century, especially for people with disability linked to chronic disease. As of January 1986, there were nearly 16,000 long-term care facilities participating in Medicare and Medicaid (Health Care Financing Administration, 1987). The government, provider groups, and consumers are expressing concern about the quality of care and have suggested changes to improve nursing home services. Standards recommended by professional organizations and consumers as well as formal government regulations should be considered by staff in their self-monitoring activities.

Government regulation of nursing homes focuses on consumer protection and control of the public funds paid for care, mainly Medicaid. Although both federal and state governments are involved in regulating nursing homes, states play a larger role. The Institute of Medicine (IOM) has published a

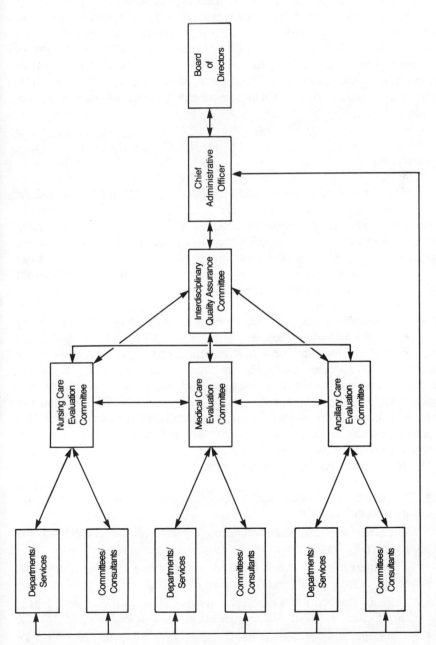

Figure 1-1 Example of Information Flow for Facility's Quality Assurance Program

study (1986) of government regulation of nursing homes, which was undertaken at the request of the Reagan administration, with the support of the Congress. The study found that government regulations for quality assurance in nursing homes encompass three main components: (1) development of conditions of participation and standards governing nursing home operations, (2) development of procedures for the survey process and determination of the extent of compliance with defined performance criteria, and (3) enforcement of compliance with performance criteria when unsatisfactory performance is found.

Certification

After the passage of Medicare and Medicaid legislation in 1965, the federal government became involved in the certification of homes participating in these two federally funded programs. Before that date, regulation of nursing homes was entirely a state responsibility. But since the certification survey was incorporated into state licensure survey processes, it is really the states that inspect long-term care facilities to determine the extent of compliance with certification standards. States differ greatly in their enforcement of standards.

Federal regulations recognize two types of nursing homes: skilled nursing facilities (SNFs) and intermediate care facilities (ICFs). Residents of SNFs require skilled nursing care; those in ICFs supposedly require less nursing care and more personal care services. States have not been consistent in making distinctions between these two types of nursing homes. The IOM report (1986) found that the mix of characteristics and service needs of SNF residents in states with few ICFs did not appear to differ significantly from ICF residents in states with few SNFs. Appendix A of the IOM report contains a history of federal nursing home regulation.

The IOM report contains the following major conclusions:

- "The quality of care and quality of life in many nursing homes are not satisfactory" (p. 21).
- More effective government regulation (especially at the federal level) can substantially improve quality in nursing homes (pp. 21–22).
- The regulatory system needs to "focus on care being provided to residents and the effects of the care on their well-being" (p. 22).
- "There are opportunities to improve the quality of care that are independent of changes in Medicaid payment policies or bed supply" (p. 22).
- "Regulation is necessary but not sufficient for high quality care" (p. 24).
- "A system to obtain standardized data on residents is essential" (p. 24).

- "The regulatory system should be dynamic and evolutionary in outlook" (p. 24).

Licensure

Licensure is a mandatory process permitting the legal existence of a facility. State licensure requirements show much variation. Rules and regulations associated with licensure identify minimum standards that should be met both before and during the provision of long-term care services. The IOM report (1986) contains the results of a survey of state licensure and certification agencies in its Appendix C. The IOM found that about one quarter of the states had licensure standards identical to the federal certification standards, and another quarter had standards that were lower than federal requirements. The rest had more stringent licensure standards.

Accreditation

A voluntary program of accreditation in long-term care has been developed by the Joint Commission. Joint Commission standards generally surpass the minimum standards of licensure and certification. Periodic revision of these long-term care standards enhances their applicability to contemporary long-term care settings. The Joint Commission has taken leadership in providing staff development programs for long-term care personnel related to their standards. They have also developed a publication to assist facilities in meeting their quality assurance standards (Joint Commission on Accreditation of Hospitals, 1986).

The monitoring and evaluation process supported by the Joint Commission is especially useful for nursing homes. Staff can, if necessary, begin quality assurance activities before there is formal development of standards of care. Members of a department are asked to identify the things they do that have the greatest impact on resident care, or aspects of their care/services that have tended in the past to produce problems for staff or residents. Next, "indicators" of good or poor care/services should be identified for each of the defined important aspects of care. These indicators may actually be standards, or they can just be such variables as infection rates, participation in Resident Council activities, unconsumed food returned to the kitchen, and broken care equipment. An indicator may need further definition in order to be measurable, a requirement for data collection and evaluation of department performance related to an indicator. Joint Commission surveyors want to find that quality assurance activities are well integrated into the functions of an organization. Quality assurance needs to be everyone's job.

Consumerism

Consumer influence on the quality of nursing home care has grown. National organizations such as the American Association of Retired Persons and the National Citizens' Coalition for Nursing Home Reform are actively involved in lobbying efforts for legislation affecting the quality of nursing home care. Voluntary ombudsman programs also have been initiated.

It was a consumer lawsuit filed on behalf of nursing home residents of a Denver, Colorado, facility in 1975 that shifted the focus of the federal survey from a facility's ability to provide care to whether residents are actually receiving the care that they need. After ten years of litigation, a court decision has required that the federal government develop a better means to assess whether facilities receiving federal funds actually are providing quality care.

A recent project of the National Citizens' Coalition for Nursing Home Reform surveyed over 400 nursing home residents to identify markers of quality of care and quality of life in nursing homes and to promote the use of this information for inclusion in the certification of nursing homes (National Citizens' Coalition for Nursing Home Reform, 1985). Staff factors ranked first in discussions of quality. Staff's help and care were important, but equally valued were staff members' personality characteristics and attitudes. Residents surveyed wanted adequate numbers of qualified, well-trained, and well-supervised staff. Some of the other quality markers identified were, in order of descending frequency of responses, environmental factors, food, activities, and medical care. The study report, *A Consumer Perspective on Quality Care: The Residents' Point of View,* validated that quality concerns are varied and numerous.

AUTHORITY AND ADMINISTRATIVE SUPPORT

The chief administrative officer of a long-term care facility receives a mandate for quality assurance activities from the facility's owner or board of directors. The chief administrative officer then delegates authority to the appropriate managers or department heads, who are responsible for developing the quality assurance plan for their individual areas. This plan should guide the growth of quality assurance activities and their integration into a department's functioning. Department heads such as the director of nursing can define quality assurance roles in staff position descriptions and delegate quality assurance functions to staff members. (However, the delegation of quality-monitoring and evaluation functions by department heads does not mean delegation of ultimate accountability for standards of care in their areas.) Department-linked care evaluation committees and a facility's interdisciplinary quality assurance committee receive administrative authority from the manager(s) to whom they report. Some organizations may want individual departments/services to report quality assurance activities directly to the chief administrative officer, in addition to reporting to the interdisciplinary quality assurance committee.

Individual facilities may define the authority, responsibility, and scope of activities of various components of their quality assurance program in different ways. The following gives suggestions for different participating groups.

Board of Directors
- mandates program
- delegates authority to chief administrative officer
- reviews reports of quality assurance activities

Chief Administrative Officer
- delegates authority to department/service heads
- provides administrative authority for the interdisciplinary quality assurance committee
- approves the budget for quality assurance activity
- initiates initial educational programs for department/service heads and the interdisciplinary quality assurance committee
- receives and reviews quality assurance reports of the interdisciplinary quality assurance committee and department/service heads
- approves or amends the recommendations of the interdisciplinary quality assurance committee
- assures that quality assurance efforts support the focus of the organization's efforts or its mission
- assures program compliance with the rules of regulatory agencies
- makes final decisions about financial priorities for the resolution of problems identified by quality monitoring that will require significant expenditures

Department/Service Head
- responsible for evaluating the care or services provided by a department/service
- delegates quality assurance functions to appropriate department-linked staff, committees, and consultants
- participates on or consults with the interdisciplinary quality assurance committee
- administers quality monitoring and evaluation processes within his or her area of responsibility
- defines department standards, criteria, and norms in conjunction with staff and quality assurance committees

- incorporates quality assurance action plans into department policy, procedures, and care delivery
- communicates facility and department quality assurance goals, structures, and processes to staff
- allocates department resources as required for the quality assurance program

Staff
- participate in quality monitoring as appropriate
- participate in quality assurance education programs
- provide feedback to the interdisciplinary quality assurance committee and department heads concerning the quality assurance program
- participate in the development of standards, criteria, and norms
- participate in the development of action plans for the resolution of problem areas identified by the monitoring process

Interdisciplinary Quality Assurance Committee
- develops a plan for the facility's quality assurance program
- implements facility-wide education concerning quality assurance
- develops interdisciplinary standards, where appropriate, with department heads/services
- coordinates interdisciplinary activity for the resolution of continuing problems that involve more than one department
- designs program reporting forms
- reviews department/service reports and makes recommendations to the chief administrative officer
- prepares periodic quality assurance reports for the chief administrative officer
- communicates recommendations from the chief administrative officer to department heads/services
- investigates long-standing, unresolved department/service problems
- manages facility-wide quality monitoring projects, such as investigating resident or family satisfaction
- revises the facility's quality assurance plan based on experience with monitoring and evaluation
- coordinates preparation for and evaluation of external regulatory surveys

Department-Linked Care Evaluation Committee
- implements area-specific education concerning the quality assurance program
- prepares periodic quality monitoring reports for the interdisciplinary quality assurance committee and department heads/services

- participates in quality monitoring as appropriate
- participates in the development of standards, criteria, and norms
- participates in the development and evaluation of action plans for the resolution of problem areas identified by the monitoring process.

Small nursing homes or those with limited financial resources may choose to manage quality assurance monitoring efforts mainly at the level of the interdisciplinary quality assurance committee; department heads are likely to serve as its committee members. A large interdisciplinary quality assurance committee can divide into work groups. These work groups may cluster personnel in related work areas so that they can serve purposes similar to a department-linked care evaluation committee. One of the work groups could develop the plan for facility-wide interdisciplinary monitoring activities. Staff may respond to the draft of the plan as well as to defined standards, criteria, and norms. Facility secretarial and medical records personnel can participate in aspects of monitoring that do not require clinical judgment. A part-time professional nurse who has a clinical background can assist both departments with limited resources and the interdisciplinary quality assurance committee with monitoring efforts.

Authority and administrative support may be linked to quality assurance activities that ensure regulatory compliance. Certainly, the board of directors and the chief administrative officer want to see that their organization avoids citations. Given the federal regulations' emphasis on quality of care, quality of life, and resident rights, authority and resources for a program that assists a facility to work toward regulatory compliances can provide a satisfactory basis for initiation of self-monitoring activities.

OVERVIEW OF THE BOOK

This introductory chapter has emphasized evaluation as an integral component of resident care. Chapter 2 provides an overview of quality assurance systems. The development of a dynamic model for defining standards, setting measurable criteria, implementing the system, and evaluating it is outlined. The various options for designing quality assurance programs are reviewed. Chapter 3 focuses on the development of a quality assurance program derived from the facility's defined purpose and standards. Sources of standards, the development of measurable criteria, and important considerations related to monitoring and evaluation processes are discussed. Chapter 4 describes the implementation of a quality assurance monitoring program. Factors that facilitate staff acceptance and involvement are identified. Specifics concerning scoring, analyzing, and reporting data are presented. An example is given of a concurrent process monitoring model that was developed at the Rush-Hines VA Teaching Nursing Home site. Chapter 5 discusses ethical considerations. Chapter 6 suggests directions for the future of quality monitoring in nursing homes.

Nursing Quality Assurance in Long-Term Care is a practical guide for the development and evaluation of quality monitoring activities in long-term care facilities. The nursing department can play a leadership role in quality monitoring, since nursing is the major service provided. Departments and services related to medical care and ancillary support activities must also evaluate the quality and appropriateness of their involvement in resident care. The role of nursing home staff as reviewers of resident care is enhanced by implementation of a formal, facility-wide quality assurance program.

REFERENCES

Beyerman, K. (1987). Developing a unit-based nursing quality assurance program: From concept to practice. *Journal of Nursing Quality Assurance*, 2(1), 1–11.
Brown, B.J. (1983). Editorial. *Nursing Administration Quarterly*, 7(3), viii–ix.
Chambers, L.W. (1985). *Quality assurance in long-term care: Policy, research and measurement*. Paris: International Center of Social Gerontology.
Health Care Financing Administration. (1987). Medicare and Medicaid: Conditions of participation for long term care facilities. *Federal Register*, 52, 38594.
Institute of Medicine. (1986). *Improving the quality of care in nursing homes*. Washington, DC: National Academy Press.
Joint Commission on Accreditation of Hospitals. (1985). *LTC/86: Long term care standards manual*. Chicago: Author.
Joint Commission on Accreditation of Hospitals. (1986). *Quality assurance in long term care*. Chicago: Author.
Lodge, M.P. (1985). *Professional practice for nurse administrators/directors of nursing in long-term care facilities (Phase I)*. Kansas City, MO: American Nurses' Association.
National Citizens' Coalition for Nursing Home Reform. (1985). *A consumer perspective on quality care: The residents' point of view*. Washington, DC: Author.

Chapter 2

Quality Assurance Systems Overview

Diana Young Barhyte

Key Points

- Quality assurance is a broad range of activities that are formed into a consistent whole through an approach–time frame combination.
- Structure, process, and outcome are the three approaches used in quality assurance programs; retrospective, concurrent, and prospective are the time frames.
- A structural approach will inform an administrator whether or not the key elements of high quality care are present; however, the approach will not yield information about whether or not the components are either appropriately configured or appropriately used.
- The process approach assesses the content and text of the health care provider's interactions with residents, and an assumption is made that key structural elements are present.
- Outcome monitoring of the measurable changes in residents' health statuses and satisfaction with their care is the third approach.
- Time frames are combined with the approach(es) used in a quality assurance program and may be retrospective, concurrent, or prospective.
- Criteria or indicators are objective, unambiguous, and quantifiable statements written in terms of standards of care that should be achieved.
- The perceptual/clinical excellence grid is a model developed by Merry (1987) that combines residents' perceptions of all aspects of their care and the environment in which it was given with objective clinical assessment of the care.

2

Quality assurance is a phrase that describes a broad range of activities. These activities have the overall purpose of evaluating the care provided to residents of long-term facilities or to patients in hospitals. They include the identification of both current and potential problems and the development of a plan of appropriate remedial and preventive actions that addresses them. In other words, quality assurance is a dynamic process that undergoes revision as problems are identified and solved. The focus of quality assurance is on the improvement of residents' care. "Care" is being used in the broad sense of the total environment in which health maintenance and promotion occurs.

The commonly accepted conventions used for quality assurance programs outline three approaches and three time frames (Donabedian, 1980; Lang, 1980). The approach–time frame combination varies across quality assurance programs, and there is no one correct combination. The approaches are termed structure, process, and outcome, and the time frames are termed retrospective, concurrent, and prospective. Building on the approach–time frame convention, Merry (1987) developed a perceptual–objective clinical model. The Merry model uses a mixture of the concurrent and prospective time frame with a process approach. The criteria or items assessing the dimensions of quality care reflect established clinical practice and patient satisfaction with their care. In the discussion that follows, the strengths and limitations of each approach and time frame will be addressed so that the readers can determine which are the better options for their particular long-term care facilities. In other words, a quality assurance program is designed or adopted by a facility because it is the better option for that particular organization and the type of residents receiving care there.

To determine which combination of the three approaches and time frames would best match a facility, there are two guidelines to assist one. The guidelines will be discussed more fully in the next chapter; however, they are introduced here to give several anchor points to the main topic. The first guideline of assistance is the mission statement of the facility. A mission statement gives the general purpose of the organization. This has been described as the best path to take to achieve the goals of an organization (Griffin, 1987). For example, a long-term care facility may have the mission of rehabilitating chronically ill aged persons. Another facility might have as its mission the care of persons having Alzheimer's disease. The mission statement is usually several sentences long and broad in scope. From the mission statement it is possible to begin deducing which approaches and time frames are the best match for a facility. Continuing with the example, a rehabilitative care facility may elect an outcome approach with a prospective time frame.

Whereas the mission statement is broad in scope, the objectives of the organization, the second guideline, specifically state how the mission will be fulfilled. The objectives are the goals of an organization and further define how the mission will be accomplished. In the preceding example, the terms "rehabilitation" and "chronically ill" would be interpreted through the facility's goals. The facility's goals are further specified into statements that are readily measurable and that may become the objectives of a quality assurance program. Defining objectives assists the quality assurance program's personnel to assess which of the approaches and time frames are the more appropriate. The quality assurance objectives also guide personnel in the development of the criteria that are the unambiguous statements or questions that directly measure specific aspects of the care given to residents (patients).

QUALITY ASSURANCE APPROACHES

Structure, process, and outcome are the three approaches used in quality assurance programs (Curtis, 1985; Hegyvary & Haussmann, 1975; Lang, 1980; Meisenheimer, 1985; Schroeder & Maibusch, 1984; Sherraud, 1985). Prior to the 1980s, most programs primarily used either a structure or a process approach. Outcome approaches tended not to be used since there were too many intervening variables. The early quality assurance program designers took the position that an outcome approach was not realistic since control over factors influencing patient outcomes was missing. For example, nurses do not fully control the treatments given to residents, since physicians write treatment orders. Therefore, statements assessing treatments were focused on when treatments were done, documentation issues, the techniques used, and so forth. Quality assurance statements were not written about the efficacy of the treatments. With changes in the federal reimbursement program, however, quality assurance experts began to re-evaluate this perspective, and the movement toward an outcome approach was begun. Similarly, the time frame used tended to be retrospective or concurrent rather than prospective. Simultaneous with the increasing interest in outcome measures, interest began to be taken in the prospective time frame.

Structure Approach

The structure approach focuses on the characteristics of the organization, such as its size (number of beds), ownership (private or public, for profit or not for profit), fiscal resources, types and qualifications of professionals, numbers and appropriateness of nonprofessionals and support personnel, physical facilities, and equipment (Joint Commission on Accreditation of Healthcare Organizations, 1988). These characteristics of a facility are relatively stable over time (Sherraud, 1985). Although ownership, the number of beds, and fiscal resources do change, it would be rare for the changes to occur frequently.

Size and Ownership

Size and ownership type are not obviously related to quality assurance if these two characteristics are studied separately. It is reasonable to question what size has to do with quality assurance, until one recalls that a facility is licensed for a specific number of beds for each service. If there are more patients admitted than there are open beds, then several quality assurance issues are relevant. Suppose, for discussion, the size for facility XYZ is 100 licensed beds, but by putting extra beds in rooms there are 120 beds open. A safety question about the facility's ability to evacuate patients in a fire or other disaster may be raised. Furthermore, if facility XYZ has adequate personnel for only 100 patients, those additional 20 patients are probably not receiving the highest quality care possible. Realistically, all 120 patients will receive a lower quality of care.

The amount and type of equipment needed for 100 patients also will be made inadequate by the addition of 20 residents. Long-term care facilities usually purchase equipment in terms of a ratio of machines to residents, plus an additional number to cover machines being repaired. If the number of residents exceeds a facility's licensed capacity, then there is no slack in the system. That is, the back-up equipment is put into service, and, should a machine malfunction, there is no replacement available. The equipment-to-resident ratio also holds true for the facility's personnel and physical plant. Size, therefore, is an important structural characteristic, especially when it is considered in conjunction with other structural characteristics.

Ownership type is relevant to quality assurance programs for several reasons. The mission statement and facility objectives reflect the owners' philosophy and influence all the characteristics of the organization. If the owners of the facility are the citizenry, then community politics will be reflected in the management of the facility. This occurs in a way analogous to the influence of politics on the management of a city- or county-owned hospital. In this type of environment, it is probable that the qualifications of the personnel hired will be influenced by a political patronage system. Additionally, since the fiscal resources of the facility will be tied more directly to the taxes paid by citizens, those available monies subsequently affect not only the condition of the physical plant but also equipment purchases and employees' salaries. These influences on structural characteristics may not necessarily be present in privately-owned institutions. Private facilities, however, are not totally free from constraints imposed by their political environments.

Privately-owned institutions have certain types of pressures on them that publicly-owned institutions do not have. Some of these pressures are financial; the bottom line of a facility's budget is important since it determines its bond rating and interest notes for loans. Although private institutions are not influenced by a patronage system, their mission statements and objectives do influence hiring by determining the qualifications of their personnel. For example, all head nurses might be required to have a baccalaureate degree and all nurses aides to have completed a training course. Religious groups owning institutions may influence the food prepared by the dietary department; the conduct expected of employees, residents, and visitors; or the medical procedures done at the facility. A facility's ownership influences the activities performed by its members in the same way that families influence the behavior of their adult members. Analogous to the family culture each of us experience is the culture of an organization (Griffin, 1987), which consists of its members' shared perception of its nature, values, norms, and style.

Fiscal Resources

The fiscal resources of a facility are considered another structural measure of a quality assurance program. The old truism "you cannot spend money you don't have" is applicable. Unless a facility has the money to purchase or rent equipment, then regardless of how needed it might be, the equipment cannot be obtained. Similarly, personnel cannot be hired, and physical facilities may deteriorate due to insufficient maintenance. Without the needed financial resources, it is difficult to deliver quality care.

Personnel

The types and qualifications of personnel may change more often, due to circumstances that cannot be controlled by the facility. For example, a nursing shortage currently exists; therefore, long-term care facilities may find it difficult to recruit nurses. On the other hand, there is a glut of physicians, so hiring physicians may be relatively easy compared to hiring qualified nurses.

In addition to the types and qualifications of personnel, the number of each type of personnel is important. There should be a sufficient number of personnel for each of the care units. The question becomes whether there are sufficient personnel—nurses, nurses' aides, housekeepers, and so forth—to care for "X" number of residents on a ward. This becomes more than a ratio of staff to residents, when the residents' levels of dependency are taken into consideration. Specifically, the more dependent a resident is, the more care will be needed by her or him. The more care required by residents, the greater the number of personnel needed. For example, fewer caregivers are needed for eight patients who each require one hour of care than for eight patients who each require four hours of care.

In summary, the structure approach to quality assurance will let administrators know whether or not the key elements are present to give high quality care. It will not tell them, however, whether the components are appropriately configured or if the elements are being used appropriately (Sherraud, 1985). It should not be inferred from the preceding comments that a structure approach to quality assurance should not be taken. Rather, the statements refer to the pitfalls that would be encountered if *only* structure is used as the approach. Certainly, structural elements need to be included because they are the foundation required for quality care to occur. They are the necessary elements upon which the other two approaches, process and outcome, build.

Process Approach

The process approach to quality assurance examines the interactions between patients and staff—the nature and sequence of events or activities in the delivery of health care (Lang, 1980). Both the content and context of the care given to residents are assessed—what the staff say to residents and how they say it, in addition to the actual activities that are done for the residents. The care activities themselves also are analyzed in terms of appropriate staff observation of policies and procedures and correct use of supplies and equipment. Patient privacy, comfort, and safety are some of the assessed elements, as are the teaching and explanations given before, during, and after any activity. By the word "activity" is meant all elements of care, from basic needs such as hygiene and nutrition to all the treatments and procedures patients receive.

Framework

One framework that is often used by nurses to organize the process of care is the nursing process. While it is labeled a nursing framework, it can be used by any discipline since it is a health care adaptation of scientific problem solving. The framework, or model, has four steps: assessment, planning, implementation, and evaluation (Yura & Walsh, 1973). Step one is the assessment of the individual who will be receiving nursing care. Assessments include physiological, psychosocial, and family support statuses and the health care problem(s) presented by the resident. Step two is the development of a plan of care for the resident that stabilizes or improves the problems identified in the assessment phase. Steps three and four put the plan into action (implementation) and evaluate the outcomes of actions, respectively.

This process of care framework is applicable to all the activities involving residents. For example, nutrition is assessed for required caloric intake and the appropriate provision of protein, fat, and carbohydrates. The caregiver also assesses the resident's ability to chew, swallow, and feed himself or herself; food preferences; and best body position for meals. After the assessment, a plan is made for a specific type of diet based upon food preferences and the frequency of feedings and the level of assistance a patient requires. The food is prepared, the resident is placed in the appropriate position and given the required assistance, and the intake of food is observed. Modifications of the plan are made if required.

The same method of assessing, planning, implementing, and evaluating may be used for any treatment, procedure, or administrative decision. An example of an administrative decision might be whether or not to have a quality assurance program. Step one would be to assess the numerous relevant factors for a program, such as state and federal requirements, the type of approach and time frame that is most appropriate for the facility, and the program's impact upon personnel and patients. Step two would be the planning of a quality assurance program. Included in the planning would be the design of the program and the establishment of its reliability and validity. The third step would be implementing the quality assurance activities and maintaining staff support of the program. Finally, step four would be evaluating the program in terms of its effectiveness and efficiency.

To summarize, a process of care framework, built on scientific problem solving, expands the areas of quality assurance that can be measured. The steps of the framework make explicit the beginning, middle, and end points that are to be considered in a quality assurance activity. Step one, assessment, directs attention to what types of information need to be gathered. Step two combines the information gathered into a logical, coherent plan. The third step focuses attention on how the plan is put into action; that is, implementation of the plan occurs. Step four examines the adequacy of the plan itself.

The process approach to quality assurance assumes that the necessary structural elements are present; however, this assumption may not be a prudent one. If support services, equipment, and supplies are not sufficient to meet the residents' care requirements, the process of giving care is harmed. The problem is how to determine the cause of less than optimal quality of care. You would not be able to establish the cause of the lower quality care if you *only* examined the process of care.

Outcome Approach

A process-only approach focuses on the activities and interactions surrounding the care residents receive. An outcome approach, on the other hand, focuses on the end results of the residents' care. What is monitored are measurable changes in the residents' states of health and satisfaction about the care they receive. Recently, the interest in developing outcome criteria has increased, in part because of the impact of Diagnosis Related Groups (DRGs) on patients' lengths of hospital stay. Health care professionals have questioned the relationship between length of stay and quality of care. Some took the position that patients who are discharged "early" are probably more debilitated and therefore may experience more negative outcomes, such as rehospitalizations. But the recent work by Krakauer (1987) demonstrated that early discharges did not lead to rehospitalizations. The reduction in length of hospital stays, however, has increased the number of patients requiring skilled nursing care after their discharge. Therefore, long-term care facilities may have a larger percentage of residents who require more intensive care.

Assessing Changes in Residents' Health

Quality assurance statements written for an outcome approach would relate to patients' knowledge about their conditions and treatment regimes and the prevention of avoidable risks. These statements might include the appropriate use of prescribed and over-the-counter medication, knowledge of dietary-drug interactions, physical therapy and occupational therapy protocols, environmental safety, appropriate use of any prostheses, and aids for activities of daily living (walkers, canes, wheelchairs). Similar to a structural approach, the resources needed by the residents would be assumed present. It would be further assumed that the resources were being appropriately used in the residents' care. The difference between a structure and outcome approach is that the latter assesses whether or not the knowledge to use a resource is present and whether use of the resource occurs.

Assessing Resident Satisfaction

The assessment of patients' satisfaction with the care they receive is another component of an outcome approach to quality assurance monitoring (Micheletti & Shlala, 1986; Sherraud, 1985). Patients' perceptions of their care include the physical plant or environment, access to the facility, visiting hours, personnel's courtesy, and the range of services offered by the facility. An analogy is the way we judge the services of the hotels we use. We expect a certain standard of service when we register at a hotel. These expectations, among others, may be for a clean room and linens, and food served in a reasonable amount of time, appropriately cooked and at the correct temperature (hot foods hot, cold food cold). We expect the staff to be courteous, dressed appropriately, and to comply with reasonable requests. Depending upon how our standards are met, we use those hotels again and recommend them to our friends. Similarly, patients and their families will return to the same facility and make recommendations about its use to others.

Initially, patient satisfaction may seem to be only a marketing tool for a facility. But although it does have a marketing component, that is not its main purpose when used as part of a quality assurance program. The information obtained through patients' perceptions is valuable because it makes us aware of parts of our work environment that we take for granted. We become used to the food service, the linen supply, the interactions between ourselves and patients, and the appearance of rooms, corridors, and hallways. We tend to forget how others are affected by this environment.

Equally important, patient satisfaction has been found to be significantly related to patients' knowledge about their conditions (Counte, Bieliausleas, & Pavlou, 1983). That is, patients who were more informed about their illnesses had more positive attitudes toward a facility where they received care and toward their caregivers. It would, therefore, seem reasonable that if a facility had a "good" environment but residents' satisfaction was less than adequate, the residents' perceptions might have been influenced by their insufficient knowledge about their conditions. This premise could be assessed by examining quality assurance scores for items that directly address residents' knowledge. A note of caution is needed here. Residents who have physiological conditions that result in poor memory functions may not be able to give accurate information about what they have been taught. Additionally, their perceptions in other areas also may be negatively affected.

In summary, an outcome approach focuses on the positive changes in the health statuses of residents. The problem one faces in designing an outcome-only approach is being able to specifically identify what factors led to the improvement or decline of the residents' health. For example, has a resident's health status improved only because of high quality nursing care? Realistically, one knows the answer is no, because nutrition and hygiene also affect health. Similarly, patient satisfaction is somewhat problematic. What exactly are patients satisfied with—staff personalities? The physical appearance of the facility? The amount of time physicians spend with them? Satisfaction may be influenced by an unusual situation that the resident remembers and has generalized to the entire length of stay. What would need sorting out would be the essential and nonessential factors affecting residents' satisfaction with their stay at a facility.

Summary of Approaches

Structure, process, and outcome are the three approaches used in quality assurance programs. When considered separately, each approach has its inherent strengths and weaknesses; however, when the approaches are combined, the result is a comprehensive program. Each is enhanced because each approach complements the others and results in a comprehensive assessment of residents' care. Process is influenced by structure; that is, unless the structural components are present, the process characteristics are either of a lesser quality or absent. It therefore is logical to conclude that outcome is affected by both structure and process. Positive end results of care will be difficult to achieve if the structural components for giving the care are not present, and even if the structural components are present, if they are not used in the care process, it would be difficult to obtain a "good" outcome. In combining the three approaches, you do not have to use all the elements of each approach or only one approach. Rather, you would select the most meaningful parts of the approach(es) for your particular long-term care facility.

QUALITY ASSURANCE TIME FRAMES

There are three time frames. A retrospective time frame is used when assessing what has occurred in the past; for example, chart reviews (audits) or an identified care issue are done for the previous six months. The concurrent time frame permits assessment of what is presently occurring; for example, personnel are interviewed to determine their knowledge about specific patients. Prospective is using a future time frame. An example is the following: You implement a new protocol that is expected to reduce the future incidence of pressure sores. The current incidence of pressure sores is then compared to the incidence of pressure sores after the implementation of the new protocol. The difference between the two incidence measures is used to determine how effective the new protocol was in preventing bedsores.

Which time frame is selected depends on what you want to measure. Which time frame makes more sense, considering the questions you want to answer? There is, however, a natural fit between some time frames and some overall approaches. Structural characteristics usually are present tense and concurrent in time, whereas outcome characteristics may fit with either the concurrent or the prospective time frame. The pressure sore protocol example given above used a concurrent (base line) and a prospective (expected a 20 percent reduction) time frame. It is common practice to use more than one time frame in a quality assurance program, because all the quality assurance criteria (questions) usually are not in the same time frame. The different time frames result from what is a logical assessment of a care area.

QUALITY ASSURANCE CRITERIA OR INDICATORS

Quality assurance criteria are the questions or statements used in examining the quality of care given to residents. The definition of a criterion is a standard, rule, or test by which a judgment can be formed (Lang, 1980); the Joint Commission on Accreditation of Healthcare Organizations (1988) calls it an indicator and defines it as "a measurable variable relating to the structure, process, or outcome of care." There are many sources of information to assist the program developer in developing criteria items or indicators. Some of these information sources include professional standards of practice, knowledge of current diagnoses and their respective treatments, and the facility's objectives.

Criteria are written in terms of what should be done, rather than what is being done. That is, the indicators often become the standards of care that are to be achieved (Joint Commission, 1988). An example might help clarify the distinction. It has been established that proper handwashing prevents the spread of infection between patients. You know, however, that personnel only occasionally wash their hands. Your handwashing criterion therefore would be "Do the personnel wash their hands between each patient contact?" not "Do the personnel occasionally wash their hands?" Again, the criteria become the expected norms or behaviors for residents' care.

In developing quality assurance indicators, there are two basic rules that should be followed: (1) The questions or statements are objective, unambiguous, and directly related to what is being measured; and (2) the criteria are stated so that there are only four possible answers: yes, no, not applicable, and information not available. The response "not applicable" is for situations where the question cannot be expected to have an answer in every case. An example would be a question about the position of a urinary catheter drainage tube; not every resident has a urinary catheter. "Information not available" is used when the indicators cannot be answered because either the required documentation or the caregiver is not available.

The second rule can be adhered to if the first rule is followed. In other words, if a quality assurance item is so written that the person doing the evaluation is unable to decide if the answer is yes or no, then the question is ambiguous. Similarly, if two people read the question and one answers yes but the other answers no, and they both are correct, the question is ambiguous.

Objectivity of the quality assurance statements also is important. Items should be free of bias or prejudice and concerned only with the actual characteristics being measured. Quality assurance criteria should measure reality—what is or is not occurring. Persons will be more receptive to results if they know the statements are objective, even when the results are not favorable. Consider which you would prefer hearing if you were the head of housekeeping: (1) The corridors were clean (no noticeable dust, spills, trash) 50 percent of the time, or (2) housekeeping does its job only 50 percent of the time. The first statement can be used constructively; standards can be set to clean up spills within five minutes of being notified, to dust floors each day, and to collect trash twice each day. The second statement is too subjective; the chief of housekeeping could not determine what was needed for improvement.

Reliability and Validity Issues

By following the two rules, the criteria or indicators should be both valid and reliable, and therefore, the quality assurance monitoring results should be better received by the facility's personnel. Additionally, administrators can confidently use the results in their endeavors to meet their organizational responsibilities. As you know, reliability means that a tool consistently gives similar results, whereas validity means that a tool accurately measures what it is supposed to measure. Rules one and two, then, are actually guidelines for assuring a reliable and valid quality assurance monitoring program.

One decision concerning reliability and validity issues will need to be made after the quality assurance criteria have been developed: whether or not copies of the quality assurance indicators should be placed on each ward and made readily available to all caregivers. If caregivers know what specific criteria are being measured, then they may consciously or unconsciously change their practices to conform to the criteria. Should this change in care-giving practices occur, neither the reliability nor the validity of the quality assurance program is affected. Actually, it has the benefit of increasing the quality of care residents receive, since the criteria reflect the level of care desired. Furthermore, personnel might be more receptive to the quality assurance program if they knew more about it.

Alternatively, sharing the quality assurance criteria with personnel could result in their changing care-giving practices only when they are being observed. Also, they might answer the questions to obtain a good score. This type of situation would affect the validity of the criteria, since the items would not reflect the actual quality of care. The caregivers, however, would know what was expected and perhaps over time would change their practice patterns. It may seem cynical, but at least during quality assurance monitoring periods, the quality of care would be improved. The benefits of sharing the quality criteria with caregivers outweigh the benefits of not sharing them.

APPROACH–TIME FRAME MATRIX

Until this point, the three approaches and time frames have been discussed without fully integrating them. Realistically, however, there are combinations of approaches and time frames, and there is no "one best way" of synthesizing them. Consider the approach–time frame matrix given in Table 2-1. The rows are the time frames, and the columns are the approaches. The cells contain the core elements to be used in writing the quality assurance criteria. In Table 2-1 the appropriate cells contain blood pressure readings, as per the example. Each cell contains some of the more critical elements; however, note that the emphasis of each time frame is slightly different.

In the first row (retrospective time frame), residents whose blood pressures exceed normal limits are identified using an audit method. The records or charts that are the primary source of the information are assumed to be accurate. The outcome of the audit is the number of occurrences (frequency) that met the criteria. This method, chart audit, is used whenever someone is trying to determine whether or not a problem exists and if it has been resolved. Whichever combination is selected, it needs to reflect a facility's mission statement, objectives, and, specifically, which aspects of patient care will be monitored.

The second row contains selected elements for a structure, process, or outcome approach using a concurrent time frame. Since the focus is on what is presently occurring, observation and interviews are used. The residents' charts also may be reviewed, but only the most recent documentation would be assessed. Some individuals define "most recent" as narrowly as the preceding 24 hours; others define it as occurring within the last seven days. A rule of thumb is to use the criteria themselves as the basis for defining "most recent"; for example, residents' blood pressures may need to be recorded daily if they are hypertensive, but only biweekly if they are normotensive.

The prospective quality assurance time frame occupies the third row. The cells in this row contain some of the elements that would be assessed if one was trying to determine the usefulness of low-sodium diets in reducing blood pressure. The structural elements that will be required are identified, permitting those currently not available to be obtained. Next, one would determine what process elements should be monitored for the program and how to go about monitoring them. Finally, the outcome indicators are established. These are the elements that should occur if the program is successful; for example what percentage of residents will have lowered blood pressures—100 percent?

Table 2-1 Quality Assurance Approach–Time Frame Matrix

Time Frame	Approach		
	Structure	Process	Outcome
Retrospective (past)	• elements are assumed to have been available	• taking and recording of blood pressure is assumed to be accurate • review residents' charts	• residents whose blood pressure readings exceed criteria identified

QA criteria: Residents who have two or more blood pressure readings above 140/90 are identified.

Time Frame	Structure	Process	Outcome
Concurrent (present)	• blood pressure cuff (size, type) • sphygmomanometer • stethoscope • caregiver	• caregiver explains procedure • resident position is appropriate • caregiver follows policy and procedure • caregiver records reading	• blood pressure reading is accurate • resident is satisfied with caregiver's explanation of procedure and the approach used

QA criteria: Residents have blood pressure readings taken each week.

Time Frame	Structure	Process	Outcome
Prospective (future)	• clinical dietitian • appropriate foods available • sodium substitutes available	• dietary history is taken, including food preferences, history of salt usage, etc. • resident is instructed on diet • blood pressure readings are taken for baseline • food served is appropriate	• resident complies with dietary plan • blood pressure is lowered

QA criteria: Hypertensive residents on low-sodium diets will have lower blood pressure readings.

75 percent? 50 percent? The findings of research studies and national standards are two useful tools to assist in setting the outcome standards.

The approach–time frame matrix illustrates the methods that have been used in the past to assess quality of care. To reiterate, quality assurance programs usually used some combination of approaches and tended to focus on either retrospective or concurrent time frames. With changes in the economic environment, specifically in methods of reimbursement, the emphasis in quality assurance programs began moving toward the inclusion of more outcome criteria. Furthermore, consumers of health care have become more vocal in their demands for access to care and for higher standards of care. These changes, among others, in the health care environment, have shifted providers' attention toward a new approach to quality assurance. The new method takes an objective-subjective approach to measuring patient care outcomes and has been named the perceptual/clinical excellence grid (Merry, 1987).

PERCEPTUAL/CLINICAL EXCELLENCE GRID

The perceptual elements of this grid are the subjective aspects of care; that is, the residents'/patients' thoughts and feelings about the care they received. You will have noted that historically in quality assurance endeavors, this was one element among the outcome measures. In this modern approach, however, the perceptual elements have been expanded so that all aspects of care and all areas of a facility are assessed. To name a few examples, patients would be asked about the efficiency of the admission, transfer, and discharge processes, their interactions with the facility's personnel, and the parking facilities and visiting hours. Since the strengths and weaknesses of assessments of patient satisfaction were discussed earlier in the chapter, they will not be reiterated at this point.

The other dimension of the grid is the objective clinical assessment of the quality of care. Similar to the perceptual elements, these measures also were part of the outcome approach. The clinical assessment also contains morbidity and mortality factors that may have been preventable, such as infection rates and drug reactions. The problem with outcome-only elements, however, is that the cause of the untoward events may not be identified. This would be especially troublesome when there may logically be multiple causes, such as in the case of infections.

Each dimension, perceptual and objective clinical, is given a score that is a composite of the individual criteria; that is, the sum categories are added together so that there is a single score for each dimension. The single score is then categorized as low or high (see Exhibit 2-1). . Then the relationship between the single two dimension scores is examined, and a decision is made about the providers.

Exhibit 2-1 Perceptual/Clinical Excellence Grid

		Objective Clinical Quality Score	
		High	Low
Perceptual Quality Score	High		
	Low		

Source: Copyright 1987 by the Joint Commission on Accreditation of Healthcare Organizations, Chicago. Adapted with permission.

This modern approach is interesting since it expands on the historical outcome approach to quality assurance. There are aspects of both patient care and the delivery of the care that have needed assessment, but for a variety of reasons have not been measured. Perhaps the most important thing about the new approach is that it has expanded our thinking.

SUMMARY

Quality assurance monitoring is a dynamic program that is designed to monitor a broad range of resident care activities. The three approaches used in evaluating residents' care are structure, process, and outcome. Structure is an examination of the characteristics of a facility that must be present for quality care to occur, for example, appropriate types and numbers of personnel. The interactions between personnel and residents, the nature of staff activities, and the sequence of the activities in the delivery of care are the critical components of the process approach. One framework used in the process approach is scientific problem solving. If the focus of the quality assurance program is on the end results of the care given to residents, then the approach is labeled outcome. Each approach, when considered individually, has strengths and weaknesses, since two of the three approaches are assumed to be present and adequate. The approaches may be used singly or in combination; whichever approach is taken, it should reflect both the mission and goals of the facility.

Concomitant with the selection of the approach(es) to be used, a decision is made regarding the time frame for the program. Again, there are three choices: retrospective, concurrent, and prospective. There should be congruence between the approach and time frame; for example, a process approach is used with a concurrent time frame. It is a common practice to use more than one time frame, since the quality assurance items within a program ask questions that cut across two time frames.

The quality assurance items are questions (criteria, indicators), which are objective and unambiguous. The answers to the criteria are "yes", "no" responses; however, most quality assurance monitoring also includes the responses "not applicable" and "information not available." The latter two categories are for criteria that will not apply to every patient; for example, not all residents will have dentures or glasses or canes. Too many not applicable and information not available responses will negatively impact on reliability and validity since those responses are considered missing data (Holt, 1988). Reliability and validity of the items are crucial and must be assessed by statistical analysis.

Finally, an approach–time frame matrix was given, using patient blood pressures as the example. The cells of the matrix contain selected elements appropriate for different approach–time frame couplets. Similar to the matrix is the perceptual/clinical excellence grid that was developed by Merry (1987). That approach measures both patients' perceptions about structure, process, and outcome elements and the objective clinical standards.

REFERENCES

Counte, M.A., Bieliausleas, L.A., & Pavlou, M. (1983). Stress and personal attitudes in chronic illness. *Archives of Physical Medicine and Rehabilitation 64* (June), 272–275.

Curtis, B.J. (1985). Auditing: A method for evaluating quality of care. *Journal of Nursing Administration*, *15*(10), 14–21.

Donabedian, A. (1980). *The definition of quality and approaches to its assessment*. Ann Arbor, MI.

Griffin, R.W. (1987). *Management* (2nd ed.). Boston: Houghton Mifflin.

Hegyvary, S.T., & Haussmann, R.K.D. (1975). Monitoring nursing quality care. *Journal of Nursing Administration*, *5*(5), 17–26.

Holt, D. (1988). Missing data and nonresponse. In J. R. Reeves (Ed.), Educational research, methodology, and measurement: An international handbook (pp. 685–689). New York: Pergamon Press.

Joint Commission on Accreditation of Healthcare Organizations. (1988). *Monitoring and evaluation—"official version."* Internal memo from P. M. Schyve to department heads.

Krakauer, H. (1987, November). *Assessment of outcomes of medical care: Mortality, morbidity, disability and cost*. Paper presented at the University of Chicago, Graduate School of Business, Center for Health Administration Studies,

Lang, N.M. (1980). *Quality assurance in nursing: A selected bibliography* (DHEW Publication No. HRA 80-30). Hyattsville, MD: Health Resources Administration, Bureau of Health Manpower, Division of Nursing.

Meisenheimer, C.G. (1985). *Quality assurance: A complete guide to effective programs*. Rockville, MD: Aspen.

Merry, M.D. (1987). What is quality care? A model for measuring health care excellence. *Quality Review Bulletin*, 298–301.

Micheletti, J.A., & Shlala, T.J. (1986). RUGs II: Implications for management and quality in long term care. *Quality Review Bulletin*, 236–242.

Schroeder, P.S., & Maibusch, R.M. (1984). *Nursing quality assurance: A unit-based approach*. Rockville, MD: Aspen.

Sherraud, H. (1985, December). Q. A. issues in long-term care—vehicle for introducing change. *Dimensions*, 8–10.

Yura, H., & Walsh, M.B. (1973). *The nursing process*. (2nd ed.). New York: Appleton & Lange.

Chapter 3

Program Development

Joan LeSage and Diana Young Barhyte

Key Points

- The same process may be used for either adapting or developing a quality assurance program.
- The purpose of a quality assurance program is interrelated to the mission statement of an organization, gives coherence to a program, and is used as the basis for developing indicators.
- Accountability for the management of quality assurance results is important in order for appropriate action to be taken to prevent or rectify problems.
- Quality assurance endeavors may be partially shaped by professional associations and external agencies and the regulations they prescribe.
- Clear definition of the purpose and the planned outcomes of quality monitoring, as well as of methods to evaluate its effectiveness, will help to educate staff, residents, and families about a facility's quality assurance program.
- A quality assurance program must be integrated within an organization's structure and functions.
- Department heads need to describe how they will identify, monitor, and resolve problems with quality monitoring and evaluation processes.
- The chief administrative officer must be prepared to support department heads in initiating changes recommended by quality monitoring that will require resources or system changes that are beyond a manager's scope of responsibility.
- Activities monitored should have an important effect on resident care. Monitoring does not have to be problem focused.
- Staff must view the topics selected for monitoring and the criteria that are developed as relevant to their work.
- The topics chosen for monitoring must consider and blend the viewpoints of nursing home administration, caregivers, and the consumer (Wilbert, 1985).
- Thorough consideration of a department's resources, functions, and contributions to resident care outcomes related to the achievement of a defined stand-

ard provides a basis for the development of measurable monitoring criteria for that standard.

- Staff must consider the availability of resources and their cost, when developing corrective action plans.
- Measurement of services alone will not enhance quality of care. Data collected must be analyzed for its impact on resident care. Evaluation of the effectiveness of corrective action plans is essential.

3

The development of a quality assurance program is easy for some people, especially after they have done it once. Other people say it is a difficult task, regardless of how many programs they have developed. Those persons who find it difficult tend to name one of the following areas as problematic: writing and testing the quality assurance items or criteria, implementing the program, or managing the reporting of results.

None of these three areas is inherently problematic. People sometimes have difficulty developing a program when they do not follow the steps of program development sequentially. If a step in the process is completed before progressing to the next step, the program development task may be accomplished efficiently. This does not guarantee that the task will be problem-free, but only that there will be a minimum of small, easily resolved difficulties.

Therefore, the purpose of this chapter is to describe the process of developing a quality assurance program. The process we describe also can be used for adapting a program. That is, one would follow the same sequential steps whether one is designing a unique program for a specific long-term care facility or adapting a program originally developed for another health care organization. For example, the quality assurance program in Appendix D was adapted from the Rush-Medicus system for monitoring the quality of nursing care (Hegyvary, Haussmann, & Cronman, 1979). The Rush-Medicus system was designed for use in the acute care setting; however, some of the items are also appropriate for nursing in long-term care facilities. Some Rush-Medicus quality assurance criteria (items) needed to be rephrased to be appropriate for use in a nonhospital setting, and other items were found to be inappropriate in a nursing home. The process described for developing a program has several sequential parts. As noted earlier, if the steps are not followed sequentially, you may find that efficiency has been reduced.

41

DEVELOP A PROGRAM PURPOSE

The first step in the process is to clearly define the purpose of the quality assurance program. A purpose is nothing mysterious. It is the answer to the question, What do you want to accomplish? The answer usually has two parts: the specific goal of the program and the part derived from the long-term care facility's mission statement. Recall that the community learns what a facility will accomplish through either hearing or reading its mission statement. For example, a statement that discusses providing rehabilitation services to the elderly informs the community that middle-aged persons are not admitted to the facility and that older persons who are residents will receive rehabilitation. Both employees and residents may use the mission statement to assist them in understanding their respective organizational roles. In the preceding example, the employees and residents know they will need to work together toward a rehabilitation goal. Part of the purpose of a quality assurance program, therefore, is to help the facility's administrators determine whether or not a facility is fulfilling its mission.

Frequently there is the misperception among facility administrators that the "real" purpose of a quality assurance program is to placate outside agencies whose regulations require the systematic evaluation of residents' care. Although it is true that the information obtained through quality assurance endeavors may fulfill regulatory requirements, that is not the purpose of a quality assurance program. Quality assurance assessments measure the efforts of a facility toward excellence and the efforts of its employees toward providing an optimal level of performance. Facilities that give high-quality care will find that there also are economic advantages, such as more client referrals and decreased costs incurred due to errors of commission and omission. Translating a long-term care facility's mission statement into a quality assurance purpose is a straightforward process that simultaneously provides the first opportunity for the facility's administrators to begin involving their personnel in the program. This involvement of personnel at the initial stage of program development will enhance their acceptance and ownership of the quality assurance program. The personnel's feelings of ownership also will facilitate implementation of the program. But more important, a clearly stated purpose gives coherence to a program, since it becomes the basis for developing the more specific quality assurance indicators. The indicators give direction in the development of objectives, subobjectives, and criteria (items).

An example of the interrelationship between a facility mission statement and a quality assurance program purpose is given below. The example also is being used to demonstrate how straightforward the process is.

Mission statement
The mission of the long-term care facility is to provide compassionate and comprehensive health care services to elderly persons.

Quality Assurance Program
The purpose of the long-term care facility quality assurance program is to systematically assess the medical, nursing, and other support services' care given to residents.

DEVELOP INDICATORS

The residents and the care they receive are the focuses of a quality assurance program (O'Leary, 1987). Indicators for the program are derived from its purpose and consist of specific measurable statements that constitute operationalizations of the program purpose. That is, the indicators are the definitions of the purpose. Remembering that definitions clarify the meanings and nuances of words will be helpful in writing quality assurance program indicators. Another point to remember is that any indicator should be within the sphere of control of the facility.

Accountability

The issue of accountability is an important consideration. Appropriate action will need to be taken to prevent or rectify problems identified by a quality assurance program. If a problem is identified but no person has the authority to take appropriate corrective action, how will the problem be resolved? It is not reasonable to ignore a problem that potentially jeopardizes residents' safety or health status. Someone must be made responsible for resolving the issue.

It is suggested that the quality assurance program has a multidisciplinary focus so that problems can be resolved by the appropriate administrative person. This multidisciplinary focus needs to be reflected in the program's purposes, which should specify responsible health care providers rather than simply naming a specific health care discipline.

For example, one long-term care facility's quality assurance program might make use of the following indicator: "A plan of care is formulated for each resident within 48 hours of admission." This indicator would be further specified when the quality assurance program's objectives, subobjectives, and criteria are written. The levels of abstraction for each indicator decrease as one goes from the major objectives to the criteria. This increase in specificity is analogous to the multidisciplinary patient/resident care management system proposed by Kugler, Nash, and Weinberger (1984). Each step requires more specificity than the one preceding it; each statement becomes more concrete and thereby more measurable.

The movement from general to specific is also followed in going from the purpose of a quality assurance program to determining the indicators. Standards of care, as followed by professional associations or by regulatory agencies, facilitate the identification of a quality assurance program's indicators.

DEFINE STANDARDS OF CARE

The purpose and the indicators you have either written or adapted become the cornerstone of your facility's quality assurance program. Standards of care set up by both professional associations and external regulatory agencies assist in defining goals. The professional associations of the various health care providers, such as the American Medical Association and the American Nurses' Association, have established standards that guide the practice patterns of their memberships. These standards are broad statements reflecting a discipline's philosophy about patient (resident) care and the conduct of its members. The professional standards can function as bench marks in quality assurance program development.

Outside agency standards are structural measures of quality care that assess whether needed parameters that facilitate quality care are in place. Examples of external agencies whose standards help shape long-term care facilities' quality assurance programs are local and state boards of health, fire and building codes, insurance companies, and the government. Board of health regulations influence both residents' care and the care environment. One example is the promulgation of regulations to prevent the spread of food-related gastrointestinal infections, whereby food service managers must maintain perishable foods at specific temperatures and food handlers must pass screening tests for selected infectious diseases. Local fire and building codes set standards of safety to protect the people living in multiperson facilities. Unless caregivers are educated appropriately, according to insurers' standards, the facility will not be reimbursed for certain procedures, and some insurance firms will only reimburse licensed physicians, even though certified nurse practitioners have been educated to do the same procedures. Other insurers will reimburse for procedures done by both groups of health care professionals. Finally, the government influences health care through its reimbursement guidelines for Medicaid (state level) and Medicare (federal level), whose regulations are types of standards since they prescribe aspects of residents' care.

The influence of external standards like those of boards of health, insurance companies, or the government is not separate and distinct from that of the earlier-mentioned professional associations. Professional organizations send their experts to testify about government regulations. Members of professional associations are employed by regulatory agencies to write, assess, and enforce health care standards and practices. These health care professionals may write standards stipulating that a quality assurance program be established. Furthermore, external agency regulations may prescribe the focus of the quality assurance program. In effect, therefore, professional groups are very influential in the development of quality assurance programs.

Professional Standards

Within the long-term care facility, adherence to the care standards of professional groups influences employees' continuing education requirements and opportunities and the types of policies and procedures that govern patient care. There is a natural evolution from professional associations' standards to the development of quality assurance. The standards of care reflected in policies, procedures, personnel qualifications, and so forth can be used as criteria within a quality assurance program. Professional standards usually describe behaviors expected of the professional, rather than the expected condition of nursing home residents. They help identify the activities of health care providers considered most important for residents' welfare. Standards serve as a model for professional practice and call for quality at a level beyond minimum regulatory standards. Practitioners should aim for the model of practice defined by their disciplines' standards.

Standards of Gerontological Nursing Practice

The American Nurses' Association has published *Standards and Scope of Gerontological Nursing Practice* (1987). The 11 standards are identified in Exhibit 3-1. They support resident care that is based on a process incorporating the following: assessment; problem identification; planning for nursing interventions that facilitate achievement of desired outcomes; implementation of care in collaboration with residents, the family, and the interdisciplinary team; and ongoing evaluation of care, including a formal quality assurance program. This publication is useful for evaluating nursing practice because each standard has defined structure, process, and outcome criteria for evaluation of its achievement. Behaviors of older adults and their family members are included among the defined outcomes. Many of the criteria, however, need to be refined in order to be measurable and objective. An important outcome criteria for Standard I, "Organization of Gerontological Nursing Services," notes the need for evidence that quality assurance activities are used to revise and improve policies, procedures, and services.

Standards of the American College of Health Care Administrators

The American College of Health Care Administrators (ACHCA), a national association for long-term care administrators, has developed standards of practice for long-term care administrators (1987). The complete standards are found in Appendix B; Exhibit 3-2 highlights the resident care section.

Exhibit 3-1 Standards of Gerontological Nursing Practice

Standard I. Organization of Gerontological Nursing Services
All gerontological nursing services are planned, organized, and directed by a nurse executive. The nurse executive has baccalaureate or master's preparation and has experience in gerontological nursing and administration of long-term care services or acute care services for older clients.

Standard II. Theory
The nurse participates in the generation and testing of theory as a basis for clinical decisions. The nurse uses theoretical concepts to guide the effective practice of gerontological nursing.

Standard III. Data Collection
The health status of the older person is regularly assessed in a comprehensive, accurate, and systematic manner. The information obtained during the health assessment is accessible to and shared with appropriate members of the interdisciplinary health care team, including the older person and the family.

Standard IV. Nursing Diagnosis
The nurse uses health assessment data to determine nursing diagnoses.

Standard V. Planning and Continuity of Care
The nurse develops the plan of care in conjunction with the older person and appropriate others. Mutual goals, priorities, nursing approaches, and measures in the care plan address the therapeutic, preventive, restorative, and rehabilitative needs of the older person. The care plan helps the older person attain and maintain the highest level of health, well-being, and quality of life achievable, as well as a peaceful death. The plan of care facilitates continuity of care over time as the client moves to various care settings, and is revised as necessary.

Standard VI. Intervention
The nurse, guided by the plan of care, intervenes to provide care to restore the older person's functional capabilities and to prevent complications and excess disability. Nursing interventions are derived from nursing diagnoses and are based on gerontological nursing theory.

Standard VII. Evaluation
The nurse continually evaluates the client's and family's responses to interventions in order to determine progress toward goal attainment and to revise the data base, nursing diagnoses, and plan of care.

Standard VIII. Interdisciplinary Collaboration
The nurse collaborates with other members of the health care team in the various settings in which care is given to the older person. The team meets regularly to evaluate the effectiveness of the care plan for the client and family and to adjust the plan of care to accommodate changing needs.

Standard IX. Research
The nurse participates in research designed to generate an organized body of gerontological nursing knowledge, disseminates research findings, and uses them in practice.

Standard X. Ethics
The nurse uses the code for nurses established by the American Nurses' Association as a guide for ethical decision making in practice.

Exhibit 3-1 continued

Standard XI. Professional Development
The nurse assumes responsibility for professional development and contributes to the professional growth of interdisciplinary team members. The nurse participates in peer review and other means of evaluation to assure the quality of nursing practice.

Source: From *Standards and Scope of Gerontological Nursing Practice* by American Nurses' Association, Inc., 1987, Kansas City, MO: American Nurses' Association, Inc. Copyright 1987 by American Nurses' Association, Inc. Reprinted by permission.

Standards are identified in the areas of general administration, resident care, personnel management, financial management, marketing and community relations, physical resource management and safety, and government/regulations. Requisite knowledge and skill areas are defined for each standard. This information can guide administrators' learning experiences and help identify needed resources for successful practice.

ACHCA is committed to the development of facility standards for resident care. Standard II, "Resident Care," recommends development of standards by identifying factors known to affect care and those variables associated with each factor that can be adjusted and measured. The importance of obtaining adequate resources, planning, implementing services, and evaluating care are recognized.

Joint Commission on Accreditation of Healthcare Organizations

The Joint Commission on Accreditation of Healthcare Organizations (Joint Commission) provides assistance to health professionals committed to improving the quality of care. The Joint Commission's *Long Term Care Standards Manual* (Joint Commission on Accreditation of Healthcare Organizations, 1988a) defines standards and their associated required characteristics for a wide variety of nursing home functions and departments and for specific individuals such as the administrator, the medical director, and the director of nursing. Exhibit 3-3 lists the four 1988 quality assurance standards. The nursing care standards, one section of a variety of patient care standards, are found in Appendix C. The nursing standards focus on the presence of a sufficient number of nursing personnel to provide defined services and the incorporation of a rehabilitative/restorative nursing program into resident care. The Joint Commission emphasizes the role of a facility's governing body, such as its board of directors, in requiring and supporting quality assurance activities. Nursing homes seeking Joint Commission accreditation must have an ongoing, organization-wide quality assurance program. Quality monitoring and evaluation is required in at least the following areas: resident activities,

Exhibit 3-2 Standards of Practice for Long-Term Care Administrators

---

II. Resident Care

A. Ensures quality resident care through planning, implementation, and evaluation of nursing services to maintain maximum health potential; social services to meet psychological and social needs and rights; dietary services to meet nutritional requirements and needs; medical services to ensure appropriate medical care; activities to meet the social recreational and therapeutic recreational needs; medical records program to ensure continuity of care; pharmaceutical program to support appropriate medical care; and rehabilitation services that will maintain and/or maximize potential of residents; auxiliary services as necessary to enhance quality of life for residents; and environmental services to provide a pleasing environment.

B. Recruits, hires, and provides ongoing education for a health care team in order to assure quality care of the long-term care resident.

C. Obtains and coordinates consultant services as needed for total care (dental, speech and hearing, pharmacist, OT, PT, mental health, etc.) by matching needs of residents with services of consultants.

D. Coordinates the development and evaluation, with the health care team, of resident care goals and policies in order to assure that adequate resources, environments, and services are available to the residents.

E. Meets regularly with health care team to assure good care is being delivered.

F. Recruits a qualified medical director and develops a professional relationship with the medical director that ensures a well planned and implemented medical care program.

G. In cooperation with the medical director, maintains strong relationships with community medical practitioners including attending physicians and physician extenders.

H. Develops communication between facility staff and the residents in order to assure a caring environment with appropriate nursing and psychosocial services.

I. Develops facility standards for resident care by identifying those factors which affect care, as well as variables within each factor which can be adjusted and evaluated.

J. Develops program to assure staff adherence to Patient Bill of Rights.

Source: Reprinted from *Journal of Long-Term Care Administration*, Vol. 15, No. 1, Spring 1987, p. 11, American College of Health Care Administrators.

---

dietetic care, medical care, nursing care, oral health care, rehabilitation care, social services, and drug usage (Joint Commission on Accreditation of Healthcare Organizations, 1988a). Each discipline or department providing resident care is expected to identify those aspects of resident care that are most important to the quality and appropriateness of their service.

Exhibit 3-3 Quality Assurance

Standard

QA.1 There is an ongoing quality assurance program designed to objectively and systematically monitor and evaluate the quality and appropriateness of patient/resident care, pursue opportunities to improve patient/resident care, and resolve identified problems.

Required Characteristics

QA.1.1 The governing body strives to assure high-quality patient/resident care by requiring and supporting the establishment and maintenance of an effective organizationwide quality assurance program.

QA.1.2 Professional and administrative staffs monitor and evaluate the quality and appropriateness of patient/resident care and clinical performance, resolve identified problems, and report information to the governing body that the governing body needs to assist it in fulfilling its responsibility for the quality of patient/resident care.

QA.1.3 There is a written plan for the quality assurance program that describes the program's objectives, organization, scope, and mechanisms for overseeing the effectiveness of monitoring, evaluation, and problem-solving activities.

Standard

QA.2 The quality assurance program addresses all major patient/resident care activities.

Required Characteristics

QA.2.1 The quality and appropriateness of care are monitored and evaluated in at least the following clinical areas:

QA.2.1.1 Patient/resident activities;
QA.2.1.2 Dietetic care;
QA.2.1.3 Medical care;
QA.2.1.4 Nursing care, including rehabilitative/restorative nursing care;
QA.2.1.5 Oral health care;
QA.2.1.6 Rehabilitation care;
QA.2.1.7 Social services; and
QA.2.1.8 Drug usage.

Standard

QA.3 The quality assurance program is planned, systematic, ongoing, and focused on those aspects of patient/resident care most important to quality.

Required Characteristics

QA.3.1 The quality assurance program consists of the following components:

QA.3.1.1 Monitoring and evaluation of the quality and appropriateness of patient/resident care in the clinical areas identified in Required Characteristic QA.2.1.

Exhibit 3-3 continued

QA.3.1.2 Organizationwide review functions, including

QA.3.1.2.1 infection control; and

QA.3.1.2.2 the appropriateness of the long term care organization for the patient/resident.

QA.3.1.2.2.1 The review includes assessment of the appropriateness of patients'/residents'

QA.3.1.2.2.1.1 admission to the organization;

QA.3.1.2.2.1.2 continued stay in the organization; and

QA.3.1.2.2.1.3 discharge from the organization.

QA.3.1.2.2.2 If the review of the appropriateness of the organization for patients/residents uses a sample of patients/residents, all categories of patients/residents are represented in the sample, regardless of payment source.

QA.3.1.2.2.3 The methods used to review and evaluate the appropriateness of the organization for patients/residents include procedures and criteria required by applicable law or regulation.

QA.3.1.3 The evaluation of

QA.3.1.3.1 interdisciplinary planning of care;

QA.3.1.3.2 patient/resident care incidents;

QA.3.1.3.3 housekeeping and laundry activities;

QA.3.1.3.4 patient/resident and family comments, and

QA.3.1.3.5 findings from patient/resident and family/visitor councils relating to patient/resident care.

QA.3.2 The monitoring and evaluation of the quality and appropriateness of patient/resident care have the characteristics described in Required Characteristics QA.3.2.1 through QA.3.4.

QA.3.2.1 Each discipline, department, or service providing patient/resident care participates in the following:

QA.3.2.1.1 Identification of those aspects of patient/resident care that are most important to the quality and appropriateness of the care the discipline, department, or service provides.

QA.3.2.1.1.1 Identified important aspects of care focus on high-risk, high-volume, and/or problem-prone clinical activities of the discipline, department, or service.

QA.3.2.1.2 Identification of clinical indicators related to the quality and appropriateness of care for the important aspects of care the discipline, department, or service provides.

QA.3.2.1.3 For all clinical indicators, identification of the level of performance related to each clinical indicator that represents the threshold at which a more intensive evaluation of the quality and appropriateness of care is initiated.

Exhibit 3-3 continued

QA.3.2.2 Data concerning the clinical indicators are collected in an ongoing manner.

QA.3.2.2.1 The levels of performance represented by these data are compared with the preestablished threshold for evaluation related to each indicator.

QA.3.2.3 When the threshold for evaluation is reached, more extensive analysis and peer review is undertaken to identify problems in or opportunities to improve the quality and/or appropriateness of care.

QA.3.2.4 Identified problems in the quality of care are resolved through actions taken, as appropriate, by

QA.3.2.4.1 the organization's administrative staff; and/or

QA.3.2.4.2 clinical staff.

QA.3.2.5 In order to assure problem correction, continued monitoring and evaluation are performed using appropriate clinical indicators and related thresholds for evaluation.

QA.3.3 Relevant findings from quality assurance activities are considered during the renewal or revision of medical staff privileges, when applicable.

QA.3.4 The findings, conclusions, recommendations, actions taken, and results of actions taken are documented and reported through channels established by the organization.

Standard
QA.4 The administration of the organization's overall quality assurance program and the coordination of quality assurance activities are designed to assure that the activities described in Required Characteristics QA.4.1 through QA.4.5 are undertaken.

Required Characteristics
QA.4.1 Each of the monitoring and evaluation activities outlined in Standards QA.2 and QA.3 and their required characteristics is performed appropriately and effectively.

QA.4.2 Information is communicated among disciplines, departments, or services when problems or opportunities to improve patient/resident care involve more than one discipline, department, or service.

QA.4.3 The status of identified problems is tracked in order to assure improvement or resolution.

QA.4.4 Information from disciplines, departments, or services and the findings of discrete quality assurance activities are used to detect trends, patterns of performance, or potential problems that affect more than one discipline, department, or service.

Exhibit 3-3 continued

QA.4.5 The objectives, scope, organization, and effectiveness of the quality assurance program are evaluated at least annually and revised as necessary.

Source: Copyright 1988 by the Joint Commission on Accreditation of Healthcare Organizations, Chicago. Reprinted with permission.

External Agency Standards: Federal Government

The Medicare and Medicaid requirements for long-term care facilities have been published (Health Care Financing Administration [HCFA], 1989). Since licensing surveys will review the areas defined by the federal government, it is logical for individual departments and services to incorporate appropriate federal requirements into their quality monitoring and evaluation efforts. The federal government's requirements related to quality of care identify the following areas that can serve as a basis for the development of standards: activities of daily living, vision and hearing, pressure sores, urinary incontinence, range of motion, psychosocial functioning, nasogastric tubes, accidents, nutrition, hydration, special care needs such as parenteral fluids, colostomy care and tracheostomy care, drug therapy, and medication errors. Examples of standard statements that could be based on the requirements are:

- Residents receive care that promotes optimum functioning in activities of daily living.
- Residents receive treatment and assistive devices to maintain vision and hearing abilities.
- Pressure sores do not develop or worsen.
- Continence of residents is promoted.
- Residents' environment is as free of accident hazards as possible.
- Residents' psychosocial adjustment difficulties receive appropriate treatment.
- Residents are protected from adverse effects of drug therapy.

These standards imply that 100 percent of residents requiring care described by the standard should receive this care. When there is no scientific evidence for specification of the desired level of achievement of a standard for a given population of residents, specification is a value judgment (Block, 1977). Individual facilities need to identify criteria to measure achievement of a standard, when they plan to monitor quality; norms defined for the criteria are used to determine the appropriateness of care related to a specific standard.

Multiple departments are often responsible for a single standard. Accountability for quality of care is enhanced by having the responsibilities of various departments identified, such as the specific roles of dietary, nursing, and physician services in achieving a standard related to nutrition. The following might be defined as a standard related to nutrition: "Residents' need for nutrition and hydration is met." Departments engaging in quality monitoring might identify the staff activities, equipment, personnel, or care provided in their areas that are crucial to the attainment of this standard. Definition of indicators of good and poor performance by a department can also help define its specific roles. Thoughtful, thorough consideration of a department's resources, functions, and contributions to resident care outcomes related to achievement of a defined standard provides a basis for the development of measurable monitoring criteria for that standard.

Resident and Community Influences on Standards

Quality assurance standards in nursing homes are the product of many factors. Resident and community characteristics must be considered. The diagram in Figure 3-1 has components of a quality monitoring system for nursing homes and emphasizes the critical role of standards derived from a variety of sources. Roberts, LeSage, and Ellor (1987) suggest consideration of resident and community values, residents' level of care, quality of life issues, and resident rights and responsibilities.

Resident/Community Values

The values of consumers of nursing home services include beliefs that are esteemed or desirable. These beliefs might affect standards concerning life-sustaining measures, food preparation (e.g., kosher kitchen), the availability of specific religious services, the observation of holidays and holy days, or the availability of private versus shared rooms. Religious and ethnic groups can and should have a significant effect on nursing home operations. Many examples of residents' values have been detailed by the National Citizens' Coalition for Nursing Home Reform (1985): choices, security, privacy, caring staff, and community involvement in nursing homes.

Residents' Required Levels of Care

Residents' health problems, the amount of care required, and the type of care needed should be considered in the definition of standards. For example, nursing and activity departments may work with alert and ambulatory residents as well as with ill individuals who are mainly confined to their beds. It is possible for a standard to define quality care for a variety of residents;

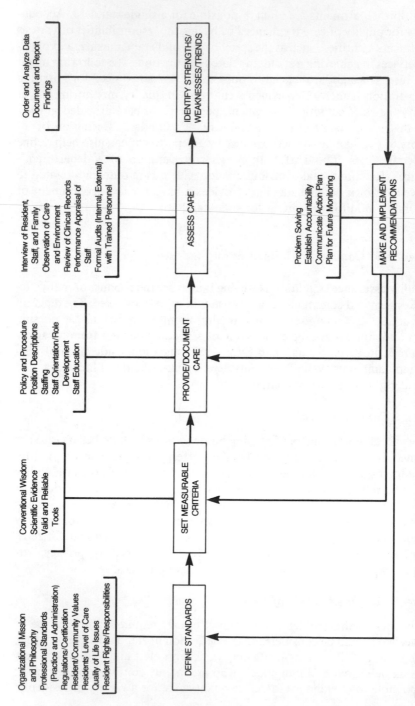

Figure 3-1 Components of a Quality Monitoring System. *Source:* From "Quality Monitoring in Nursing Homes" by K. Roberts, J. LeSage and J. Ellor, 1987, *Journal of Gerontological Nursing, 13,* p. 35. Copyright 1987 by Charles B. Slack, Inc. Reprinted by permission.

specificity can be achieved by monitoring criteria. When standards or monitoring criteria are tailored to a specific level of care, "not applicable" and "information not available" responses are minimized. This individualized approach recognizes that some groups of residents have special needs. For example, nursing home departments could develop additional standards for a population of short-term stay residents that would be different from those defined for residents who have selected a nursing home for their permanent residence.

Quality of Life Issues

The Institute of Medicine (IOM) report (1986) recommends that a new condition of participation concerning quality of life be added to certification regulations. The IOM (p. 83) suggestions for quality of life standards include statements related to the provision of a homelike environment; opportunities for residents to have choice concerning surroundings, activities, and health care; treatment with dignity and respect; and opportunities to interact with members of the community both outside and inside the home. New HCFA regulations (1989, pp. 5364–5365) include provisions for quality of life and incorporate IOM recommendations or cover their suggestions in the resident rights requirements. Requirements for activities and social services are also defined by HCFA; homes with more than 120 beds will need a full-time social worker.

Resident Rights and Responsibilities

The IOM report (1986) recommends that residents' rights be made into a condition of participation and that new residents' rights standards be added. Standards for residents' rights have been suggested in the following areas: exercise of rights as a citizen and resident of the facility; being informed about one's rights, medical condition, treatment plan, and ability to refuse treatment; management of own financial affairs; freedom from unnecessary chemical and physical restraints; freedom from abuse; assurance of privacy and confidentiality; access to telephone and mail services; ability to retain personal possessions and clothing; prior notice of transfer and discharge; participation on resident and family councils; and participation in social, religious, and political activities (IOM, 1986, pp. 27–29; HCFA, 1987, pp. 38597–38598). Comments on the 1987 HCFA proposed rules have been published (HCFA, 1989, pp. 5318–5327) and resident rights requirements defined (HCFA, 1989, pp. 5360–5362). Standards related to resident responsibilities could focus on resident knowledge of such information as facility rules, policies, charges for services, smoking restrictions, visiting hours, and participation in goal setting and evaluation related to one's care. Evaluation of staff communication of residents' rights and responsibilities is especially important.

ESTABLISH MEASURABLE CRITERIA

The terms "standard" and "criteria" are often used interchangeably (Block, 1977). A standard is an agreed-upon or desired level of performance, usually developed by professionals. Criteria, on the other hand, are the stated measurable elements of care against which actual health services may be compared (Joint Commission on Accreditation of Hospitals, 1986, p.14). Both standards and criteria can be applied to measure the structure, process, and/or outcomes of care provided to nursing home residents. The Joint Commission (Joint Commission on Accreditation of Healthcare Organizations, 1987) identifies another term, "indicator," as "a defined, measurable dimension of the quality or appropriateness of an important aspect of patient care" (p. 4). It can represent either high- or low-quality care (JCAH, 1986, p. 14). They usually are not standards, but indicators of the desired process of care may also be standards of care. A standard defining care related to nutrition might have a negative indicator of dehydration and a positive indicator of ideal body weight. Indicators can be used in the absence of standards to begin quality monitoring and evaluation; they must be measurable, guiding nursing home staff in the definition of criteria for monitoring. Indicators can describe factors such as resource utilization, complications of treatment, resident outcomes, staff activities, and family satisfaction (JCAH, 1986, p. 14).

Defining Criteria

Criteria are measurable and reflect the intent of a standard or indicator with regard to an important aspect of care. A standard can lead to the generation of any number of criteria; these criteria can measure factors related to the structure, processes, or outcomes of care. Staff planning a quality monitoring program must decide if only one type of criteria, such as process criteria, will be defined for monitoring a standard. The following are examples of four monitoring criteria defined for a standard, "The need for physical hygiene is attended to" (Rush-Presbyterian-St. Luke's Medical Center, Rush University College of Nursing, [RPSLMC, RUCN], 1986): (1) Are the resident's hands washed after using the bathroom or bedpan? (2) Is bathing equipment available? (3) Is adequate equipment for oral hygiene available? (4) Is the resident wearing appropriate, clean clothes?

Often it is not easy for a nursing home department to identify measurable criteria to determine if a defined standard of care has been achieved. It is important, however, that personnel defining criteria agree upon the individual criterion measures that will be used to determine the quality of services they provide. Because we do not always have research (scientific evidence) to prove linkages between the activities or interventions of nursing home staff and the achievement of standards, staff may need to derive criteria from department policy and procedure, common activities in their areas, and usual staff behaviors that might be found in position descriptions. Specific criteria for people requiring different levels of care can be developed.

Nursing home staff should not be discouraged from monitoring efforts because of the lack of available scientific evidence for the definition of criteria. Their defined criteria might provide the basis for a future research study. It is important that monitoring criteria have the support of the department members. When staff define criteria in their area of expertise, they can function similarly to a panel of experts, assuring that the monitoring criteria have content validity. A department should also be concerned that the monitoring criteria are reliable. After reading criteria, will two people looking at the same situation or listening to the same information respond in the same way? Wording needs to be clear so that an individual conducting quality monitoring can be objective, not subjective, in deciding the correct response for an item.

A criterion measure to determine the presence or absence of adequate equipment for oral hygiene, for example, should have written cues for the person collecting data so that there can be an objective determination of the availability of the required equipment. The definition of necessary equipment might include toothbrush or swab, toothpaste, and, if indicated, mouthwash or other solution and a denture cup. Futhermore, written cues accompanying the monitoring criteria should identify acceptable sources of information so that the person surveying will know if data must be obtained by observation of the presence or absence of equipment, by interview of a resident, or from either source. To secure a reliable interview response for a criterion measure, the exact question to ask a resident must be defined. This might be "In the past two days, when you wanted to brush your teeth (or care for your dentures), did you have the necessary toothbrush, toothpaste, gargle, etc.?" (RPSLMC, RUCN, 1986).

Information Sources for Criteria Development

After a standard has been defined, the members of a nursing home department who are developing a quality monitoring tool that measures process must identify what it is that they do or do not do while providing care that leads to achievement of the defined standard. Group identification of indicators of either high- or low-quality care for a standard might help delineate appropriate content for measurable criteria related to outcomes. Criteria that state measurable elements known to be scientifically linked to the achievement of a standard are the most desirable. Textbooks describing professional practice in the areas of nursing, medicine, pharmacology, and nutrition can assist in defining statements or monitoring questions against which actual practice occurrences can be compared. In the absence of scientific evidence for the type of care that predictably produces the attainment of a standard, staff can define criteria that they believe are highly related to standard achievement.

Rather than "reinventing the wheel," nursing home staff might look at available references containing suggestions for pertinent, measurable elements of care. When planning quality monitoring for the evaluation of nursing service in the Rush-Hines Veterans Administration (VA) Teaching Nursing Home Program (TNHP), the project's nursing leadership decided to adapt criteria from the Rush-Medicus instrument *A Methodology for Monitoring Quality of Nursing Care*, which is known to be valid and reliable in hospital settings (Jelinek, Haussmann, Hegyvary, & Newman, 1974). Also, a study by Mech (1980) was reviewed that assessed nursing care with a modified form of the Quality Patient Care Scale (Qualpacs) developed by Wandelt and Ager (1974). A wide variety of information on nursing home care is published in books and manuals. Woodson, Foley, Daniels, Landes, & Kurowski (1981) have identified recommended multidisciplinary services for common health problems of nursing home residents and suggest the appropriate care provider as well as the frequency of the service. Sometimes professional standards of practice have discussion sections following standard definitions, which may suggest appropriate criteria to measure performance.

The American Association of Homes for the Aging (AAHA) has published a workbook, *Quality of Life Assessment*, that can serve as a resource for the development of either monitoring criteria or a quality measurement instrument (American Association of Homes for the Aging [AAHA], 1983). The questionnaire format allows residents to express personal preferences and subjective assessments of the quality of their lives in a nursing home. A facility utilizing the tool will be able to determine residents' values as well as their perceptions of the home's environment. Questions are grouped into three theoretical dimensions of quality living: security, autonomy, and interpersonal relations (AAHA, 1983). Each dimension is further subdivided into four related concepts. The security section has questions regarding safety, physical comfort, structure/routine, and services. Investigation of autonomy issues explores individuality, physical independence, activities, and control. The interpersonal relations dimension focuses on privacy/respect, friendship, staff relations, and expression. Information gathered voluntarily from residents can help governing boards, managers, and staff to create a nursing home environment that enhances resident satisfaction. The workbook gives instructions for scoring.

Although *Quality of Life Assessment* was developed for residents, a facility may wish to ask staff the same questions in order to determine if there is congruence between staff and resident values and perceptions (AAHA,

1983). Since responses to the questions do not have established norms, departments or committees utilizing the tool for monitoring will have to make facility-specific judgments concerning the acceptability of the frequency distribution of responses and the correlations identified between expressed values and perceptions of quality of life.

A self-appraisal guide for long-term care facilities, *Quest for Quality*, contains ideas for criteria that can be used to monitor a wide variety of services and programs offered by nursing homes (American Health Care Association [AHCA], 1985). Areas such as the activity program, community involvement, housekeeping and maintenance, pharmacy services, and the volunteer program have monitoring plans defined, often including the definition of responsible staff, desired outcomes, and a description of evaluation procedures. Exhibits 3-4, 3-5, 3-6, and 3-7 reproduce four self-appraisal forms from *Quest for Quality*.

Additional examples of indicators and criteria for monitoring services delivered in nursing homes are found in the Joint Commission publication *Quality Assurance in Long Term Care* (Joint Commission on Accreditation of Hospitals, 1986). Specialized manuals focusing on a single nursing home service can guide in-depth evaluation. Comprehensive reviews of resident council programs (AAHA, 1982) and pharmacy services (Beverly Foundation, 1987) are available. Facilities planning to expand their self-monitoring efforts might purchase a variety of reference books. Inquiries to professional practice associations and national long-term care organizations concerning the availability of useful publications for quality assurance programs will result in lists of publications from which desired items can be selected.

Residents' perspectives of quality of care in nursing homes, which can be utilized to identify monitoring criteria, are presented in a detailed report published by the National Citizens' Coalition for Nursing Home Reform [NCCNHR] (1985). Viewpoints were obtained from group interviews with over 400 nursing home residents. Specific resident responses and their frequencies are presented for questions such as (NCCNHR, 1985), "What does "good staff" mean to you (p. 21)?" "What would make food service good in a nursing home (p. 29)?" "What kinds of activities would you like to participate in (pp. 33–34)?" "What are the kinds of choices you should be able to make (pp. 39–41)?" "What would be the ideal system for solving problems within the home (pp. 47–52)?" What would you tell inspectors to look for to know if good quality care is being provided (pp. 61–62)?" "What other factors contribute to the quality of life in your nursing home (pp. 56–57)?" "What can families do to bring about good quality care in nursing homes (p. 69)?" In addition to obtaining ideas for monitoring criteria, this book can serve as a guide for developing standards, for program planning, and for action plans to remedy deficiencies identified by facility self-monitoring programs. Resident Council members might join with staff in using ideas from this publica-

Exhibit 3-4 Activity Program Form B: Patient Activity Level

Directions: Walk through the facility and observe what patients are doing. Put a mark in the column that best describes each patient's activity. Schedule this evaluation during a time when you might expect moderate activity; avoid time when morning care is being given, meals are being served or a major activity is taking place.

Date:

Patient Activity	Tally of Patients	Comments
Reading		
Watching TV in own room		
Watching TV in group room		
Talking with staff		
Talking with other patient(s)		
Talking with visitor		
Listening to radio		
Part of organized activity		
Writing		
Needlework or craft		
Wandering		
Sleeping		
No apparent activity		

Was there sufficient staff present for each activity? _____
Do most activities fall into a few categories? _____
Were certain categories never observed? _____
Do most residents appear interested? _____

Problems identified: _____

_____

Possible reasons for problems: _____

_____

Goals: _____

_____

Action plans: _____

_____

Completed by: _____

Exhibit 3-5 Community Involvement Form A: Community Relations Activities

Directions: For each item listed, determine, if applicable, whether it occurred within the past year.

Date:

Community Relations Activities	Yes	No	Comments
Facility has contact (name) at local: Newspapers			
Radio stations			
TV Stations			
Cable TV service			
Facility has newsletter			
Newsletter circulated to: Patients, staff, families of patients, banks, churches, businesses, physicians, hospitals, schools of nursing, fraternal organizations, state legislators (Senators and Representatives), federal legislators (U.S. Senators and members of U.S. House of Representatives), social service offices, state and local agencies on aging, ombudsmen, consumer advocacy groups, consumer advocates, regulatory and rate-setting bodies, grade school principals, higher education deans, pharmacists, your suppliers, newspaper, TV and radio consumer reporters and feature editors, Mayor, City Council or equivalent			
Facility open house held			
National Nursing Home Week observed			
Rock 'n Roll Jamboree observed			
Grandparents' Day observed			
Summerfest held			
Crafts fair held			
"Family Dinners" or other family activity held			
Patients surveyed on likes and dislikes			
Family surveyed on likes and dislikes			
Administrator active in at least one civic, service or aging organization			

Exhibit 3-5 continued

Personal visit to each referring hospital by director of nursing, social worker or administrator			
"Letter to the editor" sent by head of resident council inviting community to various activities			
Advance news advisories about significant patient events (100th birthdays, 50th wedding anniversaries, marriages, etc.) sent to newspapers			
Advance advisories sent to radio and/or TV			
Staff and/or administrator have exchanged visits with at least two community organizations in last six months			
One activity per week is held outside of facility (in the community)			
Candidates for public office were invited to visit facility; follow-ups made with candidates' staffs			
Incumbent politicians invited; staff follow-ups made			
Facility participates in health career fairs; appear before school groups			
Receptionist and unit clerks are trained in and evaluated for telephone courtesy			
Community relations is a permanent budget item			
Facility maintains and displays scrapbook			
Facility has volunteer recognition program			
Facility has staff recognition program			
Facility involved with community service projects, such as sponsoring health fairs and teaching home care			
Voter registration drive conducted for residents; facility used as polling place			
Community members involved in Quest for Quality			

Problems identified: _____

_____

_____

Possible reasons for problems: _____

_____

_____

Exhibit 3-5 continued

Goals: _____

_____

_____

Action plans: _____

_____

_____

Completed by: _____

Source: From *Quest for Quality* (pp. 39–41) by American Health Care Association, 1985, Washington, D.C.: American Health Care Association. Copyright 1985 by American Health Care Association. Reprinted by permission.

tion to develop a resident satisfaction survey. Incorporation of residents' viewpoints adds to the validity of criteria selected for monitoring resident satisfaction.

Ensuring Objective and Reliable Criteria

Staff will not agree that information gained from quality monitoring is relevant unless they believe that monitoring results are reliable and objective. If special technical or clinical judgment is required to determine the correct response to monitoring criteria, then a person with the appropriate background must be involved in data collection. While this can add to the cost of a quality assurance program, the organization benefits from having reliable monitoring results.

The following are examples of process criteria that might appear on monitoring tools developed by the interdisciplinary quality assurance committee or by individual departments (RPSLMC, RUCN, 1986).

- Are resident's elimination patterns recorded upon admission to this unit? (no, yes)
- Is there a written statement with regard to the family's level of understanding, concerns, or view of the resident's condition? (no, yes, NA)
- Are nursing personnel accessible to resident during meals? (no; yes, some of the time; yes, most of the time; yes, all of the time; information not available; NA)
- Do nursing staff members and therapists introduce themselves to the resident? (no; yes, some of the time; yes, most of the time; yes, all of the time; information not available)

Some questions are best answered by yes, no, "not applicable" (NA), or "information not available." Others require a determination of frequency of per-

Exhibit 3-6 Housekeeping and Maintenance Form A: Housekeeping and Maintenance Audit

Directions: Make a walk-through inspection of the facility and note the condition
and cleanliness of all areas. Include items such as call lights, blinds
or drapes, windows, doors, lights, walls and the problem of odors.
Note specific problems, such as hinge missing, dirty, need replacement, water dripping, etc.

Date:

Facility Areas	Description of Problem
Patient rooms (include toilet room and closet)	
#	
#	
#	
#	
#	
#	
#	
#	
#	
#	
#	
#	
#	
#	
#	
#	
#	
#	
#	
#	
#	
#	
#	
#	
#	
#	
Patient bathrooms	

Exhibit 3-6 continued

Facility Areas	Description of Problem
Classroom	
Conference room	
Kitchen	
Dining room	
Patient lounge areas	
Laundry	
Chapel	
Switchboard area	
Lobby reception area	
Elevators	
Stairwells	
Public women's rooms	
Public men's rooms	
Employee lounges	
Examining rooms	
Utility rooms	
Nurses' stations	
Offices	
Activity room	
Corridors	
Closets and storage areas	
Other areas	

Problems identified: _____

Possible reasons for problems: _____

Goals: _____

Action plans: _____

Completed by: _____

Source: From *Quest for Quality* (pp. 81–82) by American Health Care Association, 1985, Washington, D.C.: American Health Care Association. Copyright 1985 by American Health Care Association. Reprinted by permission.

Exhibit 3-7 Laundry Service Complaint Form

Directions: Record all complaints made regarding laundry service by keeping an on-going record or by surveying staff members, patients and families.

Type of Problem	Week or Month			
Not enough clean linen on day shift				
Not enough clean linen on evening shift				
Not enough clean linen on night shift				
Not enough clean linen on weekends				
Not enough pillows				
Not enough blankets				
Lost personal clothing				
Damaged personal clothing				
Linen in poor repair				
Other				

Problems identified: _____

_____

Possible reasons for problems: _____

_____

Goals: _____

_____

Action plans: _____

_____

Completed by: _____

Source: From *Quest for Quality* (p. 103) by American Health Care Association, 1985, Washington, D.C.: American Health Care Association. Copyright 1985 by American Health Care Association. Reprinted by permission.

formance by nursing home staff. People engaged in monitoring need clear directions to correctly select among survey response options. Decisions may need to be made concerning how much, how many, by whom, from whom, when, where, and the acceptable time span for observation of whether defined criteria have been met. Instructions that answer these questions can be placed in the introduction to a monitoring tool or at the beginning of sections of the tool containing similar criteria. Likewise, they can be printed right in the tool along with individual criteria. Methods are combined in a situation where there are general introductory statements alerting the data collector that record reviews should include the past 30 days unless otherwise indicated in the written cues for a specific criterion. The following are examples of criteria with accompanying monitoring cues (RPSLMC, RUCN, 1986):

- Are resident's elimination patterns recorded upon admission to this unit? ("Patterns" refers to information about regularity/irregularity of bowel and bladder function. Statement of just "constipation" or "diarrhea" is not acceptable. *Code yes* only if information is present and is recorded *within three days* of admission.)
- Is there a written statement with regard to the family's level of understanding, concerns, or view of the resident's condition? (May be recorded by any member of health care team *within three days* of admission. Look for documentation in the care record or Kardex. *Code NA* if the resident has no family or significant other.)
- Are nursing personnel accessible to resident during meals? (To resident: In the past two days, have you needed or requested some help with your meal tray? If no, *code NA*. If yes, ask: "When you needed some help, did someone from the nursing staff assist you within a reasonable amount of time?")
- Do nursing staff members and therapists introduce themselves to the residents? (To resident: "Do new members of the nursing and therapy staffs introduce themselves to you?"
- Has waste been removed from the resident's room? (Check for emptied trash cans and for clutter in room. Does not apply to items left in resident's bed. Trash cans should be sufficiently empty to allow for likely accumulation of trash until next tour by housekeeping personnel.)

Frequencies associated with response choices other than "yes" or "no" should be defined for an entire instrument rather than changing for different monitoring criteria. Words like "most," "some," and "frequently" may represent different amounts to different people. (This is why yes/no responses are best.) "Some of the time" might be at least 50 percent of the time and "most" might mean at least 75 percent of the time. Anything less than a 50 percent occurrence using the prior definition of "some of the time" would be a "no" response. It is obvious that written cues to make monitoring observations more objective and reliable can still leave room for individual interpretation.

Lack of agreement concerning the meaning of various terms, such as "medical treatment" and "nursing interventions," affects reliability. A glossary of defined words may be necessary. Nursing clinical judgment is important to determine a correct response to criteria such as the following (RPSLMC, RUCN, 1986):

- Are side rails up, if the condition of the resident warrants?
- Are the goals of care current?
- Is there a plan for the maintenance of function and comfort of the resident who will not achieve a higher level of functioning?

Concurrent monitoring with two nurses to determine interrater reliability can help identify items with poor reliability. The pair can review charts (can be done separately on same shift for process audits), conduct interviews (only one person asks questions, but both listen to responses), and make observations together. Each would mark his or her own score sheet. Their results would be compared afterward and differences of opinion discussed. An agreement rate of 85 percent for items on a monitoring tool is desirable; this was the goal for Rush-Hines VA TNHP quality monitoring (Hewitt, LeSage, Roberts, & Ellor, 1985).

PLANNING THE QUALITY ASSURANCE PROGRAM

An organization's mission and philosophy guide the development of a written quality assurance plan. A clear definition of purpose and of the planned, achievable outcomes of quality monitoring, as well as methods to evaluate effectiveness, will help to educate staff, residents, and families about a facility's quality assurance program.

Authority has to be delegated to the appropriate committees and department heads in order to achieve the program's purpose. An individual facility should establish quality assurance plans and processes for monitoring based on its program purpose and facility resources. Responsibility for each component of the quality assurance process is essential. (Chapter 1 presented suggestions for the roles and responsibilities of managers, committees, and staff.) There must be clear identification of who will develop standards, indicators, criteria, and norms. Equally important is the designation of persons empowered to implement action plans resulting from monitoring. Busy staff must recognize that they will have secretarial support, mechanisms for the communication of quality assurance activities and findings, meeting time to develop corrective action plans for weaknesses, and extra staff for data collection if currently budgeted positions are inadequate to achieve defined program activities.

Small nursing homes might seek assistance from local hospital personnel when planning formal self-monitoring activities. The consultation is likely to be free, because many hospitals are strengthening their linkages with nursing homes. Maybe gratis faculty time from a nearby college could be obtained in exchange for use of the nursing home as a clinical site (Roberts, LeSage, Ellor, 1987). Students can include quality monitoring in their clinical experiences, especially those seeking advanced degrees.

The following sections are based on questions that must be considered in establishing monitoring and evaluation processes.

What Are the Program's Purpose and Goals?

The purpose should be a brief statement concerning the identification, implementation, and ongoing revision of a comprehensive, effective quality assurance program that is integrated with the organization's structure and functions. Next, there should be descriptors of the type of care that the quality assurance program will assure, such as safe, highest quality, excellent, efficient, within available resources, or consistent with achievable goals of the organization. Striving for excellence may not be viewed as realistic due to a facility's financial constraints.

The program goals should provide further definition of the purpose. Examples of information that could be included in goals are

- implementation of an objective resident care evaluation process
- involvement of all levels of staff within their areas of expertise
- facilitation of communication between departments, services, and committees, to enhance resident care
- implementation of action plans to correct deficiencies that are based on a prioritization of problems in relation to their potential for adverse impact upon resident care and the well-being of residents, visitors, and employees
- establishment of an evaluation process that uses objective criteria, provides recommendations to eliminate or minimize the occurrence of identified problems, and allows for follow-up and reassessment
- provision of assistance to individual departments in defining their scope of care and in maintaining ongoing quality monitoring activities
- maintenance of a central interdisciplinary quality assurance committee to promote coordinated, multidepartmental information and problem review,

problem prioritization and solution initiation, and participation by clinical, administrative, and ancillary staff in the quality assurance process

- reduction, where possible, in duplication of effort with regard to quality assurance activities and utilization of existing staff/resources in conducting program activities

Who Is Responsible for the Different Components of Quality Monitoring and Evaluation?

Figure 3-1 identifies six components of quality monitoring and evaluation: definition of standards; development of measurable criteria; provision and documentation of care; assessment of care; identification of strengths, weaknesses, and trends; and formation of an action plan and implementation of recommendations (Roberts, LeSage, & Ellor, 1987). Directional arrows emphasize that the process is conducted in an ongoing manner. Department heads should have responsibility for quality assurance activities. Delegation of quality monitoring and evaluation functions by department heads to committees or staff does not mean delegation of accountability. All departments or services providing resident care, as well as the administrative and ancillary support of that care, need to be involved. (Chapter 1 identified examples of the authority, responsibility, and scope of activities for different personnel and committees who may be designated to participate in quality assurance.) Nursing home staff who have not initiated self-monitoring are already spending a great deal of effort on one important component, provision and documentation of care. Commitment of resources to the other components of quality monitoring and evaluation enhances a facility's ability to provide quality care.

For best results, the departments, services, and committees involved in quality assurance activities should develop written plans defining their responsibilities and scope of activities. Department heads need to indicate how they will identify, resolve, and monitor problems. Within their areas of authority, department heads are responsible for modifying the delivery of services in conformance with recommendations for changes that emerge through evaluation mechanisms. Such changes need to be coordinated with other affected departments and personnel prior to implementation. Appropriate records of quality assurance activities, findings, recommendations, and methods of follow-up need to be maintained.

What Are the Implementation Procedures for the Quality Assurance Plans?

Although staff at a nursing home may be able to describe the kind of quality assurance program they would like for their facility, implementation can be delayed again and again, waiting for a time when people are not so busy or when all leadership positions are filled. The actual initiation of quality assurance activities requires a great deal of information sharing. Communication of the plan through the education of managers and staff is essential. Authority and reporting relationships must be clear. An interdisciplinary quality assurance committee should be established, if this group has not already been formed during the early stages of planning. Each department, service, or committee involved in quality monitoring needs to have the appropriate authority's approval of their general plan, indicating how they will identify, resolve, and monitor problems. Since extra personnel or expenses may need to be budgeted, an identification of required resources should be completed early. A tracking system of labor and expenses might be established to validate the accuracy of expense estimates. This information can be used to justify future budgeted items.

Self-monitoring might start with each of the involved areas defining a minimum of one or two indicators of high- or low-quality of services provided by their area (JCAH, 1986). An alternative would be developing department-specific standards or defining monitoring criteria based on a facility-wide multidisciplinary standard identified by the interdisciplinary quality assurance committee. The more comfortable people are with expectations for self-monitoring, the more likely the initial experience will be a positive one and encourage support of an ongoing program. The interdisciplinary quality assurance committee might want to develop forms for recording and reporting monitoring and evaluation activities so that there can be some uniformity in reporting and an early trial of the ability of these forms to communicate quality assurance activities. Exhibit 3-8 is an example of a quality assurance reporting form. Use of legal-size paper for this information would allow more room for description of monitoring activities.

Focusing on important aspects of care or services might lead to the selection of items for initial self-monitoring activities that are already being reviewed in some manner. There may be current or past written reports that might be helpful in determining how monitoring should be conducted, when, by whom, and how often. Meetings for discussing the monitoring process, reporting monitoring results, and reviewing the success of action plans are essential. Initially, it may be best to incorporate these discussions into meetings that are already being conducted.

The chief administrative officer must be prepared to support department heads in initiating changes recommended by quality monitoring that will require resources or system changes beyond the scope of responsibility of the areas conducting the initial monitoring. If staff perceive that reasonable efforts are not taken to support defined action plans, it will dampen their enthusiasm for self-monitoring activities. Managers and staff need a clear vision of how quality monitoring results are used to improve the quality of care or

Exhibit 3-8 Example of a Quality Assurance Monitoring and Evaluation Report

Quality Assurance Monitoring and Evaluation Report

Page _____ of _____

Date ____ / ____ / ____

Department/Service _____

Reporting Period _____ to _____

Signature _____ Date _____

Date	Standard/Indicator	Assessment Findings	Action Plan	Follow-Up Who/What/When/Results	Next Review Date	Date Solved

services. Staff also need feedback on their efforts to correct deficiencies identified through monitoring. If there are no plans for remonitoring on at least an annual basis, the effectiveness of action plans may be difficult to evaluate. Changes in staff, the resident population, or the organization of services beyond the control of a department may lead staff to decide that a certain action plan is no longer the best one to produce the desired results. A more detailed discussion of implementing a quality assurance program is presented in the next chapter.

What Will Be Monitored?

The purpose and goals of the quality assurance program should provide a framework for the topics selected for monitoring. The implications of a program's audit focus on structure, process, or outcome were presented in Chapter 2. The activities monitored should be those with the greatest effect on resident care. The Joint Commission (Joint Commission on Accreditation of Healthcare Organizations, 1988b, p. 2) notes that when identifying important aspects of care, staff should select activities that are high volume (occur frequently) and high risk (produce serious consequences) and that have caused past problems for residents or staff. Monitoring does not necessarily have to be problem focused. The Joint Commission has published samples of indicators to consider for monitoring several services provided by nursing homes (Joint Commission on Accreditation of Hospitals, 1986, pp. 30–37). The following are examples of potential indicators and thresholds (variable among settings) to trigger more intensive monitoring:

- pressure sores develop (stage 2 or greater)/worsen
  threshold: 0%
- fracture/hospitalization develops from falls
  threshold: 5% of falls (stage 2 or greater)
- aspiration pneumonia
  threshold: 0%
- undesired or unexpected weight gain/loss greater than 5 pounds/month
  threshold: 0%
- hospitalization for dehydration
  threshold: 0%
- medication errors
  threshold: 5% of doses dispensed
- physician visit not completed at required interval
  threshold: 0%

- emergency room use without hospitalization
  threshold: 20%
- restraint use
  threshold: 15% of residents
- no written plan for bladder training/keeping resident dry for individuals
  with urinary incontinence
  threshold: 10%
- no documentation of daily exercises for residents requiring assistance
  with ambulation
  threshold: 10%
- residents receiving both laxatives and antidiarrheal medications within
  72-hour period
  threshold: 0%
- residents receiving greater than 5 regularly scheduled medications per day
  threshold: 0%
- hours of nursing care per resident day are below 3.2
  threshold: 0%

These are negative indicators; but indicators can also be stated in a positive manner, describing dimensions of good care. Some of these dimensions of resident care might be considered as just part of the criteria for indicators of a higher conceptual level: malnutrition, infection, self-care level, hospitalization, and medication therapy. The format of the above statements, however, makes them more readily usable by readers. Standard development is appropriate for an indicator or groups of indicators (i.e., residents are protected from adverse effects of drug therapy). Nevertheless, monitoring and evaluation with indicators do not require prior definition of a standard.

Topics chosen for monitoring must consider and blend the viewpoints of nursing home administration, caregivers, and consumers. Wilbert (1985) notes that harmony must be sought among

- the administrative need for input in regard to program evaluation, staff
  productivity, or resource allocation
- the professional need for data on which to base practice decisions and
  articulate the domain of practice
- the consumer demand for timely, appropriate care that preserves dignity and independence in addition to being scientifically correct (p. 124)

The importance of the initial self-monitoring experience being a positive one has already been identified. Staff must view the topics selected for monitoring and the criteria that are developed as relevant to their work. Professional standards, when available, can be especially useful in developing department standards. The definition of standards or indicators, the development of measurable criteria, and the monitoring process should not be so complex or lengthy that staff become discouraged, believing that data will not be useful if they take a long time to collect and evaluate. A department's first monitoring efforts might survey areas noted as problematic by external regulatory agencies, or activities highlighted by residents' or families' complaints. If it is important to get the process under way quickly, it may be best to identify indicators of quality rather than to wait until standards have been defined and agreed upon. Utilizing a monitoring tool from *Quest for Quality* (AHCA, 1985) may help get things started. New indicators and criteria are not required for each monitoring period. Staff need to remember that monitoring criteria should be reused on a periodic basis to track strengths, weaknesses, and trends in care provided.

Focused monitoring can be used, instead of, or, more likely, in addition to, periodic monitoring with a defined set of standards/indicators or criteria. Whereas some monitoring tools must be used in their entirety to gain appropriate information about care provided, other instruments have a section that can be utilized by itself to gain desired information, especially when its area of focus covers the majority of problems identified by a prior quality monitoring. For example, the admission questions from the nursing quality monitoring tool (RPSLMC, RUCN, 1986, Appendix D, sections 1.1, 1.2, and 3.1) can be used separately for extra audits of the admission process. These additional quality checks should not replace regular, comprehensive monitoring if review of the entire care process is desired.

The Activity Program Form that evaluates resident activity level (AHCA, 1985), Exhibit 3-4, is an example of an instrument in which the data collected may not lead to a decision about the appropriateness of care without additional data collection and defined norms. These data could be collected for the following standard: "Residents have opportunities to participate in a variety of activities." The four questions following the form's activity tally ask about appropriateness of staffing, type and variety of activities, and resident interest. To have objective and reliable answers for the questions, a set of cues needs to be developed for a "yes" response.

Once activity department members' attention is directed toward potential problem areas identified by a monitoring instrument, more intensive audits can be conducted if necessary. To validate the areas of the activity program that might be in need of change, it would be best to repeat the activity level monitoring at specified times on randomly selected days over a period of one month. This provides information from several observations. Activity staff would need to decide at what point (defined norm or threshold) more intensive monitoring of a specific activity or unit is needed. A decision must be made about the acceptable percentage of residents who are noted in the "wandering," "sleeping," and "no apparent activity" categories. These percents might vary from unit to unit. Acceptable levels could even change from one monitoring period to another, depending upon the health problems and functional ability of residents living in the facility.

The Joint Commission (Joint Commission on Accreditation of Healthcare Organizations, 1988b, p. 3) suggests that staff set a "threshold" at levels from 0 percent to 100 percent so that department members will be aware when quality assurance data should trigger more intensive monitoring or development of a corrective action plan. Clinical indicators are used properly when they help to identify areas that need in-depth scrutiny. The more intense monitoring process will focus on standards, indicators, or criteria for which thresholds have not been achieved (below desired level of performance) or have been exceeded (safety parameters). Definition of thresholds allows busy staff to focus detailed quality monitoring efforts in areas where there are true opportunities to improve resident services. The threshold for some occurrences that have especially serious consequences for residents should be set at 0 percent. This would require special review of all cases found. An example would be facility fires or aspiration pneumonia; all occurrences receive intensive evaluation. Unsatisfactory outcome measures are likely to lead to in-depth monitoring of the care process.

When department staff determine what will be monitored, it is important for them to select standards or indicators for monitoring that are related to care or organizational structure, processes, or outcomes that the department can control. This facilitates implementation of a successful action plan. However, many aspects of care in nursing homes are interdisciplinary in nature. Take the example of the need to monitor falls and drug usage, both important because of resident risks associated with problems in these areas. If a single department, rather than the interdisciplinary quality assurance committee, undertakes monitoring of falls and drug usage, department staff need to realize that they are likely to need the cooperation and collaboration of additional departments in order to define monitoring criteria or to implement an action plan for identified problems. Beginning department quality assurance activities with monitoring items that are within the control of department staff may facilitate staff commitment to participate in self-monitoring activities. Positive changes in care will reinforce the benefit of the quality assurance program.

The Rush-Hines VA Teaching Nursing Home Program utilized a nursing quality monitoring tool adapted from the Rush-Medicus hospital tool (Jelinek et al., 1974). Exhibit 3-9 presents the structure of this process monitoring tool's objectives and subobjectives. Appendix D identifies criteria developed for each of the subobjectives, which may serve as standards. Objectives 1.0 through 4.0 are related to planning, implementation, and evaluation of standards for nursing practice. Objective 5.0 focuses on high risk areas—infection, emergencies, medical-legal procedures, and safety. Criteria developed for Objective 6.0 are often related to activities that nursing does not control, but these fac-

Exhibit 3-9 Methodology for Monitoring Quality of the Care Process: Objective and Subobjective Structure

---

1.0 The plan of care is formulated.
    1.1 The condition of the resident is assessed on admission.
    1.2 Data relevant to health care are ascertained on admission.
    1.3 The current condition of the resident is assessed.
    1.4 The written plan of care is formulated.
    1.5 The plan of care is coordinated with the medical plan of care.

2.0 The physical needs of the resident are attended to.
    2.1 The resident is protected from accident and injury.
    2.2 The need for physical comfort and rest is attended to.
    2.3 The need for physical hygiene is attended to.
    2.4 The need for supply of oxygen is attended to.
    2.5 The need for activity is attended to.
    2.6 The need for nutrition and fluid balance is attended to.
    2.7 The need for elimination is attended to.
    2.8 The need for skin care is attended to.
    2.9 The resident is protected from infection.

3.0 The nonphysical (psychological, emotional, mental, social) needs of the resident are attended to.
    3.1 The resident is oriented to the facility on admission.
    3.2 The resident is extended social courtesy by the staff.
    3.3 The resident's privacy and rights are honored.
    3.4 The need for psycho-emotional well-being is attended to.
    3.5 The resident is taught measures of health maintenance and illness prevention.
    3.6 The resident's family is included in the care process.
    3.7 The need for psycho-emotional well-being is attended to by therapeutic milieu.

4.0 Achievement of care objectives is evaluated.
    4.1 Records document the care provided for the resident.
    4.2 The resident's response to therapy is evaluated.

5.0 Unit procedures are followed for the protection of all residents.
    5.1 Isolation and decontamination procedures are followed.
    5.2 The unit is prepared for emergency situations.
    5.3 Medical-legal procedures are followed.
    5.4 Unit safety and protection procedures are followed.

6.0 The delivery of care is facilitated by administrative and managerial services.
    6.1 Nursing reporting follows prescribed standards.
    6.2 Nursing management is provided.
    6.3 Clerical services are provided.
    6.4 Environment and housekeeping services are provided.
    6.5 Professional and administrative services are provided.

Source: Adapted from *A Methodology for Monitoring the Quality of Nursing Care*, DHEW Publication No. HRA 76-25, (p. 63) by R. C. Jelinek et al., 1974, Washington, D.C.: U.S. Government Printing Office.

---

tors have a significant impact on the delivery of nursing services. Information concerning the availability of support personnel, equipment, and other care providers is important in analyzing data related to the delivery of nursing services. Action plans to remedy problems involving non-nursing departments require communication among all personnel involved. It is important that nursing homes have an interdisciplinary forum for discussion of quality assurance activities.

How Will Monitoring Be Conducted?

Ideally, quality monitoring is comprehensive, coordinated, systematic, and ongoing. Excellent communication among departments and services is important to avoid duplication in plans to implement monitoring. Each area planning quality monitoring should file a quality review plan, such as that outlined in Exhibit 3-10, with the person to whom the area reports. The interdisciplinary quality assurance committee or a care evaluation committee that has representation from several related departments or services should also receive this plan. The written quality review plan needs the support of all departments and services involved in monitoring and evaluation activities. The quality review plan outlined in Exhibit 3-10 requires a listing of participating departments or services as well as the signature of a responsible individual from each area.

To be comprehensive, a quality assurance program has to include all areas of nursing home functioning that are related to resident care. New programs may initiate activities in only a few target areas at the start. Quality of care might be monitored by a department, service, committee, or a group of practitioners. Assessment of indicators or standards that are important facility-wide can be the responsibility of the interdisciplinary quality assurance committee. Examples of possible facility-wide topics are

- environmental safety
- infection control
- drug therapy
- resident satisfaction
- employee satisfaction
- family satisfaction
- community involvement in the home
- loss of belongings (residents and staff)
- staff educational programs

Several steps must be considered in designing a monitoring activity. The first and third have already been reviewed in this chapter; the second is presented in Chapter 2. First, the responsible department, service, or com-

Exhibit 3-10 Example of a Quality Review Plan

Quality Review Plan

Date: _____
Department/Service/Committee: _____

A. Standard/Indicator

B. Monitoring criteria (attach copy if appropriate)

C. Source(s) of data

D. Frequency and duration of data collection

E. How/By whom will data be collected?

F. Sampling and analysis plan

G. All involved departments/services (list)
    —implementation of monitoring
    —responsible for action plan

H. Signatures of all involved departments/services

---

mittee must select the standard(s)/indicator(s) that will serve as a basis for monitoring. Second, the focus of evaluation (structure, process, outcome, or a combination of these) and the time frame (retrospective, concurrent, or prospective) for an audit must be selected. Third, objective, measurable criteria must be defined; norms or thresholds for acceptable performance are identified. Other steps that are described are determination of frequency and duration of audit, choice of time for data collection, identification of data sources and data collection strategies, selection of person to collect data, obtaining consents for interview (if applicable), and determination of sampling technique. Evaluation activities are reviewed later in this chapter.

Determination of Frequency and Duration of Audit

The frequency of monitoring activities for a standard or indicator is affected by turnover of staff or nursing home residents, the frequency of performance or occurrence of the factor being monitored, the risk associated with the lack of performance of an activity or the occurrence of an outcome, and the number of people affected by the standard or indicator. Safety issues such as staff needle sticks, staff back injury, and resident injury may be monitored and reported on a monthly basis. Quarterly evaluation based on ongoing monitoring or determination of prevalence at a point in time might be adequate for the following unless a high percentage of residents are adversely affected: falls, pressure sores, and infection due to urinary catheters. Process monitoring of important care-related activities frequently performed by various departments might be completed one or two times a year, possibly more often if there is a high turnover of residents or staff. Audits of records of hospitalization, emergency room use, and drug utilization can take place every six months. Monitoring of community involvement, volunteer programs, staff development, and family involvement might be completed annually. Of course, complaints or identification of increasing problems and risks to residents or staff would call for more frequent monitoring and evaluation activities than might be identified in the annual quality review plan.

Monitoring schedules from quality review plans (see Exhibit 3-10) submitted to the interdisciplinary quality assurance committee can be displayed on a 12-month form developed to note the planned monitoring schedule for an indicator or standard. Exhibit 3-11 gives an example of monthly distribution and display of a facility's quality assurance activities. The facility's plan should be developed so that monitoring is spread as evenly as possible throughout the year, rather than requiring intense activities during a few months. Individual departments, services, or committees could also produce a similar 12-month quality monitoring plan. It is likely, however, that those actually responsible for monitoring would want a plan dealing not only with months but also showing required activities by week.

Exhibit 3-12 gives an example of the format for a one-month weekly plan. Departments may not want to limit the weekly plan to just a listing of the standards/indicators to be monitored. The weekly plan may cue a department to accomplish activities related to preparation for monitoring and reporting of monitoring, as well as noting the actual monitoring time period. Week four of a month prior to monitoring might be given over to activities such as random selection of potential subjects for a resident survey, preparation of forms, and the posting of notes to staff concerning upcoming quality assurance activities. The weekly plan should note the person responsible for the activity (see initials in Exhibit 3-12). Notations of due dates for reports should identify to whom the formal report is sent, as well as other required distribution.

Decisions about the duration of data collection or review related to a monitoring criterion must be indicated in quality monitoring instructions, no matter what the time frame. For retrospective monitoring, which frequently involves audits of medical records, the person obtaining old charts must know if the review extends back 6 months, 12 months, or 18 months. Concurrent

Exhibit 3-11 Monthly Distribution and Display of Annual Plan for Quality Monitoring and Reporting

Page _____ of _____

Standard/Indicator	JAN	FEB	MAR	APR	MAY	JUN	JUL	AUG	SEP	OCT	NOV	DEC
Resident involvement in activities	*	*	* X	*	*	* X	*	*	* X	*	*	* X
Family involvement in facility	*	*	*	*	*	*	* X	*	*	*	*	*
Nursing process implemented		*	X			*	X			*	X	
Residents protected from adverse effects of drug therapy	* X	*	*	*	*	*	* X	*	*	*	*	*
Safe environment provided	* X	* X	* X	* X	* X	* X	* X	* X	* X	* X	* X	* X
Residents protected from pressure sores	*	* X	*	*	* X	*	*	* X	*	*	* X	*
Residents protected from falls and injury	* X	*	*	* X	*	*	* X	*	*	* X	*	*
Other												

Note: * = Collect; X = Analyze/Report

Exhibit 3-12 Weekly Activity Plan for Quality Monitoring

Nursing Service Quality Assurance Schedule

Page _____ of _____

Month: January

Week One
- Obtain occupancy and actual resident days per unit for past month and calendar year (BG).
- Resident acuity data for December sent to activities program (BG).
- Check units for any fall reports not forwarded (AO).
- Check units for any medication error reports not forwarded (AO).

Week Two
- Describe fall and injury by unit/area; calculate fall and injury rates. Tally data on predictors of falls and injury (AO).
- Calculate past six-month turnover rate and review exit interview/reason for leaving data. Report distributed to units, administrator, and interdisciplinary quality assurance committee (AO, JD).

Week Three
- Job satisfaction survey distributed to staff (AO).
- Reminder sent to head nurses that past quarter's pressure sore monitoring data due in nursing office the first week of next month (BG).

Week Four
- Reminder sent to units that nursing process audit will be conducted in February (BG).
- Report of past quarter fall and injury audit sent to safety committee. Copy to administrator and interdisciplinary quality assurance committee (JD).
- Job satisfaction data forwarded to interdisciplinary quality assurance committee (AO).
- Random selection of potential residents, days, and shifts for nursing process audit (AO).
- All staff/resident injury data forwarded to safety committee (BG).

Note: Initials of responsible person in parentheses.

---

audits involving observation of the environment, interviews of residents or staff, or observation of staff providing care to residents can be conducted on a single day, daily for one week, or on randomly selected days over a time period such as four weeks. If data collection for concurrent audits is extended beyond four weeks, there will be a delay in tally, analysis, and evaluation of monitoring data. Such delays can hinder staff recall of unit, resident, and personnel issues that might affect monitoring results. Furthermore, since concurrent audits are meant to benefit those actually working and living in the facility, rather than to evaluate care given to those discharged or deceased, it is important to obtain data and develop action plans in a timely fashion. Prospective studies, such as surveys of falls and pressure sores, involve periods of ongoing data collection that are reviewed at intervals of one to three months.

Usually the more infrequent or low-risk the problems, the longer the period of time between monitoring and/or reporting.

Duration of data review is also an issue for evaluation of individual monitoring criteria. Data collectors searching a chart for the presence or absence of information that will dictate choice of a criterion's "yes" or "no" response must know if they are searching the entire medical record (likely in retrospective audits) or reviewing records for data related to the past 24 hours, 72 hours, week, or 30 days. Limiting concurrent chart reviews to a period not extending beyond the past 30 days does help to keep monitoring information related to current practice. Exceptions to this time limit might be one-time notations, such as the presence of a family member's emergency phone number or the listing of a resident's allergies.

Choice of Time for Data Collection

The time of day and the day of the week chosen for data collection can affect the results of quality monitoring. The National Citizens' Coalition for Nursing Home Reform's survey (1985) of nursing home residents found that perceptions of quality were decreased on weekends when regular managers had time off. Significant reductions in staff or support services on weekends or the use of part-time staff hired just for weekends are signals that the care process should be surveyed at this time. Night shift monitoring, with resident interviews delayed until morning, is possible. Obviously, observation of specified activities must occur at times when there is a high probability that the activity will be performed. Activity patterns of staff or residents must be considered if they are to be available for interviews. The Rush-Hines VA Teaching Nursing Home Program conducted its concurrent nursing process audits on randomly selected day and evening shifts during weekdays over a 28-day period.

Identification of Data Sources and Data Collection Strategies

Criteria developed to measure achievement of a standard or indicator of quality may require a data collector to obtain data from either single or multiple sources. Varied data sources for the evaluation of a standard give an opportunity for more than one group (e.g., staff and residents), where appropriate, to contribute to the process. Monitoring of medical records, especially patient charts, was popular in the early 1970s. Now other records are used, such as the following: the patient care Kardex, medication books, nurse staffing schedules, physician coverage schedules, records of unusual occurrences, meal plans, housekeeping's cleaning schedule, pharmacy order sheets, attendance records of orientation and other educational offerings, hospital transfer forms, culture and sensitivity reports, and the interdisciplinary care plan.

Minutes of infection control and safety committees also can be sources of information.

Chambers (1986, pp. 77–79) recommends use of a criteria map (decision tree) approach for monitoring health records. Criteria mapping includes an examination of relationships among resident characteristics, caregiver actions, and resident outcomes. The branching criteria can follow care provider actions based on decision making that utilizes information about resident characteristics.

Interviews of nursing home residents are especially important because of the significance of their perceptions of the adequacy of care provided. However, all quality monitoring must not be based on interviews, due to the inability of residents who are very ill, disoriented, non-English speaking, or suffering from communication disorders to answer questions. Staff, visitors, and volunteers can also provide answers to interview criteria.

Data collectors obtain valuable information from the observation of residents' rooms, the general unit environment, staff job performance, and dining room activities at mealtime. Sometimes an observer must make an inference about a positive or negative response to a monitoring criterion based on printed schedules and the like using the schedule to infer that the person or activity noted was really present at the appointed time.

Data collection strategies will become more creative as staff involvement in self-monitoring increases. Face-to-face interviews may be replaced with telephone interviews or with questionnaires that can even be sent through the mail to families and others in the community who may be involved in nursing home operations. In some instances, time-consuming record reviews can be replaced by computer printouts of certain variables from data sets.

It is most important that the data collection strategy produce information that is effective in evaluating a standard or indicator. Staff new to the self-monitoring process should give consideration to appropriate data sources in their planning. The relationship of the method of data collection to the evaluation of standard attainment may be easier to understand than the relationship of the monitoring approach (structure, process, outcome) to the type and meaning of quality assurance data.

Selection of Person To Collect Data

Plans for quality monitoring need to designate the person(s) responsible for data collection. Staff may help collect data through ongoing entries in log sheets or department records that note the frequency of the occurrence of certain factors, as well as actual performance of interviews, observations, and record review. In order to promote anonymity and honest responses to interviews, staff should not conduct resident or staff questioning in areas where they regularly work. Furthermore, nurses should not monitor the records of residents for whom they provide care. The involvement of several staff members in the completion of monitoring instruments may reduce the reliability of data collected unless there is training to ensure reliability.

If clinical judgments about the adequacy of nursing services are required to respond to monitoring criteria, then a nurse must collect data. This consideration of having a knowledgeable person conduct audits holds, moreover, for monitoring any area where special expertise is required to make a judgment concerning the presence or absence of desired performance. However, if data collection does not involve inference and mainly needs calculations such as frequency counts, percents, or averages and listing of available data, it is likely that a support person, possibly a secretary, can assist. Examples of such data are length of stay, discharge status of residents, descriptions of resident case mix, unit occupancy, staffing levels, and staff characteristics. Sometimes survey criteria, especially environmental observations and record review, only require a monitor to have a health care background, rather than be an area expert. Trained volunteers also can provide valuable assistance, but they may not be the best choice in family interview situations. Although criteria may only require a "yes" or a "no" response, family members often request information about their relative or facility operations during monitoring interviews (Neubauer, LeSage, & Roberts, 1989).

Planning to implement a quality assurance program includes making a decision about hiring an extra person to assist with its implementation. It may not be a full-time job unless a nursing home is quite large or self-monitoring plans are extensive. Since nursing is the major resident care service provided in long-term care facilities, combining the role of quality assurance coordinator with a staff development position would be very useful. Staff education is often an important component of corrective action plans. A suggested position description for a quality assurance coordinator who is a registered nurse is found in Exhibit 3-13. It incorporates leadership responsibilities in the areas of staff development, quality monitoring and evaluation, and policies and procedures.

Department heads may be responsible for some data collection. Cost information, staffing levels, student rotations, community involvement, and participation in staffing levels continuing education are data most likely kept by managers.

Obtaining Consents for Interviews/Participation in Quality Monitoring

The following discussion is based on Rush-Hines VA TNHP experiences and publications (Hewitt, LeSage, Roberts, & Ellor, 1985; Neubauer, LeSage, & Roberts, 1989; Roberts, LeSage, & Ellor, 1987) as well as the *Orientation Manual for Observers, Nursing Quality Monitoring Methodology* (1980) developed by the Nursing Systems Management Program at Rush-Presbyterian-St. Luke's Medical Center.

Exhibit 3-13 Position Description for a Quality Assurance Coordinator

---

Quality Assurance Cooordinator

The quality assurance coordinator is responsible for coordinating nursing quality assurance activities and performing monitoring delegated by the medical care evaluation committee and the interdisciplinary quality assurance committee. The coordinator reports to the director of nursing. Responsibilities shall include the following:

1. Monitors utilization of resident classification system to ensure reliability of data.
2. Collects data used for monitoring the quality of nursing care.
3. Assists with analysis and follow-up of quality assurance data.
4. Collaborates with health care team to assess, plan, implement, and evaluate resident care.
5. Participates in the development, interpretation, and implementation of standards of nursing practice, including policy and procedures.
6. Identifies educational and practice needs of staff and makes recommendations to department heads/services.
7. Participates in the development, implementation, and evaluation of orientation and inservice programs.
8. Serves as chairperson of the nursing care evaluation committee and member of the interdisciplinary quality assurance committee.
9. Performs other related activities as assigned.

Qualifications: A registered nurse with clinical experience in a nursing home setting. Has demonstrated management and communication skills. Evidence of previous leadership experiences.

Data collectors should dress professionally and identify themselves as participants in the facility's quality assurance program, when approaching residents, staff, and others about quality monitoring. An identification badge is important in face-to-face contacts. A box-style clipboard can hold required forms and provide an easily transportable writing surface. Verbal consents are adequate in most cases. Surveyors should carry a prepared written statement of introduction to ensure that required information is transmitted or collected in preparation for monitoring contacts. The heterogeneity of the nursing home population as well as sensory and cognitive deficits can affect residents' understanding of information; therefore, some interviewer improvisations may be tolerated. General environmental observations outside of resident rooms can be made without permission, but it is best for the data collectors to introduce themselves. Facility policy should be followed to determine whether consent for entrance into resident rooms for environment observations is necessary. Obviously, residents or staff in the room should always be told when data collectors are conducting observations related to quality monitoring. When criteria require observation of residents' belongings that are likely to be inside drawers (e.g., items for oral hygiene and bathing), such data may have to be forfeited to ensure the right of privacy and to secure resident support and participation in quality monitoring. In contrast to hospital patients, nursing home residents are less likely to be readily available, because they are not restricted to the bedside area. Another resident should be selected for monitoring if the person originally chosen for the audit cannot be located, is not present in the building, or declines to participate. The data collector and the person being interviewed should talk in a private area.

Posted notices concerning quality monitoring and data collector's introductions should include the following components: the name of the data collector; department membership, if appropriate; notification that the person is a representative of the facility's quality assurance program; information about the method used to select participants (most likely random selection) so that they will not feel they have been labeled as someone who has complaints about care; a guarantee of anonymity, the anticipated time it will take to answer questions; notification of the right to decide not to answer some questions; and an actual request for participants' assistance. If there will be follow-up contacts or phone calls from the facility, this should be noted on the questionnaires. When overview letters explaining the quality assurance program's monitoring plans are sent to residents' significant others, it may not be necessary to give prior, written notification of each specific monitoring activity involving families. The name and phone number of a contact person associated with the quality assurance program may be included with written information so that concerned individuals can request additional information or give feedback concerning the monitoring process.

Protocols for obtaining subjects and consent for monitoring need to be considered during the planning phase. The following is a protocol for interviewing family members or the significant others of residents randomly selected for regular, in-facility monitoring. Coupling the responses of family members and residents may assist in the evaluation of collected data. Rush-Hines VA TNHP found it most effective if the data collector for telephone interviews was the same person who had surveyed the nursing home residents, because family members often requested information about them. This example provides steps of a protocol used for family telephone interviews.

1. The nurse quality assurance coordinator will discuss family interviews with residents participating in quality monitoring who have lived in the facility for at least 30 days.
2. The observer, upon completion of the resident interview portion of the audit, will say to the resident, "I would like to contact your closest family member or friend who is involved (*or concerned*) with your care and who has visited you at the home in the past month. I will call him or

her on the telephone to ask some questions about the care here at (*name of facility*)."

3. If the resident seems amenable, the observer will request a name, address, phone number, and best time to call, saying, "I'll send him (*or her*) a letter stating who I am and that I'll be calling within a week."

4. For residents who cannot provide this information (confused, unresponsive), obtain it from the care record and/or staff.

5. Send the letter on the day of the resident interview.

6. Call five days after the letter is sent. Leave a message if the person is not at home and get a time to return the call. Keep calling if there is no answer. Try another time of day.

7. When the person is reached, say "My name is (*give name*). I am working with the staff at the (*name of facility*). You should have received a letter from me this week. I would like to ask you some questions about the care (*resident name*) is receiving at the home. Anything you say is confidential and will be used to try to improve care for *all* residents. Would you mind if I ask you a few questions? It should take about 20 minutes. If you don't want to answer any of the questions, that is okay." After positive response, begin survey.

Determination of Sampling Technique

"Sampling is taking any portion of a population or universe as representative of the population or universe" (Kerlinger, 1973, p. 118). A sample drawn, however, is not necessarily representative. The population for quality monitoring might be residents on a specific unit or all people living in a nursing home. It is important in evaluation of quality assurance data that data obtained from a sample be representative of the population being studied.

There are two approaches to sample selection, probability and nonprobability sampling. Three methods of probability sampling that might be utilized by quality assurance programs are simple random sampling, stratified random sampling, and systematic sampling. Convenience sampling and purposive sampling are types of nonprobability samples.

In simple random sampling, each member of the population has an equal chance of being selected. Random selection is free from biases so samples of adequate size are likely to be representative of the population under study. The selection process requires listing of the complete population (all cases). This list can be cut apart so that each name is on a separate piece of paper. The slips of paper are placed in a bowl and the sample is selected by drawing out the number of slips that equal the desired sample size. A less time-consuming process for obtaining a random sample involves numbering each case on the list and utilizing a table of random numbers, often found in statistics texts, to obtain the sample. The process is described in research texts such as Nieswiadomy (1987).

Sometimes a population includes subgroups (strata) based on different characteristics, for example functional ability, level of care required, or sex. For stratified random sampling, the population is divided into subgroups and a simple random sample is drawn from each subgroup. The sample size for each subgroup may be in proportion to the size of the subgroup's representation within the study population. Stratified random sampling assures that subgroups are adequately represented in the sample.

In systematic sampling, the first sample case must be randomly selected (blindfolded person can just point to name on list) and subsequent cases are chosen at a specified interval (such as every fourth name) until a predetermined number of cases is drawn for the sample. This can be a time-saving technique. One must be careful to avoid systematic bias when ordering the list of names; the population listing has to be random for the characteristic being studied.

Nonprobability samples do not use random selection so the likelihood of bias is increased. Subject selection requires judgment to obtain cases typical of the study population. Convenience sampling involves use of readily available cases, such as all residents with family visits during the prior month. These residents may or may not be representative of residents receiving family visits during the past year. Purposive sampling requires selection of specific, typical cases to acquire knowledge about a population. The selection process needs an expert. Sampling for a specific purpose might include investigation of problems experienced by residents receiving dental care in the community.

Nonprobability sampling techniques weaken one's ability to state that a sample is representative of a population. A very small sample size also lacks representativeness. A general guideline for sample size noted by the Joint Commission is no fewer than 20 cases or less than 5 percent of the population, whichever is greater (Joint Commission on Accreditation of Hospitals, 1986, p. 106). The Rush-Hines VA TNHP nursing process monitoring studied 15 residents on each 60-bed unit.

How Will Monitoring Results Be Evaluated?

Reports of monitoring and evaluation (see Exhibit 3-8) should be completed within six weeks of the end of data collection. This allows staff to become involved in the evaluation and implementation of action plans while there is still high interest in producing change based on monitoring results. It also allows prompt feedback about "good news" or staff strengths, rewarding excellent performance. Calendars similar to monitoring timetables can be developed for reporting dates or both shown on the same form (see Exhibit 3-11).

Figure 3-1 identifies the evaluation component in the box "Identify Strengths/Weaknesses/Trends." Nursing home staff involved in the development of a quality assurance program often ask questions about how they will interpret information obtained from quality monitoring. The quality review plan presented in Exhibit 3-10 notes that a plan for analysis must be developed prior to monitoring. In general, there needs to be a match between norms defined for standards or criteria and the actual information concerning care or services identified in the monitoring process. When indicators of high- or low-quality care are used, rather than standards, the department, service, or committee conducting monitoring must decide on a threshold level to determine if more intensive monitoring is required (Joint Commission, 1988b). The more in-depth audit can provide a basis for evaluation.

Scoring might involve determining a tally of frequency, such as the number of pressure sores that have developed in a facility; a rate of occurrence or incidence, new events occurring during a reporting period divided by the population at risk of event (Hanlon, & Pickett, 1984, p. 235), such as the number of falls per 1,000 patient days; or averages, such as the mean number of regularly scheduled drugs per resident. Narrative descriptions may be appropriate in some cases. If monitoring instruments have been developed, staff need to decide if all items on the tool have equal weights, or if some items have higher value than others in determining a final score, considering their impact on quality of care.

Presentation of data in an understandable fashion is important. The reading ability and language skills of some staff in nursing homes hinders their comprehension of written reports. Clearly labeled line graphs and bar graphs can provide visual aids to show a rise or fall in values obtained from sequential quality monitoring, such as the number of articles of clothing reported lost in the laundry, the performance rate of various required activities in the admission procedure, the percent of different types of served food consumed on monitoring days, the number and type of employee injuries, the percent of residents and staff prepared for fire emergency, and the percent of resident satisfaction with housekeeping services. Number scores should be spaced and described so they can be easily interpreted. If data obtained for monitoring criteria are summarized in a fashion that conceals results for individual criterion measures, the raw data should be available so that evaluation and corrective action plans can focus on specific problem areas.

Exhibit 3-14 has an example of a reporting form for nursing quality assurance data from the monitoring instrument in Appendix D. Scores for each of the 32 subobjectives approximate the number of "yes" responses as a percentage of the total valid responses for all survey criteria developed to measure each of the subobjectives (For hand scoring, no = 0; yes = 1; and

Exhibit 3-14 Example of Reporting Form for Nursing Quality Assurance Data

---

Unit Quality Report

Unit Name: _____

ID Number: _____

Period Reported: _____

Quality Criteria	Total Score
1.1 Condition is assessed on admission.	86
1.2 Data relevant to care are ascertained.	87
1.3 Current condition is assessed.	88
1.4 The written plan is formulated.	85
1.5 Plan is correlated with medical plan.	53
1.0 Nursing care plan formulated.	<u>80</u>
2.1 Resident protected from accident and injury.	86
2.2 Need for physical comfort and rest is attended.	87
2.3 Need for physical hygiene is attended.	95
2.4 Need for supply of oxygen is attended.	63
2.5 Need for activity is attended.	100
2.6 Need for nutrition and fluid balance is attended.	75
2.7 Need for elimination is attended.	78
2.8 Need for skin care is attended.	92
2.9 Resident is protected from infection.	72
2.0 Resident physical needs attended to.	<u>83</u>
3.1 Resident is oriented to facility on admission.	88
3.2 Resident is extended courtesy by staff.	97
3.3 Resident privacy and rights are honored.	90
3.4 Psycho-emotional well-being attended.	95
3.5 Resident taught health maintenance and illness prevention.	75
3.6 Resident's family included in care process.	54
3.7 Psycho-emotional well-being attended: therapeutic milieu	83
3.0 Nonphysical needs attended to.	<u>83</u>
4.1 Records document care provided.	87
4.2 Resident response to therapy is evaluated.	79
4.0 Achievement of objectives evaluated.	83
5.1 Unit procedures followed for resident protection.	83
5.2 Unit is prepared for emergency situation.	100
5.3 Medical-legal procedures are followed.	100
5.4 Unit safety and protection procedures followed.	75
5.0 Unit Procedures are followed.	<u>90</u>
6.1 Nursing report follows prescribed standards.	80
6.2 Nursing management is provided.	100
6.3 Clerical services are provided.	75
6.4 Environment and housekeeping services are provided.	87
6.5 Professional and administrative services are provided.	65
6.0 Delivery of care facilitated.	<u>81</u>

Note: Based on the monitoring instrument found in Appendix D.

Source: Objective and Subobjective Structure adapted from *A Methodology for Monitoring the Quality of Nursing Care* (DHEW Publication No. HRA 76-25, p. 63) by R.C. Jelinek, et al. Washington, D.C., U.S. Government Printing Office, 1974.

---

partial performance is .5 or .75). The numerator in calculations is the point total of positive responses over a denominator that is the number of all valid responses, positive or negative. Criterion measures have equal weights. "Not applicable" and "information not available" are excluded from the calculation. The scores for major objectives 1.0, 2.0, 3.0, 4.0, 5.0, and 6.0 were obtained by averaging (equal weights) the scores obtained for their subobjectives.

An individual department or facility must decide how it wants to interpret scores. Monitoring results of 80 or above might be noted as strengths. Scores below 70 might be identified as areas with opportunity for improvement. Very low scores, such as 50 or below, could be designated as definite weaknesses requiring the development of a corrective action plan. Raw scores for each of the criteria would need to be utilized to pinpoint specific problems. These score levels guided staff feedback at the Rush-Hines VA TNHP (Roberts, LeSage, & Ellor, 1987, p. 39).

A simple way to determine trends involves the comparison of current monitoring results with data from past audits. Facilities initiating self-monitoring may not have available data for comparison unless some studies of areas monitored were conducted in the past. A form based on data presented in Exhibit 3-14 could be developed to show not only scores for the current monitoring period but also those of past monitoring periods, displaying results from different monitoring periods in separate columns on the right.

Exhibit 3-15 is an example of combining a monitoring tally sheet with a reporting tool. Criteria are listed on the left side; results by monitoring periods are on the right. The frequency with which various criteria are violated is prominently displayed. Criteria listed identify that the right dose of a medication must be given to the right person, at the right time, and by the correct route. Other criteria defined by staff can also be listed. Information on doses distributed by staff each month is important in determining an error rate. When the error rate exceeds the threshold, more extensive monitoring can be initiated. Causes of criteria violations are determined in order to develop an effective action plan to remedy deficiencies. Details about errors are usually described in unusual occurrences reports.

Evaluation of monitoring results definitely requires more than just noting the rise or fall of attained scores, frequencies, means, or rates. The important question in cases of noted deficiencies is, what caused the problem? Staff members evaluating data must consider if there have been changes in staff, the resident population, or the organization of services since the last data collection period. Discussions with staff and interaction among the members of care evaluation or interdisciplinary committees can be valuable in detecting the roots of identified weaknesses. A paper presenting an overview of the Joint Commission's "Agenda for Change" (Joint Commission on Accreditation of Healthcare Organizations, 1987, p. 8) notes that there are six major classes of variables that exert important influences on the quality of

Exhibit 3-15 Medication Error Frequency Tally Sheet, Based on Monitoring Criteria

The medication error violates the following monitoring criteria:	JAN	FEB	MAR	APR	MAY	JUN	JUL	AUG	SEP	OCT	NOV	DEC
Right drug	1											
Right patient	2											
Right time (a) unit problem	4											
(b) pharmacy problem	2											
Right route	—											
Right dose	3											
Agency nurses follow proper procedures	1											
PRN drug given for correct purpose	2											
Other												

resident care: practitioner variables, health team variables, organizational variables, clinical care variables, health care policy variables, and patient variables. A single score or a decrease in a score may not just represent a measure of clinical care or staff performance. A score can also reflect changes in resident case mix, a new director of nursing, a recently implemented policy or procedure, or the effects of the consolidation of two separate services into a single department. Exhibit 3-16 has examples of variables that have the potential to affect quality. Plans for a quality assurance program should include maintenance of data sets to assist in the evaluation process.

Accurate interpretation of the meanings of the "numbers" generated by quality monitoring is important in the development of a workable corrective action plan. If staff do not take the time to evaluate monitoring data, they will not be able to make value judgments about the quality of care they provide. Furthermore, improvement in care or services will only be achieved when the specific problems causing unsatisfactory results are corrected.

Sometimes monitoring findings cannot be adequately evaluated by a single department or care evaluation committee (representation from related departments, services, and committees). Review of data may be beyond the expertise or authority of the group conducting quality monitoring. In this case, plans for referral to obtain interpretation and action plan recommendations from the interdisciplinary quality assurance committee must be included in a facility's quality assurance program. This committee should also conduct an annual review of the activities of each group participating in the quality assurance program.

How Will Corrective Action Plans Be Developed, Implemented, and Reported?

If evaluation of monitoring data identifies problems, individuals reviewing the data must specify opportunities to improve care and resolve identified problems. Figure 3-1 emphasizes this component of quality monitoring in the box labeled "Make and Implement Recommendations." Staff are not meeting their responsibilities to residents, the facility, the public, their professions, and regulatory agencies if they are not committed to change. Quality review plans (see Exhibit 3-10) and quality monitoring and evaluation reports (see Exhibit 3-8) must require groups involved in the development, implementation, and reporting of corrective action plans to assign responsibility, identifying responsible individuals, departments, or committees.

Evaluation reports can describe means to maintain quality. However, many action plans will likely address deficiencies in knowledge, performance, or systems. Staff initiating self-monitoring must understand that the availability of resources and costs must be considered when developing corrective

Exhibit 3-16 Examples of Variables That Might Affect Outcomes of Quality Monitoring

---

Facility Variables
Number of beds—Medicare skilled, skilled, intermediate, sheltered
Average occupancy by level of care
Revenue sources—percent type for each level of care
Average daily cost of care
Medicare and Medicaid reimbursement rates
Facility accreditations
RN, LPN, NA staff (hrs/resident day)—daily, monthly
Average occupancy by "type" (resident classification system)—unit, facility
Average hourly salary for various nursing positions
Social activities provided—residents, family, staff
Safety Committee activities
Infection Control Committee activities
Resident days per month, year—unit, facility
Number of admissions per month, year
Admission program
Position descriptions
Employee benefits
Policy and procedures—department specific, operational
Resident Council activities

Resident Variables
Level of care required (resident classification)
Length of stay
Sex, average age, marital status
Percent admitted from various sites
Discharge status (dead/alive)
Number of hospitalizations and number of residents involved; number of repeats;
   length of hospital stay
Number utilizing emergency room (ER), excluding persons admitted to hospital
   through ER, and number of residents involved; number of repeats
Average number of doses of medications dispensed per day
Percent of residents at various functional levels (ambulation, dressing, feeding,
   elimination, bathing)
Reasons for hospitalization
Reasons for ER use, day of week and time sent, unit sending to ER
Percent residents with enteral feedings
Common health problems

Staff Variables
Percent part-time to full-time staff—RN, LPN, NA, other
Average length of time employed—RN, LPN, NA, other
FTE budgeted; positions filled
Educational level of staff in various departments
Number of staff enrolled in formal educational programs
Number and type of specialty certification
Turnover, stability, percent scheduled time as sick time per type of position
Reasons for staff leaving
Inservice attendance of staff

action plans. It is imperative to involve those who will be affected by change in the planning process. There should be measurable objectives (expected results) for each action designed to produce change, as well as a time frame for its implementation and reassessment. Obviously, cost will need to be one factor to consider in prioritizing for implementation of the various components of an action plan.

Minutes of staff or committee meetings that have discussion of corrective action plans are useful in drafting final recommendations. Coordination and communication of plans for implementation and follow-up of a corrective action plan can be facilitated by a form to record the corrective action plan report (see Exhibit 3-17). To keep paperwork to a minimum, the same form can be used to seek approval for an action plan from superiors, to obtain approval sign-offs of groups involved in the plan, to monitor progress toward the achievement of expected results, and to serve as an attachment to periodic and annual reports of quality assurance activities. Printing the form lengthwise on a legal-size sheet of paper expands the room available for typing the report.

When a quality assurance program is being developed, decisions must be made about instances when corrective action plans need approval at a level above that of the group developing the action plan. It has already been suggested that when the group conducting quality monitoring does not have the expertise or authority to develop and implement a corrective action plan, monitoring results might be sent to the interdisciplinary quality assurance committee for that group to perform these tasks.

Implementation of action plans can include a variety of methods: staff meetings, discussion at the Resident Council or family groups, inservice education, development of new forms for medical records, or revision of policy and procedure. When several departments are involved, or a single large department such as nursing, it is important that one individual, preferably the quality assurance coordinator, monitors the observation of deadlines, report completion, staff education, and whether required inspections are conducted. Periodic reminders help ensure the compliance of individuals who are responsible for carrying out different parts of the action plan.

Action plans might include recommendations to develop new standards or to change the threshold for the evaluation of an indicator. New monitoring criteria may be defined, or changes may be made in current criteria and monitoring tools. These changes must be noted in reports of the follow-up of action plans, since scores are no longer directly comparable when they are based on different sets of monitoring criteria. Furthermore, alterations in the plan for quality monitoring related to a standard or indicator should require involved groups to file a new quality review plan (see Exhibit 3-10) with the interdisciplinary quality assurance committee and appropriate managers.

Program planning must include a determination of reporting frequency. Department heads, practitioners, managers, and the facility's governing body

Exhibit 3-17 Example of a Corrective Action Plan Form

Corrective Action Plan Report

Page _____ of _____

Standard/Indicator: _____ Date ___/___/___

Date of plan development: ___/___/___
Person coordinating action plan/follow-up: _____

Plan/Follow-Up	Who	When	Expected Result
1.			
2.			
3.			

Signatures of Representatives of Groups Involved in Implementation:

_____ _____ _____

_____ _____ _____

need information concerning quality assurance activities. Quarterly and annual reports sent to designated managers and the interdisciplinary quality assurance committee may be adequate. A reporting form like that shown in Exhibit 3-8, with required attachments, is adequate for quarterly reports. The interdisciplinary quality assurance committee might request that due dates for the quarterly reports of various groups conducting quality monitoring be staggered so that all reports do not arrive at the same time. The annual reports, however, could all be due on the same date. The annual report can be a summary of the quarterly reports, plus a listing of quality assurance activities that are already planned for the next year.

How Will the Effectiveness of the Program Be Evaluated?

Plans for quality monitoring need to include an annual evaluation of the effectiveness of a facility's quality assurance program. The interdisciplinary quality assurance committee is an appropriate group to carry out program appraisal, including review of annual quality assurance reports of all departments, services, and committees. In addition, individual departments or services should evaluate their own activities. Reports are shared with the chief executive officer and the board of directors. Evaluation of the effectiveness of quality assurance activities determines if the purpose of the program was accomplished. The facility's annual plan for monthly monitoring (see Exhibit 3-11) provides the interdisciplinary quality assurance committee with a basis to identify the completeness of survey activity. Quality assurance monitoring and evaluation reports (see Exhibit 3-8) can be utilized to assess what was actually monitored, areas identified as problems or in need of improvement, and whether quality monitoring and evaluation activities led to maintenance or improvement in the quality of care. Revision of a quality assurance program might be an outcome of the annual review process.

Those conducting the evaluation process might want to define a list of questions about program effectiveness and compare the facility's quality monitoring experience and data to this information-gathering instrument. Overall, evaluation will determine how the outcomes of a quality assurance program have affected the care and services a nursing home provides for its residents. Evaluation of program effectiveness is discussed further in Chapter 4.

SUMMARY

Chapter 3 focuses on planning for a quality assurance program. The development of a purpose and standards was emphasized. Sources of standards, the use of indicators, the development of objective and measurable criteria, and important considerations related to monitoring and evaluation processes were discussed. The involvement of representatives from a variety of groups in the design of a quality assurance program, especially when they work together as members of an interdisciplinary quality assurance committee, will enhance support of the program. Individual departments, services, and committees can define their own monitoring activities. There needs to be formal approval of plans by the nursing home's governing body. Facility-wide educational programs are a key factor in informing staff about the quality assurance program and in obtaining commitment to quality care.

REFERENCES

American Association of Homes for the Aging. (1982). *Resident decision-making in homes for the aging*. Washington, DC: Author.
American Association of Homes for the Aging. (1983). *Quality of life assessment*. Washington, DC: Author.
American College of Health Care Administrators. (1987). Standards of practice for long-term care administrators. *Journal of Long-Term Care Administration, 15*(1), 11.
American Health Care Association. (1985). *Quest for quality*. Washington, DC: Author.

American Nurses' Association. (1987). *Standards and scope of gerontological nursing practice.* Kansas City, MO: Author.

Beverly Foundation. (1987). *Pharmacy manual.* Pasadena, CA: Author.

Block, D. (1977). Criteria, standards, norms: Crucial terms in quality assurance. *Journal of Nursing Administration, 7*(7), 20–30.

Chambers, L. W. (1986). *Quality assurance in long-term care: Policy, research, and measurement.* Paris, France: International Center of Social Gerontology.

Hanlon, J., & Pickett, G. (1984). *Public health: Administration and practice.* St. Louis: Times Mirror/Mosby.

Health Care Financing Administration. (1987). Medicare and Medicaid: Conditions of participation for long term care facilities. *Federal Register, 52,* 38596–39606.

Health Care Financing Administration. (1989). Medicare and Medicaid; Requirements for long term care facilities. *Federal Register, 54,* 5316–5373.

Hegyvary, S.T., Haussmann, R.K.D., & Cronman, B. (1979). *Monitoring quality of nursing care: Part IV: The nursing process framework in four specialty areas.* Washington, DC: U. S. Department of Health, Education, and Welfare.

Hewitt, S., LeSage, J., Roberts, K., & Ellor, J. (1985). Process auditing in long-term care facilities, *Quality Review Bulletin, 11,* 6–15.

Institute of Medicine. (1986). *Improving the quality of care in nursing homes.* Washington, DC: National Academy Press.

Jelinek, R.C., Haussmann, R.K.D., Hegyvary, S.T., & Newman, J.F. (1974). *A methodology for monitoring quality of nursing care* (DHEW Publication No. HRA 76-25). Washington, DC: U. S. Government Printing Office.

Joint Commission on Accreditation of Healthcare Organizations. (1987). *Overview of the Joint Commission's "Agenda for Change."* (Available from Joint Commission on Accreditation of Healthcare Organizations, 875 North Michigan Avenue, Chicago, IL.)

Joint Commission on Accreditation of Healthcare Organizations. (1988a). *Long term care standards manual.* Chicago: Author.

Joint Commission on Accreditation of Healthcare Organizations. (1988b) *Monitoring and evaluating the quality and appropriateness of care.* (Available from the Joint Commission, 875 North Michigan Avenue, Chicago, IL.)

Joint Commission on Accreditation of Hospitals. (1986). *Quality assurance in long term care.* Chicago: Author.

Kerlinger, F. (1973). *Foundations of behavioral research.* (2nd ed.). New York: Holt, Rinehart, and Winston, Inc.

Kugler, D., Nash, T., Weinberger, G. (1984). Patient/resident care management and quality assurance. *Quality Review Bulletin, 10*(8), 109–111.

Mech, A.B. (1980). Evaluating the process of nursing care in long term care facilities. *Quality Review Bulletin, 6*(3), 24–30.

National Citizens' Coalition for Nursing Home Reform. (1985). Summary Report. *A consumer perspective on quality care: The resident's point of view.* Washington, DC: Author.

Neubauer, J., LeSage J., & Roberts, K. (1989). Making the family a partner in quality assurance. *Geriatric Nursing, 10,* 35–37.

Nieswiadomy, R. (1987). *Foundations of nursing research.* Norwalk, CT: Appleton and Lange.

Nursing Systems Management Program. (1980). *Orientation manual for observers, nursing quality monitoring methodology.* (Available from Nursing Services Research and Support, 1743 W. Harrison St., Chicago, IL.)

O'Leary, D.S. (1987). President's column: Studies needed to support clinical standards. *Joint Commission Perspectives, 7*(11/12), 1–3.

Roberts, K.L., LeSage, J., & Ellor, J.R. (1987). Quality monitoring in nursing homes. *Journal of Gerontological Nursing, 13*(10), 34–40.

Rush-Presbyterian-St. Luke's Medical Center, Rush University College of Nursing [RPSLMC, RUCN]. (1986) *Nursing quality monitoring tool for nursing homes*. Chicago: RPSLMC, RUCN.

Wandelt, M., & Ager, J. (1974). Quality patient care scale. New York: Appleton-Century-Crofts.

Wilbert, C.C. (1985). Selecting topics/methodologies. In C.G. Meisenheimer (Ed.), *Quality assurance: A complete guide to effective programs* (pp. 103–131). Rockville, MD: Aspen.

Woodson, A.S., Foley, S.M., Daniels, P.J., Landes, D.P., & Kurowski, B.T. (1981). *Long-term care: Guidelines for quality*. Denver, CO: University of Colorado Health Science Center.

Chapter 4

Implementation of a Quality Assurance Program

Joan LeSage and Diana Young Barhyte

Key Points

- Management support of quality monitoring efforts needs to be highly visible.
- Successful implementation of a quality assurance program requires the development of a staff education program that will involve all nursing home personnel. Each staff member can be a catalyst for change, since quality is everyone's job.
- When a department initiates quality monitoring related to areas that are within its sphere of influence, successful implementation of corrective action plans is enhanced.
- The following are a manager's responsibilities to a quality assurance program: provide structure, analyze resources, utilize data, monitor staff activity and productivity, and budget for the program (Lewis, 1985).
- Position descriptions can note staff responsibility for identification of opportunities to improve care and the nursing home environment, for participation in monitoring activities, and for involvement in the implementation and evaluation of corrective action plans.
- Special training is necessary for personnel engaged in data collection, to ensure reliability and objectivity.
- Repeated monitoring with defined criteria provides a foundation for the identification of practice trends, strengths, and weaknesses.
- Scoring the quality assurance monitoring tool (Appendix D) is basically the same regardless of which phase (major objective, subobjective) is being scored; it is the percentage of "yes" responses among all the valid responses.
- The subobjectives usually are scored first, and it is the average of the criterion scores (Appendix D).
- Scoring the major objectives requires a decision about whether or not to use an average of averages (Appendix D).
- After scoring is completed, interpretation of the results is begun, using the minimal acceptance score as the bench mark.

- The results of quality assurance monitoring should be disseminated to the appropriate persons responsible for the respective care units.
- Staff involvement in the development of corrective action plans and the evaluation of the success of these plans is an important means of promoting staff commitment to quality monitoring.
- The nursing process monitoring tool (Appendix D) is published to provide ideas for those initiating self-monitoring. It needs further development and testing before the criteria provide valid measures of the defined standards (subobjectives).

4

After the individual with authority makes the decision to initiate facility-wide self-monitoring (quality assurance program), managers responsible for implementation (department heads, area directors) must prepare themselves, their department operations, and their staff for quality assurance activities. Quality monitoring and evaluation should be integrated within an organization's structure and functions. Quality assurance is consumer driven (e.g., residents, staff, families, referring physicians, affiliated hospitals) and management supported. Managers need to learn how they can best support quality assurance efforts. The following are essential steps in implementing a quality assurance program:

- Manager clarifies the purpose and goals of the quality assurance program.
- Manager familiarizes herself/himself with the quality assurance plan (organization of program; department, committee, and staff responsibilities; implementation timeline; reporting requirements and schedule, including standardized forms; program evaluation; and confidentiality policy).
- Manager provides needed supports.
- Staff members are educated.
- Data collectors are trained.
- Monitoring is conducted.
- Monitoring results are scored, analyzed, and reported.
- Corrective action plans are developed, implemented, and reported.
- Program effectiveness is evaluated.

This chapter focuses on management support, educating staff, training data collectors, scoring data and analyzing results, and evaluating program effectiveness. An example of the implementation of nursing's monitoring of the process of care at the Rush-Hines VA Teaching Nursing Home Program is presented.

MANAGEMENT SUPPORT

A major issue in health care for the 1990s is the quality of care. Individuals in management positions in nursing homes are accustomed to operating in an environment of constant change. Federal and state laws related to nursing homes have been rewritten frequently in the 1980s. Decisions regarding care delivery, such as increasing the number of licensed nursing personnel, have economic impacts as well as an effect on quality. And the current and future demand for quality care is likely to occur in an environment of limited resources. Self-monitoring activities associated with a quality assurance program provide a means for managers to clarify expectations regarding accountability and performance. Data collected can assist managers to assess the effectiveness of resource utilization linked with varying levels of care provided. Lewis (1985) identifies the following managers' responsibilities to a comprehensive quality assurance program: provide structure, analyze resources, utilize data, monitor staff activity and productivity, and budget for the program. The role of the director of nursing, a facility's nursing administrator, will be reviewed as an example of management support.

Provide Structure

The director of nursing has important roles and responsibilities related to organizational management and the management of personnel in her or his department. Eliopoulos (1983) recognizes the great potential of this individual to enhance care in nursing homes. A listing of the director of nursing's roles and responsibilities was developed by the Professional Practice for Nurse Administrators/Directors of Nursing in Long Term Care Facilities project (Lodge, 1985, pp. 36–37); these are reprinted in Appendix A. The nurse administrator manages her or his department in an environment that includes not only the nursing home but also the community, consumer expectations, and government regulations, and she or he must develop nursing services that are sensitive to these needs and expectations. Furthermore, the nursing department must be integrated into the organizational structure, promoting organizational effectiveness by delivery of quality nursing care and by collaboration with other components of the nursing home organization to promote nursing's mission.

The nurse administrator helps structure the quality assurance program by defining nursing's purpose and philosophy; this definition should include a statement about quality assurance. Exhibit 4-1 contains an example of purpose and philosophy statements. The nursing department's philosophy provides a foundation for its quality assurance program.

Position descriptions for unit staff (nurse aide, L.P.N., R.N.), supervisors, the assistant director of nursing, staff development personnel, the nurse quality assurance coordinator, and the director of nursing must include statements of their responsibilities for quality assurance activities. This is also true for position description of consultants and other personnel reporting to the nurse administrator. Departmental or interdisciplinary committees for which the director of nursing is accountable need clear quality assurance expectations. Since quality is everyone's business, all job descriptions can note responsibility for identification of opportunities to improve care and the nursing home environment, participation in monitoring activities, and involvement in implementation and evaluation of corrective action plans. Responsibilities such as development of standards, design of quality assurance studies, data collection, data analysis, participation on committees that are part of the quality assurance program, evaluation of a department quality assurance program, and annual appraisal of the facility's quality assurance program should be assigned to appropriate personnel. A quality assurance coordinator does provide important coordination functions and allows the director of nursing to have a single individual responsible for implementation of the department's quality assurance plan.

The nursing department's written quality assurance plan must incorporate significant components of the facility-wide quality assurance program and specific structures or processes mandated by the interdisciplinary quality assurance committee. The plan should include descriptions of the following (Joint Commission on Accreditation of Hospitals, 1986; Lewis, 1985, p. 21):

- purpose and goals
- the scope of the program
- authority and responsibility
- the process for problem identification, analysis, corrective action, and follow-up of quality issues
- department committees with responsibilities and membership
- reporting mechanisms, including standardized forms
- program evaluation

Implementation of the plan will require the coordinated effort of unit staff, unit leadership, and nursing administration. Nursing staff should be surveyed

Exhibit 4-1 Purpose and Philosophy Statement

Purpose

The purpose of the department of nursing is to provide therapeutic, preventive, and restorative care to nursing home residents that will assist them to attain and maintain an optimum level of health and well-being or, when inevitable, provide support for a peaceful death.

Philosophy

We believe:

1. Each resident has worth and dignity and rights as a citizen and member of the nursing home community and society.

2. Each resident has the rights and responsibility to participate in planning, implementing, and evaluating his or her nursing care.

3. The essence of nursing practice is "the nursing diagnosis and treatment of human responses to health and illness" [American Nurses' Association, 1987, p. 2]. Nursing care is delivered utilizing a systematic process, including assessment, diagnosis, planning, intervention, and evaluation [American Nurses' Association, 1988].

4. The department of nursing staff provides care that maximizes resident independence in the activities of everyday living; promotes, maintains, and restores health; prevents disease; and maintains life in dignity and comfort until death. Nursing administration will offer orientation and staff development programs to support the achievement of such resident care.

5. The nursing staff has a commitment to work harmoniously and productively with all departments and services to promote a positive nursing home environment, interdisciplinary resident care within the facility, and continuity of care as residents move to the hospital, community, or other care settings.

6. The department of nursing has the responsibility to provide a nursing quality assurance program that is an integral part of nursing services and the facility-wide quality assurance program.

7. The department of nursing has a responsibility to create and maintain an environment in which employees can develop and progress according to their ability and initiative.

8. The department of nursing has a responsibility to participate in formal educational programs for all levels of nursing personnel, preparing them to practice in nursing homes. It also has an obligation to be supportive of educational programs of other health disciplines.

9. The department of nursing has a responsibility to participate in research, to disseminate research findings, and to utilize research findings in practice.

for interest in serving on formal committees. Communication between department and unit quality assurance committees is enhanced if a representative from a unit committee serves on the department committee. Small facilities may only have a single department committee. Re-appraisal of the quality assurance program on an annual basis may lead to changes. Alterations are definitely necessary if quality assurance activities are not having a positive impact on nursing care provided for the nursing home's residents.

Analyze Resources

The resource analysis performed by managers establishes the availability of human, financial, and other resources for implementation of a quality assurance plan. Organizational deficiencies that might have an adverse effect on quality monitoring and evaluation processes need to be identified early, in the planning stage if possible. Consideration of the nursing department's scope of care (services performed by the department, the recipients of services, sites of care, and types of practitioners) can help to identify resources as well as provide a basis for monitoring and evaluation processes.

Human resources can include nursing staff (number and educational background), nursing home consultants, resident council members, volunteers, secretarial staff, families, legal services, contact personnel in community agencies, and salaried professionals in other nursing home departments who can provide consultation. Material resources might be office equipment, audiovisual equipment, facility structure, supplies, storage areas, computer, word-processing and reproduction capabilities, meeting rooms, staff offices, and privacy room for residents. The department budget and family donations may comprise the only financial resources. Some nursing departments will have research and other grant income.

Analysis of systems resources should cover the adequacy of the organizational structure, the utilization-review program, peer review activity, staff performance appraisal, standing committees, staff development programs, operational policies and procedures, budgeted positions, position descriptions, recruitment and retention activities, and organizational commitment to quality assurance program. Is there potential to utilize or build on committees or meetings that are already in place? Availability of resources alone will not guarantee a successful quality assurance program. The utilization of these resources is a critical factor (Lewis, 1985, p. 24).

Utilize Data

Some managers have little data on which to base decisions about data collection, analysis, and utilization for a quality assurance program. Other organizations have large amounts of information, but it is not readily available or in a usable form. Useful data are reported and displayed so that nursing home personnel can easily evaluate their actual performance in relation to the defined, desired performance (standards).

Ethical considerations concerning data obtained from quality monitoring are reviewed in Chapter 5. Quality assurance reports should provide anonymity for individuals participating in audits. State laws to ensure that documents are not subpoenable need to be followed. When records cannot be kept confidential, it is important that a facility develop and implement corrective action measures and perform remonitoring according to its defined schedule. Liability has been found to increase in cases when a facility "(1) adopted a quality assurance program and failed to follow it or (2) identified a problem and failed to take proper corrective measures promptly" (American Health Care Association, 1985, p. 10).

The majority of data readily available for a director of nursing deal with staffing. Ideas for quality monitoring data sources were presented in Chapter 3. The following are examples of information that potentially could be useful in providing management support for quality assurance programs:

- unusual occurrence reports (injury, medication errors, lost belongings)
- personnel records, including annual performance appraisal
- reports of fire and disaster drills
- facility recruitment and retention information
- financial reports
- utilization-review reports
- resident transfer records
- research studies
- reports of external licensing and certification surveys
- Joint Commission on Accreditation of Healthcare Organizations standards
- professional standards
- infection control reports
- policy and procedure committee reports
- safety committee reports
- drug utilization reports
- quarterly or annual reports on non-nursing departments
- past quality assurance data
- resident and family surveys
- staff job satisfaction surveys
- employee injury reports

We have already recommended that a department initiate quality monitoring related to areas that are within its sphere of control or influence; this enhances implementation of needed corrective action. Sometimes, however, nursing staff note instances of low-quality care being provided by other services that places residents at risk. Ideally, nursing should encourage joint data collection with the other involved department or refer the quality issues to the interdisciplinary quality assurance committee. If other services do not desire to engage in self-monitoring in these instances, the nursing administrator may need to document the existence of a problem outside the framework of the quality assurance program. The seriousness of problems may range from such situations as the unavailability of on-call physicians to lack of an adequate resident transport system within the facility. These situations are controllable and changeable yet may not be within the authority of the nursing department.

Good managers can abstract significant facts from the many reports they receive concerning their facilities' operations. Nurse managers should make an effort to see that quarterly and annual reports distributed by the nursing department contain data that are easy to interpret and readily usable by other nursing home managers. Exhibits 4-2 and 4-3 display examples of formats for the presentation of data.

Monitor Staff Activity and Productivity

The director of nursing needs to collect and share data concerning staffing, care delivery, staff characteristics, resident characteristics, recruitment and retention, and staff development. Such information can play a significant role in the interpretation of data obtained from quality monitoring as well as in the formulation of corrective action plans. Exhibit 4-3 contains an example of a quarterly report form for a nursing unit. This might be completed by a head nurse or a member of the director of nursing's office, in consultation with unit staff. Small nursing homes with a homogeneous population could have a single report, combining data from more than one unit. Data concerning areas of risk for residents and staff, such as those presented in Exhibit 4-2, should be a part of quality assurance information. Exhibit 4-3 does contain a quality assurance section for reporting scores of the six major objectives of the nursing process monitoring tool in Appendix D. Presentation of current information alongside past data helps identify changes and trends.

Personal computers with word-processing capabilities and statistical packages can decrease the time required for preparing reports. Nurse managers who do not have access to computers can develop blank forms, make photocopies, and just fill in data as required, rather than completely retyping forms each time they are needed. Using the size-reduction capabilities of photocopiers, one can line up data from several reporting periods on a single sheet of paper. A summary of nurse staffing can be recorded and tallied easily on a form such as Exhibit 4-4 when computer assisted record-keeping is not available.

The director of nursing is responsible for collecting information concerning the department's operation. Serious consideration needs to be given to

Exhibit 4-2 Information Report Form, Summary Format

Special Occurrences	Present Quarter	Previous Quarter	Same Quarter Last Year
Resident falls per 1,000 resident days			
Fractures per falling incidents (rate)			
Medication errors per doses dispensed			
Lost resident belongings (frequency)			
Hospitalizations (frequency)			
Emergency room transfers without hospitalization (frequency)			
Resident death in facility (frequency)			

Discussion:

Pressure Sores	Present Quarter	Previous Quarter	Same Quarter Last Year
Present on admission (frequency)			
Stage 1 or 2 (on admission)			
Stage 3 or 4 (on admission)			
Developed in facility (frequency)			
Stage 1 or 2 (current status)			
Stage 3 or 4 (current status)			

Discussion:

Staff Injuries (frequency)	Present Quarter	Previous Quarter	Same Quarter Last Year
Back injury			
Needle stick			
Other			

Comments/Trend Analysis:

Source: Adapted from unit reports, Geriatric/Gerontological Nursing Department, Rush-Presbyterian-St. Luke's Medical Center, Chicago, Illinois.

Exhibit 4-3 Quarterly Report Form for a Nursing Unit

Unit _____

Quarter _____

Goals/Plan/Status

Goal	*Plan*	*Status*
1.	1a.	1a.
	1b.	1b.
	1c.	1c.
2.		
3.		
4.		

	Present Quarter	Previous Quarter	Same Quarter Last Year
Unit Utilization Average census			
Average occupancy (percent)			
Average resident acuity (from classification system)			
Average length of stay			
Number of admissions			
Number of discharges			
Comments/Trend Analysis:			

	Present Quarter	Previous Quarter	Same Quarter Last Year
Staff Coverage Average actual staff hours/resident day			
Budgeted hours/resident day			
Vacancies (full-time equivalent)			
Overtime (shifts/wk)			
Per diem (shifts/wk)			
Agency use (shifts/wk)			
Absenteeism (shifts/wk)			
Comments/Trend Analysis:			

Exhibit 4-3 continued

Quality Assurance/Process Audit	Current Scores	Prior Scores	Same Quarter Scores Last Year
Nursing care plan formulated			
Resident physical needs attended			
Nonphysical needs attended to			
Achievement of objectives evaluated			
Unit procedures followed			
Delivery of care facilitated			

Quality assurance issues identified/activities initiated:

Quality assurance audits/activities:

Staff Promotions	Previous Position or Level	New Position or Level

Staff Development

Name	Description

Continuing Education (Out of Department)

Name	Topic	Location	Date

Exhibit 4-3 continued

**Indicates individual presented a paper or poster at the conference

---

Recruitment/Retention Activities

Interviews	*Number Interviewed*	*Number of Offers*
R.N.		
L.P.N.		
N.A.		
Other		

New Staff

Name/Position	*Status (FTE)*	*Start Date*	*Comments*

Resignations

Name	*Status (FTE)*	*Length of Employment*	*Comments*

Preceptors

	New Staff Member	*Comments*

Inservices Presented

Name	*Topic*	*Number Attending*	*Date*

Exhibit 4-3 continued

Certifications/Validations
Name   *Type of Certification*

Formal Education Enrollment
Name   *Degree Program*   *Institution*   *Course*

Educational Programs Using Unit Facilities
School   *Level of Students*   *Course*   *Dates*

Tours:

Consultations:

Other:

Research Activities:

Organizational Utility (discuss support and environmental services):

Conclusions/Summary

Head nurse signature: _____ Date: _____

Source: Adapted from unit reports, Geriatric/Gerontological Nursing Department, Rush-Presbyterian-St. Luke's Medical Center, Chicago, Illinois.

Exhibit 4-4 Monthly Staffing Sheet

Unit _____   (Month/Year) _____   Staffing Sheet Summary

	Day			Eve			Noc			Total Staff			Resident Type				Hours/ Resident Day
Date	N.A.	L.P.N.	R.N.	N.A.	L.P.N.	R.N.	N.A.	L.P.N.	R.N.	N.A.	L.P.N.	R.N.	I	II	III	IV	
1																	
2																	
3																	
4																	
5																	
6																	
7																	
. . . .																	
30																	
31																	
Average																	

the content and format of information shared with other departments, in order to communicate the best possible data concerning nursing services. Reports of staff activities should recognize the educational involvement of staff (staff development) both within and outside the nursing home. The director of nursing and chief administrative officer can utilize staff activity data to provide positive feedback to those showing exceptional achievement.

Budgeting

In a 1986 lecture in Chicago focusing on the price of quality, Dr. Avedis Donabedian said:

> The relation between quality and cost, though capable of breeding endless complexity, is also simple in its fundamentals. Three aphorisms can encompass it. First, quality costs money. Second, money does not necessarily buy quality. Third, some improvements in quality are not worth the added cost.
> It should be clear to everyone, though sometimes we seem to forget it, that more quality must cost more: in technical resources, creature comforts, knowledge, skill, time, attention, dedication. Being so precious, it does not come cheaply; but I am convinced that people, if informed, are willing to pay the price. (p. 1)

Managers in nursing homes must be aware of the cost of operations in their spheres of responsibility. Indeed, there is a cost attached to quality monitoring and evaluation. Records concerning costs and benefits are essential for the director of nursing to continue or possibly even to expand her department's quality assurance program. Quality assurance trend data noting improvement are important. Documentation of costs provides information that can be utilized to control costs and justify expenses.

Eliopoulos (1983, p. 167) notes that budgeting skills may be nurse administrators' strongest asset. When budgeting for quality assurance, the director of nursing must make as complete a listing as possible of resource utilization. Having staff keep track of time spent in quality assurance efforts (e.g., data collection, compilation of reports, development of tools, quality assurance meetings [department and interdisciplinary], quality assurance inservices, research time) will assist in the determination of labor costs. The efforts of volunteers, the secretarial staff, consultants (paid and unpaid), and the director of nursing should not be forgotten. Other possible expenses included in costing are paper, photocopying, notebook binders, printing, travel, phone, computer time, audiovisual aids used in staff education, food served at staff meetings, office space for added personnel, file cabinets, and postage for mailing letters and questionnaires.

The nursing administrator is accountable for the delivery of nursing care and the cost of these services. It is important to ensure that dollars spent on monitoring, recording, evaluating, and reporting on quality do produce quality. Time and effort is needed to focus on areas with known opportunities to improve services and care.

EDUCATING STAFF

Successful implementation of a quality assurance program requires the development of an educational program that will involve all of the nursing home staff. Staff education should stimulate understanding of and commitment to quality care and self-monitoring. Information presented in an overview session should be easy to understand and cover, at a minimum, the following:

1. The facility is implementing a quality assurance program and has defined quality and the program's purpose for its staff.
2. There are important reasons for the development of a quality assurance program within the nursing home.
3. Everyone is expected to participate.
4. The nursing home is providing a clear description of how individuals can participate in the process.

To emphasize the commitment of senior management to the quality assurance program, the chief administrative officer, the director of nursing, or the medical director should be a co-leader of the scheduled initial overview educational session. The quality assurance coordinator might be the second leader.

If possible, educational sessions should be scheduled on day and evening shifts, with groups limited to 20 or fewer people so that there can be discussion. The length of an individual session and the number of sessions may vary, but it is likely that the overview, which should be attended by everyone, can be completed within one hour. Program planners must decide if managers and supervisors will attend a special "kick-off" session separately from the rest of the staff or if managers and other staff will attend the overview session together. It is best, however, that there be representation from more than one department at each session (difficult to achieve on night shift) in order to stimulate discussion among the various disciplines working in the nursing home. The focus on interdisciplinary responsibility for program success is important. If the orientation plan only calls for each department head or area director to communicate the overview information to her or his own staff, the interdisciplinary perspective may be lost.

The definition of the key concept *quality* is very important, and it needs to be communicated to employees. The following definition recognizes the needs and wants of administration, residents, and staff: Quality is optimum utilization of the nursing home's resources to meet the expectations of consumers of its services, to support professional standards, and to promote a positive work environment. This definition might complement a program purpose, such as the following: The purpose of the nursing home's quality assurance program is to have a systematic and ongoing self-evaluation process to improve programs and services that support and provide resident care, as well as to enhance the environment in which care is delivered.

After informing staff that a quality assurance program will be implemented, reasons for its development should be explained. A major reason is to promote the coordination and effectiveness of any quality monitoring and evaluation activities that are already in place; it is cost effective to prevent duplication of efforts. Meeting obligations to the consumers of facility services is a second important reason. The nursing home's desire to be proactive in defining opportunities for improvement, rather than just reacting to reports of deficiencies identified by external regulatory agencies, might serve as a third reason. Finally, a nursing home could want to take on a leadership role in defining much-needed indicators of quality in nursing home settings; this is a way for a nursing home to meet its responsibility to society.

The third important message to communicate to staff is that everyone is expected to participate. Each individual can be a catalyst for change, since quality is everyone's job. In general, employees must understand that it is their job to identify opportunities to improve services or care and to be willing to participate in action plans to make care and support services more effective. At this point, the co-leaders of the overview session might divide the educational program's participants into groups of four to five people for discussion of questions related to the facility's definition of quality. A possible question is, who are the consumers of nursing home services? Besides residents and families, staff should identify that groups such as attending physicians, students in the facility, and the staff themselves are consumers. A second question might be, What expectations do the various groups of consumers have of the facility? This discussion can stimulate thought about different individuals' roles in the provision of quality.

The fourth message is the description of how staff can participate. The general process can be described; it would be helpful if staff could have a written copy of the program's information flow following a staff member's identification of an opportunity to improve either care or the nursing home environment. Figure 4-1 is an example. Emphasize that everyone has a responsibility to recognize and report opportunities to improve care. A suggestion box can be made available for those hesitant to report problems. Families and residents also might use the suggestion box. Potential roles for staff at different steps in the process can be identified. Some changes are implemented without involvement of quality assurance committees. Limited numbers of individuals, serving as formal staff representatives, will participate in discussion groups, serve on quality assurance committees, or provide consultation for the development of corrective action plans.

The overview session should end with questions and answers. The leader needs to thank staff members for attendance and for future services they will be providing for the facility's quality assurance program. The teaching plan developed for the overview session can be utilized repeatedly as a part of orientation for new staff. Periodic inservices concerning the quality assurance program, possibly quarterly, can provide information to staff about progress made toward implementation of the quality assurance program. Inservices can also serve as a method to obtain feedback from staff concerning the effectiveness of quality assurance efforts.

Additional special educational sessions will be required for staff participating on quality committees. These people need information on such topics as data sources, methods of data collection, sampling techniques, data analysis, and the development of corrective action plans. Furthermore, there must be a commitment to inservice education related to knowledge deficiencies identified by quality monitoring. An investment in staff education has the potential to make important contributions to resident well-being (Ullmann, 1985).

Ongoing enthusiasm for quality assurance efforts can be maintained not only through educational programs but also through other activities to heighten awareness of quality assurance. The facility newsletter might print articles about the quality assurance program. Special talks could be presented to resident and family groups. Contests focusing on quality of care slogans or poster preparation can be conducted. Individuals receiving recognition for their contributions to quality assurance in employee-of-the-quarter programs highlight staff roles. Departments that have implemented effective corrective actions resulting in improvements in quality could receive some type of special recognition. Individuals who have identified opportunities to improve care that have been implemented might receive special pins. Events such as a "quality day" might help establish enthusiasm for the new self-monitoring program. Whatever activities are planned, it is very important that staff recognize that management supports the quality assurance program.

TRAINING DATA COLLECTORS

Staff who will be collecting data need to receive training concerning data collection protocols, the use of monitoring instruments, sample selection, and

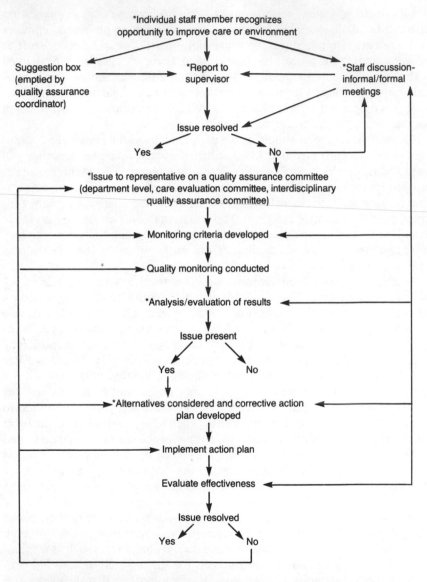

*Point in information flow where it is possible to identify opportunity to improve care or environment.

Figure 4-1 Information Flow Following Identification of an Opportunity To Improve Care or the Environment

approaching residents, families, and staff about participating in monitoring. When data collection tools contain items for which there could be disagreement in rater responses, such as occur in the nursing process monitoring tool for nursing homes in Appendix D, data collectors will need training to ensure their interrater (or interobserver) reliability. The person who trains others as data collectors must be familiar with a tool and the instructions for its use. To become a reliable observer, the new data collector trains with this expert in the tool's use, who functions as a "standard." The person in training needs to perform simultaneous data collection with the "standard" until the two people, collecting data from the same sources at the same time, agree at least 85 percent of the time on what they observe (Nursing Systems Management Program, Rush-Presbyterian-St. Luke's Medical Center, 1980, p. 20).

The accuracy of information recorded on quality monitoring forms may be poor if tools are not developed with explicit instructions and cues for ratings. Just handing a person a form and asking her or him to fill it in, even if the person has special expertise in the area being monitored, will not guarantee reliable and objective data. Not only must monitoring criteria be developed with care, persons must be trained to rate them.

The Rush-Hines Veterans Administration (VA) Teaching Nursing Home Program (TNHP) project utilized a variety of people to collect data concerning resident care: a quality assurance coordinator, student nurses, secretaries, and special nurse TNHP data collectors. Student nurses completed a post-discharge assessment on residents for whom they cared who had been discharged. This allowed staff to receive feedback on the appropriateness of the discharge planning process. The form was developed jointly by the students' nursing instructor and TNHP staff. The students did not just pick up a copy of the form and go out to complete it; they received instruction from their teacher concerning the form's use, the information that was being sought, and their role in the home.

Office staff were trained to collate from logs data regarding emergency room use and hospital stays. Since pharmacy records were not computerized, office staff also used medication record books to abstract desired information concerning drug use. Individuals were trained in the use of the forms, which usually entailed filling in data in labeled columns, and their work was monitored for accuracy. There were standing instructions that any questionable data should be marked so that they could be verified by one of the nurse managers. They were also instructed how to tally frequencies, calculate means, and determine percents.

A nurse quality assurance coordinator was utilized by the Rush-Hines VA TNHP to collect most of the data used to evaluate the quality of nursing care and of certain defined areas of care nursing shared with other disciplines. Kibbee (1988) identifies the quality assurance nurse as an emerging professional. The nurse in the quality assurance coordinator position needed to be trained to conduct the modified Rush-Medicus process audit, complete family phone calls, review incident reports for medication errors and falls, and collaborate with medicine in the study of antibiotic utilization. Each of these monitoring processes required specialized skills in data collection and reporting. The antibiotic audit was done quarterly and involved review of all residents taking antibiotics on the survey day. The sample size was always less than ten, and every case was selected for review. A physician trained the first nurse, and she trained the next. The process involved the following: use of medication records to identify each resident taking antibiotics; review of chart to determine drug type, dose, method of administration, frequency, length of therapy, and the exact reason for therapy; review of lab slips for evidence of culture and sensitivity; identification of resident health problems other than the reason for antibiotic therapy; and discussion of findings with the physician linked to the infection control committee, to evaluate data. Results were shared with appropriate people, including each unit's gerontological nurse practitioner, so that deficiencies could be corrected. No resident names appeared on reports.

Training for the family telephone interview was based on the protocol described in Chapter 3. The quality assurance coordinator stopped mailing letters because families were willing to respond to the telephone questionnaire after a brief description and request to participate over the phone. A limit on the number of attempted calls and the time period for calling had to be defined. Randomly selected residents participating in the regular process audit who had been at the nursing home over 30 days and had been visited in the past 30 days had a family member or significant other contacted. Only about half of the eligible residents had visitors, and the quality assurance coordinator was generally able to reach 65 percent of the identified relatives after one to four phone calls. Sampling involved every eligible case agreeing to participate who could be contacted. Calling extended into the evening, in order to reach people who worked. Scoring used pooled data for each of the 16 criteria (see Appendix E). Some of the items family members were asked were similar to those that had been reviewed with their relative. The quality assurance coordinator did additional analysis to look at the percent agreement between family and resident perspectives on these items. (Neubauer, LeSage, & Roberts, 1989).

Data collection protocols for falls and injuries involved reviewing both incident reports and medical records. At times, the staff member reporting the fall was approached for data. Information was reported for the following variables:

- number of falling incidents during the quarter and number of residents involved

- average age, age range
- sex of fallers
- reason for admission
- day of week, time of day, shift involved, unit
- location of fall
- number of previously reported falls per involved residents
- days since admission that falling occurred
- whether fall was witnessed by staff
- resident activity preceding fall
- injury, type of injury
- type of follow-up required for injury
- documentation of pertinent information regarding the fall in progress notes
- information concerning use of restraints or side rails documented in records
- safety precautions addressed on care plan
- number of different medications (used to calculate range and average number of medications for faller group)
- average nursing hours per resident day for each month audited

Analysis also involved calculation of the falling rate per 1,000 resident days, injury rates for different types of injury per 1,000 resident days, and the percent of falls resulting in fractures. Staff and the quality assurance coordinator need to be aware of methodological concerns related to different methods of calculating fall rates (Morse & Morse, 1988). Reports noted comparison of current quarter data to past quarter occurrences. Although it would have been desirable to set threshold rates and just review falling or injury incidents according to a few defined monitoring criteria, reserving in-depth analysis for monitoring periods when thresholds were exceeded, nursing leadership had decided to build a database related to falls. The quality of the data and reports was dependent upon the data collection skills of the quality assurance coordinator. Analysis was completed by the nursing leadership group; only occasional corrective action plans were required.

The TNHP secretary collecting information related to drug use recorded data from all residents on each unit on the date of the survey. Drug usage is most likely surveyed by pharmacists in other settings. Frequency lists of all drugs prescribed, both regularly scheduled and PRN, were developed. Descriptive data concerning residents, such as sex, age, and unit census, were also collected. The data reported by unit and displayed in Exhibits 4-5 and

Exhibit 4-5 Drug Usage Reporting Form

	6/86	12/86	6/87	12/87	6/88	12/88
Unit B						
Census	60	58	59	60	57	58
Mean number of drugs/resident						
Regular	5.3	5.5	5.1	4.5	4.8	4.3
PRN	.98	1.5	1.6	1.8	1.0	1.2
Unit C						
Census	58	57	60	59	60	59
Mean number of drugs/resident						
Regular	4.1	4.8	4.6	4.2	4.4	4.9
PRN	1.8	1.7	1.9	1.8	1.7	1.8

4-6 were calculated by office staff. Much can be done by computer rather than by reviewing unit records when pharmacy services are computerized. The drug usage reports were analyzed later by a member of the nursing leadership group, who considered the ten most frequently used drugs, the current health problems of residents, and the frequency of use for specific drug categories such as laxatives, sedatives, tranquilizers, and sleeping medications. Professional judgment is required to note instances of possible excess usage. Some reports showed comparisons to past monitoring periods, demonstrating changes and trends (Exhibit 4-5). An indicator that a certain percent of residents will not have more than five regularly scheduled drugs would lead to more in-depth evaluation of drug usage by residents with more than five when the threshold percentage was exceeded (Exhibit 4-6). Physicians and pharmacists can be involved in this review. A corrective action plan should be developed as appropriate.

A TNHP nurse data collector who assisted the quality assurance coordinator obtained information concerning use of indwelling and external catheters. Information was collected twice a year on the usage on a particular day. The sample was all cases, and data were reported by unit. Most nursing departments would only want to investigate each case with a catheter if more than a defined percentage (threshold) of residents had catheters or infections associated with catheter use. The data collection form for indwelling catheter use had five columns:

- bed and room number of resident with catheter
- setting in which catheter use was initiated
- reason for catheter
- appraisal of potential to discontinue use
- history of urinary tract infection

Data were mainly obtained through interview of the head nurse on a unit. Medical records were consulted as necessary. The form for survey of external catheter use repeated the five columns of variables used to monitor internal catheters and added two more: time of day used and determination of whether usage represents a downgrade (from an indwelling catheter or a decrease in hours of use per day). Reports used as the basis for analysis also noted the percent of residents requiring catheters, the type and frequency of bowel or bladder incontinence in the resident population, and the percent of residents with either written bladder-training programs or plans to keep them dry. Careful data collection and reporting was required for the evaluation process to lead to accurate judgments about the adequacy of care and to effective corrective action plans.

In addition to the ongoing documentation of all cases of pressure sores, a facility can do in-depth evaluation of residents with pressure sores on any designated survey day. These data were collected by a nurse data collector at the TNHP and reported by unit. Data collection forms had six columns for recording data. The headings were

- site of decubitus
- initial stage and current stage

Exhibit 4-6 Drug Usage Reporting Form

Unit B	
Regularly Scheduled Drugs	*PRN Drugs*
N = 59	N = 59
Range: 0–10	Sex: male, 12; female, 47
Mean: 4.6	Range: 0–4
Mode: 6	Mean: 1.2
Age range: 22–97	Mode: 1
Age mean: 78	21% of population has no PRN drugs
14% have no regularly scheduled drug.	53% have 1 PRN drug
41% have more than 5 drugs	14% have 2 PRN drugs
	12% have 3 or more PRN drugs
Unit C	
Regularly Scheduled Drugs	*PRN Drugs*
N = 60	N = 60
Range: 0–10	Sex: male, 15; female, 45
Mean: 4.2	Range: 0–7
Mode: 3	Mean: 1.5
Age range: 36–92	Mode: 0
Age mean: 76	37% of population has no PRN drugs
8.7% have no regularly scheduled drugs.	31% have 1 PRN drug
30% have more than 5 drugs	14% have 2 PRN drugs
	18% have 3 or more PRN drugs

- place of initial development (hospital, home, nursing home)
- probable cause and health problems related to cause
- history of sore infection
- current treatment

Data sources were interviews of head nurses and medical records. Staff were consulted if necessary. Other data also had to be collected for the analysis process, including descriptive data about the resident population, such as the percent of residents requiring special skin care and the functional level of residents in regard to ambulation ability (no assistance, some assistance, total assistance, bed/chair/toilet transfer only). Data regarding incontinence were sometimes pertinent to evaluation of the pressure sore information. Reports included frequency information, the percent of affected residents, and a comparison of current data with information from past audits. Professional nursing judgment determined the adequacy of practice for individual cases.

The best time of day to interview staff and residents or unit leadership needs to be determined, so that data collection does not interfere with resident needs or place undue time pressure upon staff. Individuals collecting data should be aware of times of days when records required for review are not needed by personnel for record review and charting. Head nurses appreciate advance scheduling for their interviews. Data collectors should avoid resident meal hours (if appropriate), change of shifts, and staff break times. The physical plan of the unit area where records are stored can hinder or facilitate the audit process. It is very helpful to have desk space close to areas where records are kept. If this desk space does not interfere with the functioning of unit staff, the data collector can work in this area without removing records to another location. When records must be moved to another location for review, the appropriate staff and unit clerks need to know the location and what records the data collector is taking. The availability of an area with privacy for staff interviews is also important.

Pre-audit reliability training for the TNHP quality assurance coordinator was conducted initially by representatives (serving as standards) of Rush's Nursing Systems Management Department who were knowledgeable, experienced, and reliable in the use of the Rush-Medicus hospital tool. Orientation to the audit process and a review of tool criteria were followed by concurrent observation sessions scheduled on three or more days. Once the nursing home obtained a quality assurance coordinator who had high inter-rater agreement with Rush's "standard", this person conducted reliability training at the nursing home for others utilizing the process monitoring tool. The hospital reliability training process included the following steps (Nursing Systems Management Program, Rush-Presbyterian-St. Luke's Medical Center, 1980, pp. 18–20):

1. The learner and expert observer (standard) schedule approximately three hours for each reliability testing session.

2. Three patients on a selected unit are chosen for review, and the appropriate questionnaire is selected for each patient depending on patient "typing" or time since admission. (New admissions need admission questionnaire).

3. Each observer needs a copy of the same selected questionnaire, so that both have the same list of criteria. (At least two alternate forms of questionnaires were defined for each of the four resident types at the TNHP. There were also subsets of the criteria for unit survey and new admissions. Hospital training sessions utilized a hospital classification system, whereas VA reliability testing used a modification of the VA resident classification system. Both divided patients into four types. Not all monitoring criteria are used to evaluate each selected person and the unit. Questionnaires consist of 30 to 50 items; audit time is about one hour per resident.)

4. Records are obtained for three patients. All observations for interrater reliability testing are made at the same time.

5. Each observer takes one of the three medial records and searches for the information necessary to answer the questions on the questionnaire. A separate recording sheet is used rather than marking responses on the questionnaires, so that they can be reused. When each observer completes questions from her or his medical record, they trade records with each other and begin to answer questions for the next patient. This saves time. Observers do not discuss their responses with each other until all criteria for a questionnaire have been answered.

6. Observers proceed to other sources of information when record review is completed. When interviewing or observing, they go together, but only one person asks questions (so as not to burden staff and patients). The other listens or observes and records responses without consulting her or his partner. Each question should have its answer recorded immediately, before going on to the next.

7. When completed, the two observers should count the number of questions on which there was complete agreement on the answers. The number of items on which there was agreement should be divided by the total number of questions to find the percent agreement.

8. The two observers should discuss criteria on which the same answer was not recorded. Disagreements concerning the meaning of a questions or terms that cannot be resolved should be referred to the person with responsibility for managing the quality assurance program.

9. The two observers keep scheduling three-hour testing periods until 85 percent agreement between them is achieved. It is important that any ambiguities regarding criterion measures are cleared up at this time. The new quality assurance coordinator may begin collecting data in the nursing home setting once there is an 85 percent agreement between the two raters.

The objectivity and reliability of data reported to quality assurance committees, managers, and staff is a critical factor in developing an effective quality assurance program. Development of data collection tools and training of data collectors need to receive careful attention.

SCORING THE DATA

After all of the data have been collected, it is time to score the information. Scoring can be done "by hand" using a calculator, but it is much easier to use a computer. Computers do not make mathematical errors or mis-enter a number the way we humans do; therefore, its answers are always mathematically correct. The scoring process is done in three phases: (1) scoring of each criterion, (2) scoring of each subobjective, and (3) scoring of each major objective.

The score, regardless of which phase is being scored, is basically the same. It is the percentage of "yes" responses among all the valid responses, where any "not applicable" and "information not available" responses have been excluded. A step-by-step example would be helpful. Suppose, for the example, that ten documentation sources (chart, flow sheet, etc.) have been examined to answer the criterion "Is there a written statement about the condition of the skin." (Jelinek et al., 1974). Further suppose that there are three possible answers to the question—yes, no, and not applicable—and that the responses are given the following values: yes = 2, no = 1, not applicable (or information not available) = 0. One would then do as follows:

Step 1 Multiply the value of each response (V) by the number of times it occurred, or its frequency (f): (V × f).
Step 2 Multiply the number of valid responses by the value given to the yes response.
Step 3 Divide the value × frequency figure for yes responses (yes V × f) by the number obtained in step 2.

The scoring process described above is depicted in Exhibit 4-7.

The score for this criterion that was used ten times is .67 or 67 percent. If a criterion is written so that there are several categories for yes—"yes, 100 percent of the time"; "yes, 75 percent of the time"—the score is calculated the same way. Remember, however, that *each* category of yes must receive

Exhibit 4-7 Scoring Process

Response	Value	Frequency	Value × Frequency
Yes	2	6	12
No	1	3	3
NA/INA*	0	1	0
		(10)	Σ = 15

12 ÷ 18 = .67 or 67%

*Not applicable/information not available; not used in scoring
Source: Rush-Presbyterian-St. Luke's Medical Center, Nursing Systems Management Program, 1982.

a different value, for example, "yes, 100 percent of the time" = 3; "yes, 75 percent of the time" = 2.

The scoring of the subobjectives follows scoring of the criteria associated with each of the subobjectives. Each criterion is scored as described, then the scores for each criterion are added together, and that answer is divided by the number of criteria. In other words, the subobjective score is the *average* of the criterion scores. Mathematically, the formula is

$$\overline{X} = \frac{\Sigma x}{n}$$

where $\overline{X}$ is the subobjective score. An example of this would be the following.

Criterion a score =   .800
Criterion 2 score =   .675
Criterion 3 score =   .780
Criterion 4 score =   .450
Criterion 5 score =   .950
Total (Σx)   = 3.655
3.655 ÷ 5 (number of criteria) = .731

Major objectives are the last computations done. Although the scoring of the major objectives is straight-forward, it does require a decision before proceeding: Will the score be the average of the subobjective score, or, will it be the average of the individual criterion scores? If the first option, average of the subobjective scores, is selected, then the method described above is used. That is, the subobjective scores are added together and divided by the number of subobjectives. Note, however, that actually this is an average of an average, since the subobjective scores are themselves averages. An average of an average is considered "bad" mathematics by some statisticians. On the other hand, persons who use averages of averages give the rationale that it is appropriate because subobjectives having many criteria do not unduly influence the major objective score (c.f. Hegyvary & Haussman, 1975). The influence Hegyvary and Haussman are attempting to control could be done by using a weighted average. Another method of controlling the influence would be to have a more even distribution of criteria across subobjectives.

Averages are measures of the central tendency of scores and are influenced by extreme scores. An example of this phenomenon occurred in the example of scoring a subobjective. Criterion 4 had a score of .450; this low score lowered the subobjective score. Let us examine what would happen if that criterion were withdrawn. The subobjective score would be .800 + .675 + .780 + .950 = 3.205 ÷ 4 = .801. The score is higher.

The second option would be to take the average of all the criteria for the major objective. In this case, each criterion is given equal weight. All of the criterion scores are added together and divided by the number of criteria for the major objective; this is exactly the same procedure as used for obtaining a subobjective score.

After all the scoring has been completed, analysis of the results (scores) begins. First, each institution needs to determine what is the minimally acceptable score for a subobjective and a major objective. The selection of the minimal score is a sensitive issue since it will be used to judge the performance of a work group against a bench mark (minimal score), of work groups against one another, and of the institution itself (Joint Commission on Accreditation of Healthcare Organizations, 1988). Will it be .50 (50 percent of the responses) or a higher number? To use 1.0 (100 percent) may be too high for every subobjective. Similarly, using .20 (20 percent) may be too low for any subobjective. Further, not every subobjective needs to have the same minimal acceptable score. Lastly, it may be decided that a minimally acceptable score will not be set until several monitoring periods have been completed.

ANALYZING RESULTS

Whatever percentage of "yes" responses is used as the bench mark (minimally acceptable score), it is used in the analysis of the scores. Each subobjective and major objective score initially is examined against the bench mark. Scores exceeding the bench mark are judged as "good"; those less than the bench mark are judged as "not good." Any score lower than the minimally acceptable score should be analyzed further so the reasons for its inadequacy can be determined and action can be taken to correct the deficiency. After the scores have been examined against the bench mark, it is useful to inspect the scores for each subobjective across time. The purpose is to discover the trend for a particular subobjective. It is useful to ask whether the scores are steadily increasing, decreasing, not changing, or showing both increases and decreases. Some people plot the scores on graph paper to get a better picture

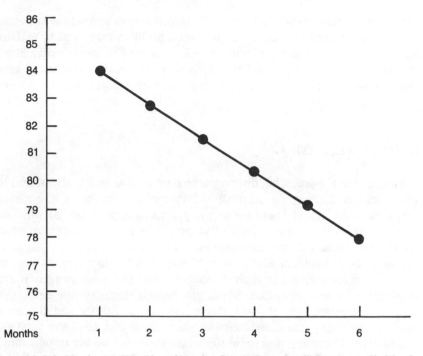

Figure 4-2 Subobjective 1.0 "The Plan of Nursing Care Is Formulated" Scores over Six Months

of the trend, since minor changes often go unnoticed. Figure 4-2 is a pictorial representation of minor changes.

Both the vertical and the horizontal scales of the figure have been increased, to demonstrate the point, since the usual distance between points of a scale may be too small and thereby mask any change. The decline of six points over six months may be more difficult to recognize when the data are not in graph form. In addition, scores that increase one period and decline the next, giving a sawtooth pattern, may be more readily understood as increasing, decreasing, or not changing, once the scores are plotted.

The rationale for examining all subobjectives of the same major objective together is to determine if any outlier scores (very high or very low scores) are influencing the major objective score. This is an analogue of the computation of the subobjective score. Recall that criterion 4's score of .450 lowered the subjective score from .801 to .731. More important, the subobjective scores are used in both problem definition/problem resolution and education planning. This is possible because the subobjective scores are finer gradations of a major objective. An example may be useful. Say that a major objective 2, "The patients' physical needs are attended to," has several subobjectives. Each of the subobjectives is part of the major objective, and each subobjective has its own score. These differences among the subobjective scores are used to focus attention upon problem areas and to reaffirm nonproblem areas. Suppose subobjective 2.1 (i.e., the first subobjective of major objective 2) scores .52, and subobjective 2.2 scores .95. You would know that the part of the major objective examined by 2.2 was "good," whereas 2.1 needed attention.

RESULTS REPORTING

Throughout the preceding discussion on data scoring and analyses, nothing was mentioned regarding who should receive the results of the quality assurance monitoring. There are several groups of appropriate persons who need to receive the results. The patient care units need to receive the scores for their units so that they can take action to resolve problem areas, assess the outcome of problem-solving activities that had been taken, and receive positive reinforcement for their "good" scores. The management person responsible for several units needs to get the unit scores so that each unit's progress can be followed. Finally, the facility's administrator and director of nursing also require the individual unit scores, since they have a facility-wide perspective. Ultimately, it is these top administrators who are responsible to residents, the families of residents, legal entities, and the community. All levels of personnel can more effectively work together in improving the quality of care when everyone has the information.

EVALUATING PROGRAM EFFECTIVENESS

One task associated with a quality assurance program is evaluation of the program's effectiveness. Some aspects of effectiveness have been discussed earlier, for example, problem recognition and resolution through examining the quality assurance scores (results). Staff who perceive the usefulness of a quality assurance program will be supporters; therefore, the design, development, and implementation of quality assurance endeavors need staff involvement. The system should become their program, which means that staff should participate in the data-gathering process without being threatened, review their results without being defensive, and use the results to benefit patients. A sign of program effectiveness is the facility staff giving constructive criticism of the quality monitoring instrument, data collection methods, and results reporting. In so doing, staff are attempting to enhance the reliability and validity of the program by their critiques, which may vary from suggesting a word change in a criterion to adding or deleting criteria. Should the suggestions change the intent of criteria, then staff involvement in the decision is a useful way of maintaining effectiveness.

Effectiveness is defined in *Webster's New World Dictionary* as producing a desired result. This should not be interpreted, however, as having criteria set at such a minimal level that every score is 100 percent. Nor should criteria be consistently scored as 0 percent or consistently scored as "not applicable" or "information not available." If those results are consistently produced, then the criteria are meaningless. Furthermore, the quality assurance tool would not be effective because it would not be validly assessing the quality of care received by residents.

The effectiveness of a quality assurance program cannot be taken for granted. A systematic review of the program should be done yearly. Technological advancements and changes within the health care delivery system may result in some criteria becoming antiquated. Similarly, changes in policies and procedures may require changing the wording of criteria or adding new criteria.

EXAMPLE OF ADAPTING A QUALITY ASSURANCE MODEL

Some people have decided that an effective long-term care quality assurance monitoring program can be adapted from an acute-care setting program, among them this chapter's authors. We believe that some of the standards of care are the same; for example, personnel are assigned tasks based upon their educational experience. We also subscribe to the philosophy of not reinventing the wheel. That is, if there are valid and reliable criteria in a quality assurance program that has been successfully used in multiple settings throughout the world, it is more efficient to use that program. The following example is our adaptation of a nursing concurrent process model for quality assurance to a long-term care environment.

Original Criteria for Acute Care Setting	Adapted Criteria for Long-Term Care Setting
1. If the patient depends on prosthetic devices for activities of daily living, is this recorded upon admission to this unit?	If the resident depends upon . . . admission to this unit?

*The word "patient" is changed to "resident," which is more applicable to long-term care facilities.

2. Does the nursing history include the following information . . .	Does the history include the following information . . .

*A multidisciplinary approach is appropriate; therefore the restrictive "nursing" was deleted.

3.   Is there a statement written on ad-
                                  mission indicating a tentative
                                  discharge arrangement?

A new item is needed that reflects a facility's goal, in this care rehabilitation and discharge to community. The criterion changes we made constitute
modifications of the time frame, make use of the term "resident," and take
a multidisciplinary approach. New criteria had to be written. The complete
quality assurance tool can be found in the Appendix D.

INITIATING CONCURRENT PROCESS MONITORING
OF NURSING CARE

The Extended Care Center (ECC) at Edward Hines, Jr., Hospital opened
its 120-bed first floor just three months before the Teaching Nursing Home
Program linkage (January 1983) with Rush University College of Nursing.
The VA medical center already had a well-developed quality assurance program, and each of the separate services had its own quality assurance program. It was decided that each of the disciplines functioning at the ECC would
extend its quality monitoring into that setting. Furthermore, an interdisciplinary quality assurance committee had been formed at the ECC. That
group had already defined goals for the ECC quality assurance program. These
goals clearly defined commitment to a systematic process of care, encom-
passing assessment; problem identification; planning, including goal setting;
intervention; and evaluation. This commitment to the care process com-
plemented TNHP plans to implement a modification of the Rush-Medicus
nursing process monitoring tool, which had been developed for hospitals
(Jelinek, Haussman, Hegyvary, & Newman, 1974). Its objective and subobjective structure (see Exhibit 3-9) supported the current American Nurses'
Association's standards of gerontological nursing practice (American Nurses'
Association, 1976).

Dr. Sue Hegyvary, then Associate Vice President of Nursing at Rush, had
already explored this tool's modification for nursing home settings (Hegyvary
& VanMaanen, 1981). She served as the initial consultant for development
of the monitoring tool at the ECC. The Rush-Medicus tool focuses on the
nursing process (problem assessment, development of a plan, implementation of the plan, evaluation of results) and patient needs, concepts that are
important in both acute care and long-term care settings (Hegyvary & Haussman, 1975). Consideration is also given to unit management and support services. The Rush-Medicus instrument has over 350 audit items for medical/
surgical, psychiatric, nursery, emergency room, and pediatric units, grouped
into homogeneous clusters to define six objectives: "Plan of care is for-

mulated," "Physical needs are attended," "Nonphysical needs are attended," "Achievement of objectives is evaluated," "Unit procedures are followed for the protection of all patients," and "Delivery of nursing care is facilitated by administrative and managerial services." These six objectives were originally further delineated by 30 subobjectives (a more recent form of the hospital tool has 32 subobjectives). Separate scores are obtained for individual subobjectives, as well as for the major objectives. Scoring is discussed in a prior section in this chapter.

Classification of patients by "type" reflects a patient's nursing needs, and each audit item is coded according to the types of patients for whom it is most applicable. The master item list is divided into subsets of 30 to 50 item questionnaires for different patient types, an admission questionnaire, and unit observation questionnaires in order to keep the monitoring process manageable, about one hour per person. Sampling in hospital settings calls for data collection from 10 percent of unit census or a minimum of ten randomly selected people, whichever is greater. Computer programs are available for scoring the hospital instrument. Document review, patient interview, staff interview, and observation are part of the original methodology. Validity and reliability, well established for acute care settings, had not been tested in nursing homes.

The TNHP was also fortunate to receive support from the Nursing Systems Management (NSM) Program within the Division of Nursing at Rush. NSM had ten years of experience with process audit methodology. They could support audit implementation, provide consultation for the project, orient the TNHP quality assurance coordinator to the tool, and train and test for reliability.

Dr. Hegyvary presented a set of criteria plus recommendations for patient type and source of information to the TNHP nursing leadership. Next, a panel of reviewers, including directors of nursing in community nursing homes, critiqued this information. The process was repeated two times. During tool development, many hospital items were deleted, some were reworded, and new criteria were written (Hewitt, LeSage, Roberts, & Ellor, 1985).

While ECC nursing leadership were still reviewing criteria, the ECC interdisciplinary quality assurance committee conducted its first facility-wide audit, an assessment of whether interdisciplinary care plans contained measurable goals, with the assistance of a nursing student. Unsatisfactory results led to a staff education program, and plans were made for future remonitoring. The interdisciplinary quality assurance committee was very pleased when the new nurse quality assurance coordinator informed them that the planned nursing process audit had a criterion measure, 1.401, which would be used to see if goals were measurable. The interdisciplinary group decided that nursing could do the follow-up monitoring as a part of its quality assurance activities and report back to the interdisciplinary group.

Planning for the initial monitoring required clear communication among administration, nursing leadership, and staff. Unit personnel were informed that an established methodology for assessing the quality of nursing care would be utilized in their setting. Staff did not have access to criteria before the first monitoring period, but criteria were placed in notebooks on each unit for staff reference and comment following the first audit. Staff were asked to agree to be interviewed if approached and assured that it would take less than ten minutes of their time. Anonymity was guaranteed since data were reported as group data for their unit. Staff were also assured of confidentiality regarding their responses. When monitoring was implemented, it was gratifying that very few staff members refused to participate. The reason for refusal was usually a lack of time because of resident care responsibilities.

Notices were sent to each unit to remind nurses of the process monitoring that would be taking place during an upcoming 28-day period. Randomly selected day and evening shifts were utilized initially; weekend times were dropped after only one trial period. The ECC did not have part-time weekend staff, and unit questions regarding support services did require recall of support services for the past 48 hours, so weekend coverage problems could be reported in Monday audits.

The Resident Council was informed about the planned care process monitoring when the TNHP Project Director (Joan LeSage) went to a Resident Council meeting to discuss the TNHP program and its goals. Residents responded positively, and although only about a third of the residents were at the meeting, those in attendance stated that they believed residents would welcome the opportunity to give feedback about their care.

Issues regarding policy and procedure, the sampling process, and resident classification had to be settled. The ECC had well-defined nursing and operational policies and procedures, so the quality assurance coordinator only had to validate them rather than help develop or revise guidelines for care. Examples of policies and procedures that had to be clarified were the policy for changing various types of tubing; the procedure for disposal of soiled supplies and equipment, both isolation and nonisolation; the required frequency of nursing notes; how nursing staff should sign notes (by initials, full name, etc.); the list of acceptable abbreviations; the correct order of chart forms; the procedure for recording medications; and forms routinely present in the chart.

The initial sample size was 20 residents from each of the two 60-bed units. The hospital methodology of using a table of random numbers to select two residents for each monitoring session was followed. Because of the need to conduct reliability testing of the tool, approximately half of the observations were conducted simultaneously by two nurses during the first two monitoring periods. The studies of inter-rater agreement for the original adapted quality tool ($N = 54$) yielded an average agreement of 84 percent with a range of 83 percent to 87 percent. Reliability was similar across resident types. Residents were "typed" using a VA classification tool that had reliability higher than 95 percent. The quality assurance coordinator made quarterly checks of the reliability of staff classification of residents with this tool.

Monitoring was planned to be conducted three times a year. It was not necessary to develop a new worksheet control form for recording the date, name, room number, classification type, and code number of the questionnaire used for each resident selected for monitoring. The hospital response recording sheet, which could be used with any questionnaire, also did not need modification. This sheet contained a heading for detailing data concerning the unit, the ID number of the data collector, the questionnaire number, the sex and age of the person being monitored, the date, and the shift. The rest of the sheet was divided into boxes numbered from 1 to 50 so that the code numbers of responses to a questionnaire's criteria could be recorded for future planned computer analysis. Numbers recorded were always 1, 2, 3, 4, 8, or 9 (see Appendix D).

Hand analysis was done at first. Exhibit 4-8 is an example of a worksheet to determine response frequency for individual criterion measures. When scoring was completed, scores were available for individual criterion measures, subobjectives, and objectives. Objective and subobjective scores were printed on a form like the one displayed in Exhibit 3-14. After the second monitoring period, head nurses not only received objective and subobjective scores for the most recent monitoring period, but, on a second form, the current data also were lined up next to scores for the past periods. Data from one unit were not shared with another unit. Rather than encouraging competition between units, we wanted the staff on a single unit to work together as a team to improve their own resident care.

The quality assurance coordinator met privately with head nurses to discuss their unit scores. There was an attempt to evaluate scores in terms of a variety of factors, such as the average hours of nursing care provided per day during the monitoring periods, the acuity of residents, the presence of new personnel, the absence of key personnel, the health problems of residents, and the adequacy of support services. Information from scores for individual monitoring criteria had to be consulted frequently in order to pinpoint problem areas. These data were readily available on the hand scoring sheets. By the third audit, head nurses were receiving a listing of all criterion measures that were definite problem areas, that is, those with a score of 50 or less. The score from the most recent past monitoring period was always printed alongside the current poor performance score to determine changes and trends. At times, the quality assurance coordinator also shared other information that was obtained throughout the data collection period. Problems identified, resident criticisms, or praise for staff were communicated to the appropriate people, with confidentiality being protected.

Exhibit 4-8 Scoring Worksheet Admission Questionnaire

			SCORING WORKSHEET ADMISSION QUESTIONNAIRE			
CRITERION	NO	YES	YES: 1-3 YES: ORAL YES: SOME YES: INC	YES, MOST	YES: >3 YES: GREAT DEAL YES: WRITTEN YES: ALL YES: COMP	NA
1.102						
1.103						
1.104						
1.105						
1.111						
1.114						
1.115A						
B						
1.116A						
B						
C						
1.120A						
B						
1.123						
1.124						
Other						

Information concerning the process monitoring experience and nursing's quality data were presented at the TNHP nursing leadership meetings, the interdisciplinary quality assurance committee, and the medical center's Nursing Service's Quality Assurance Council. The major component of analysis, however, took place in meetings at the unit level, where the quality assurance coordinator discussed scores with staff. Each monitoring period, staff became more and more comfortable with discussion of monitoring results, and they increased their participation in developing action plans to improve scores. Recognition was given for subobjectives with scores of 80 or more by praising staff for high-quality nursing practice in these areas. Action plans, following discussion of the lists of specific criteria with scores less than 50 (problem areas), assigned staff, the head nurse, or the quality assurance coordinator as the responsible party for implementing the action plan and its follow-up. Each unit had a notebook for quality assurance data and reports so that this information was available to staff on all three shifts.

Refinement of Monitoring and Evaluation

Repeated monitoring and evaluation using the process monitoring tool led to identification of the current nursing home tool's 233 items, which are found in Appendix D. The criteria require document review (38 percent), resident and nurse interviews (40 percent), and observation (22 percent) as data sources. Revision of the tool led to concurrent interrater agreement of 86 percent. Eighteen of the criterion measures for data obtained from resident records now allow the quality assurance coordinator to use data recorded by any member of the health care team. Busy nursing staff should not have to repeat documentation of information recorded by other disciplines. The nurse quality assurance coordinator reports scores for these 18 items to the interdisciplinary quality assurance committee, and this group assists in analysis of scores from these criteria.

Staff feedback that the list of questions concerning the unit (criterion measures from subobjectives 5.0 and 6.0) was too long led to a division of those items into two questionnaires, with an alternate form being used each scheduled monitoring time. Additional information concerning the revised tool has been obtained following its utilization for monitoring in four different community nursing homes. The resident classification system was changed when a new classification system was implemented in the ECC. Since the new classification only identified three "types" of residents, it needed to be modified for four "type" designations. The authors are considering reducing type categories to just two. In 1986 the TNHP began selecting only 15 residents per unit, but at least three had to have been admitted within the last 30 days for the admission questionnaire.

Statistical analysis has focused on reviewing correlations of the individual criterion measures with their subobjectives, as well as the distribution of item responses. This information was evaluated for VA data, community nursing home data, and combined data. We found 134 criterion measures that appear to be appropriate for quality monitoring in nursing homes. The other 99 need further testing to make decisions concerning whether they should be dropped, kept, rewritten, or linked with another subobjective. Of the 99 items that did not have a statistically significant correlation with their subobjective, 31 are new items written for the tool, 26 are revised old items, and 42 are items identical to the original hospital tool. Their data sources approximated distribution of data sources for the total tool. After removal of noncorrelated items, 10 of the 32 subobjectives have less than 4 significantly correlated items remaining, a number considered inadequate: 1.3, 1.5, 2.1, 2.6, 2.7, 3.2, 3.5, 3.6, 5.3, 6.1 (see Exhibit 3-9). The 134 criterion measures that were significantly correlated with their subobjectives had the following origins: 38 (28.4 percent) new items, 23 (17.9 percent) hospital tool items, and 73 (54.5 percent) revised items from hospital tool.

The most significant practice change based on process monitoring involved alterations in the admission process and program. Orientation booklets were developed for residents and families. A slide-tape program describing the ECC and its services was produced for potential residents and their families. The weekly family support group began incorporating information that was useful for families of new residents. As a result of the evaluation of scores for admission-related criteria, a new nursing admission database was developed and implemented to cue the nurse to include important assessment items. Scores improved following the initiation of action plans.

Repeated process monitoring provided a firm foundation for identification of practice trends, strengths, and weaknesses. It allowed residents who participated to benefit from audit findings. Process monitoring scores began to be used in analysis of data related to outcome measures (e.g., criteria from subobjective 2.8 for pressure sores, subobjectives 2.1 and 5.4 for accidents, subobjective 2.7 for catheter use). Staff recognized that care had been improved simply as a result of the audit process itself. By answering the nurse interview items and reviewing monitoring results, staff began increasing their awareness of factors contributing to quality care. This is especially important when working with nonlicensed staff. The process offers staff feedback on their nursing efforts and gives specific information as a basis for modifying practice. Because the framework for monitoring is the nursing process and resident needs, scores have diagnostic value for components of practice; this enhances the development of successive action plans. Roberts, LeSage, & Ellor (1987) note:

> As more nursing services attempt to evaluate the care they provide, there will be better information about criteria to use and the most

effective monitoring systems. Eventually nurses will have scientific evidence about quality nursing care. Sharing this data with licensing and accrediting agencies that review the care provided in their facilities could change the content of these surveys and make them more meaningful. (pp. 39–40)

SUMMARY

Implementation of a successful quality monitoring program requires an educational program involving all nursing home staff. Management support of quality monitoring efforts needs to be highly visible. Consumer and staff feedback and monitoring data must be utilized for revision of the facility's quality assurance plan. As the program is refined, it is likely to focus on the most problematic or high-risk areas. The frequency for monitoring certain standards can change. Automation and use of nonprofessional staff decreases time involvement of professional staff for scoring. Tool development and the training of data collectors requires significant attention, and there must be a commitment to the evaluation and follow-up of monitoring reports in order to improve quality.

While the tool printed in Appendix D (RPSLMC, RUCN, 1986) still needs more testing and revision, it is published to provide ideas for those attempting to initiate self-monitoring activities in their nursing home. This process tool is important for nursing practice because it incorporates professional standards. Process, in many cases, is outcome-to-date. While there is great concern about the outcomes of care, practitioners need to remember that consumers often focus on the everyday processes of care and living in nursing homes and that they recognize the important effects of the care process on the quality of their lives.

REFERENCES

American Health Care Association. (1985). *Quest for quality*. Washington, DC: Author.
American Nurses' Association. (1976). *Standards of gerontological nursing practice*. Kansas City, MO: Author.
American Nurses' Association. (1987). *The scope of nursing practice*. Kansas City, MO: Author.
American Nurses' Association. (1988). *Standards and scope of gerontological nursing practice*. Kansas City, MO: Author.
Donabedian, A. (1986). *The price of quality and the perplexities of care*. Chicago: University of Chicago, Center for Health Administration Studies.
Eliopoulos, C. (1983). *Nursing administration in long term care*. Rockville, MD: Aspen.
Hegyvary, S.T., & Haussmann, R.K.D. (1975). Monitoring nursing care quality. *Journal of Nursing Administration, 5*(5), 17–26.
Hegyvary, S.T., & VanMaanen, H. (1981). *Nursing care and patient adaptation in Dutch nursing*

homes: An exploratory study. Unpublished manuscript, National Hospital Institute, Utrecht, The Netherlands, and Rush-Presbyterian-St. Luke's Medical Center, Chicago.

Hewitt, S., LeSage, J., Roberts, K., & Ellor, J. (1985). Process auditing in long term care facilities. *Quality Review Bulletin, 11*, 6–15.

Jelinek, R.C., Haussmann, R.K.D., Hegyvary, S.T., & Newman, J.F. (1974). *A methodology for monitoring quality of nursing care* (DHEW Publication No. HRA 76-25). Washington, DC: U.S. Government Printing Office.

Joint Commission on Accreditation of Hospitals. (1986). *Quality assurance in long term care.* Chicago: Author.

Joint Commission on Accreditation of Healthcare Organizations. (1988) *Monitoring and evaluating the quality and appropriateness of care* (Available from the Joint Commission, 875 North Michigan Avenue, Chicago.)

Kibbee, P. (1988). An emerging professional: The quality assurance nurse. *Journal of Nursing Administration, 18*(4), 30–33.

Lewis, E.M. (1985). Administrative support. In C.G. Meisenheimer (Ed.), *Quality assurance: A complete guide to effective programs* (pp. 17–43). Rockville, MD: Aspen.

Lodge, M.P. (1985). *Professional practice for nurse administrators/directors of nursing in long-term care facilities (Phase I)*. Kansas City, MO: American Nurses' Association.

Morse, J. & Morse, R. (1988). Calculating fall rates: Methodological concerns. *Quality Review Bulletin 14*, 369–371.

Neubauer, J., LeSage, J., & Roberts, K. (1989). Making the family a partner in quality assurance. *Geriatric Nursing, 10*, 35–37.

Nursing Systems Management Program, Rush-Presbyterian-St. Luke's Medical Center. (1980). *Orientation manual for observers: Nursing quality monitoring methodology*. (Available from Nursing Services Research and Support Services, 1743 W. Harrison, Chicago.)

Roberts, K., LeSage, J., & Ellor, J. (1987). Quality monitoring in nursing homes. *Journal of Gerontological Nursing, 13*(10), 34–40.

Ullmann, S. (1985). The impact of quality on cost in the provision of long-term care. *Inquiry 22*, 293–302.

Chapter 5

Ethical Considerations

Diana Young Barhyte

Key Points

- There is a distinction between using performance appraisals as part of a quality assurance program and using quality assurance results as part of employees' performance evaluations.
- There are ethical considerations in the collection and use of quality assurance data.
- Involvement of elderly residents in the evaluation of the quality of their care should consider the ethical issues involved.

Currently there is a heightened awareness of the appropriateness of the behavior of presidential candidates, officers of Fortune 500 corporations, and government officials. The actions of administrators in the health care industry as regards patient care issues are also scrutinized and have been reported by members of the press. Since the early 1980s, hospital ethics committees have been reviewing decisions affecting patient care; other committees protect the rights of the mentally and physically handicapped (Gibson-McIver & Kushner-Kimbrough, 1986). The discussion of ethical issues is not a new phenomenon among health care workers; however, the focus has been on the patient, not on the employee. The shift in focus partially resulted from employees' responses to hospitalized patients who had disease processes that posed a threat to caregivers, such as AIDS, or patients who were having procedures that posed ethical dilemmas for caregivers, such as elective abortions. A second stimulus was the evolution of quality assurance programs that yielded information that was objective and reflected the caregivers' knowledge, skills, and adherence to the institution's policies and procedures. It became possible for the quality assurance information to be used in a different way and in a way that was not part of the original design and implementation of quality assurance programs. The resulting shift in focus and purpose of the quality assurance information has begun to pose an ethical dilemma for persons in charge of quality assurance programs. However, it has only been recently that the use of quality assurance information has been discussed within an ethics framework (Barhyte, 1987).

The popularity of ethics as a topic did not lead, however, to the decision to include it in this book. Rather, the decision was made because of one specific incident that occurred at a meeting where quality assurance results were being discussed. The incident epitomized the ethical concerns about the use of quality assurance information. One participant, a middle manager, said that quality assurance scores were particularly useful in evaluating individual staff nurses since they were objective and nonrefutable. For several seconds there was silence. Then other managers began to agree with her. One person, however, said that quality assurance results were *not* meant to either reward or punish individual caregivers. Quality assurance programs evaluate residents' care, not their caregivers.

The conversation among the meeting participants revealed their implicit assumptions that (1) selected structural elements of a quality assurance program and performance appraisal program are interchangeable, (2) individual employee evaluation is an appropriate quality assurance program goal, and (3) it is ethical to use quality assurance results to evaluate individual employees. All these assumptions, however, were not necessarily correct.

Before continuing, however, definitions need to be given so that communication is clear. Morals refers to "standards of behavior actually held or followed by individuals and groups" (Thompson, Melia, & Boyd, 1983, p. 3; Veatch & Fry, 1987). These authors then define ethics as "the science or study of morals" (p. 3). Ethical principles are actions described as benefiting people, serving justice, and enhancing autonomy and as entailing truth-telling, fidelity, and the avoidance of killing (Veatch & Fry, 1987). The final definition is for dilemma: a choice between two equally desirable or undesirable alternatives. An ethical (moral) dilemma is one in which each of the alternatives can be justified by moral (ethical) principles (Benjamin & Curtis, 1986).

USING QUALITY ASSURANCE FINDINGS TO EVALUATE EMPLOYEE PERFORMANCE

Administrators have multiple responsibilities, among which are the monitoring of patients' care and the appraisal of employees' performance (Simms, Price, & Pfoutz, 1985). Performance appraisal is a program used by administrators to measure and evaluate employees' behavior and accomplishments for a finite period. Appraisals are judgments concerning the employee and are used for counseling and career development. In addition, performance appraisal is used to defend demotions and firings (Banner & Cooke, 1984; Ganong & Ganong, 1984). These decisions affecting employees are both the responsibility and the right of administrators.

The items comprising performance appraisals may be normative statements that have been mutually determined between the administrator and employee. This means that one or more items can be *unique* to each employee. On the other hand, there may be an employee appraisal form that is used for all staff. The generic appraisal form has the advantage of being standardized. Everyone is evaluated with the same items; however, the appraisal form may not match all job descriptions. The issue, however, is not what type of appraisal is used but the intent of the evaluation. Performance appraisals are used to evaluate employees. In contradistinction, quality assurance programs evaluate the care received by residents. The two programs assess separate and distinct entities: residents and caregivers.

It should be noted that using performance appraisals as part of a quality assurance program is not the same as using quality assurance results as part of employees' performance evaluations. The systematic and objective evaluation of employees to attest to their competency as caregivers is an appropriate quality assurance goal. It is one of the Joint Commission on Accreditation of Healthcare Organizations' (Joint Commission) quality assurance standards for physicians with hospital admitting privileges (Joint Commission on Accreditation of Hospitals, 1986). The goal is to improve the practice patterns of good physicians (Weinberg, 1987). Hospitals are expected to evaluate each doctor's care and determine whether or not appropriate standards of care were upheld. This type of physician evaluation can be both a structural and an outcome measure. One structural measure would be the determination of the appropriate certification of physicians and evidence of continuing education endeavors to maintain currency in their practice. An outcome measure would be the morbidity and mortality patterns of each physician having admitting privileges. Doctors who exceed the facility standard for the incidence of morbidity or mortality may be denied privileges. In the preceding situations, the performance appraisals of doctor's care were a part of a facility's quality assurance program.

Arguments against Use

The more difficult question to answer is raised by the other side of the issue, which is the use of quality assurance results as part of employees' evaluations. The reasons given for not using quality assurance information in this manner can be categorized into two positions. The first may be labeled a level of analysis problem. This type of problem occurs when a quality assurance instrument is designed to gather information about a unit or department. Since the purpose of the instrument is to obtain an overall unit-level evaluation, the information obtained will not be accurate about any one individual working on the unit. The inaccuracy occurs because the sample does not correspond to the population about whom an administrator is generalizing. This type of inappropriate use of results is labeled the *ecological fallacy* by researchers (Robinson, 1950; Selvin, 1958).

The second commonly voiced position against using quality assurance results to judge individual performance is sample size. Proponents argue that the amount of information is insufficient to make a judgment about an employee. They point out that when a random sampling strategy is used to obtain a sample of patient care activities, rather than a sample of an individual caregiver's work, it is unlikely that more than one piece of information about the individual caregiver's work would be in the sample. The basic argument is that neither rewards nor punishments should be based on only one assessment from the entire range of an employee's patient care activities.

Arguments in Favor of Use

In opposition, there are proponents of using quality assurance results to evaluate employees. As these persons usually use one or more of Veatch and Fry's (1987) ethical principles in their reasoning, all the principles outlined by these authors will be covered below.

The arguments for using quality assurance results to evaluate employees are as follows. Using the results benefits caregivers since those who are performing their jobs well can thereby be rewarded and those who are not performing to the set standards can be counseled appropriately. All employees, therefore, benefit, since the "good" caregivers can maintain or improve their level of care and the "poor" caregivers can learn what is wrong with their care so that they can improve it. Ultimately, the residents benefit from the improvements.

The principle of justice also is fulfilled. Each caregiver's rights have been protected, and each person is given some form of merit according to individual effort. The autonomy of the individual is preserved since caregivers' consent to quality assurance monitoring is implied by their participation. The principle of truth telling is met because neither the quality assurance questions nor the answers are covert. Each question is directly soliciting the information. The staff know how the results were obtained and how the information will be used in their evaluations.

Another argument is that using quality assurance results to evaluate caregivers assists in maintaining a safe and healthful environment, which satisfies the ethical principle to avoid killing. Society assumes that the willful killing of patients (residents) will not occur; consequently, the obligation of a long-term care facility to provide a safe and healthful environment for residents is a proxy for the principle of avoiding killing. Facilities also have a duty to act in accordance with the rules and regulations governing their activities, and one part of this duty is to ascertain that caregivers are following prescribed standards of care. Following predetermined standards of care is expected to result in a decreased incidence of morbidity and mortality (which may be used as outcome measures for a quality assurance program). Support for this position is found in the Joint Commission standards referred to earlier in this chapter. However, the logic of this argument is faulty in that it shifts from the facility level to the individual level. This is the ecological fallacy (error) noted earlier.

In summary, the proponents argue for using quality assurance results in the evaluation of individual caregivers. They express the opinion that both employees and residents benefit, caregivers' rights and autonomy are protected by their consenting to participate, and killing has thereby been avoided. The principle of truth telling is adhered to by honestly informing caregivers of how the information will be used and by having the questions be overt in content. Serving justice occurs because each employee receives some form of merit based upon performance.

Impact on Residents

The preceding sections presented both a proponent and opposition view of using quality assurance information in the evaluation of employees' performance. The earlier discussion focused on the employees. But there is another source of opposition to using quality assurance information for employees' evaluations and these persons focus only on its impact on the residents. They may be labeled residents' advocates since they are evaluating situations that residents may encounter and taking positions to safeguard residents.

The most compelling part of the residents' advocates' argument is the principle of autonomy. Autonomy is defined by *Webster's New World Dictionary* as self-government. Basically, autonomy is one of our human rights. That is, we have personal liberty, and we determine our own actions regardless of how those actions are perceived by others. This includes actions perceived by others as not being in our own best interests (Veatch & Fry, 1987). Humans have the innate right to be both recognized and respected. Incorporated into this premise is the explicit assumption that no one is free to negate the rights of others (Curtin & Flaherty, 1982).

Unfortunately, the principle of autonomy is not fully extended to the elderly. The general public has negative views of the elderly and characterizes them as less than fully mentally capable. Older persons are perceived as being childlike. These misperceptions are readily seen in caregivers who interact with the elderly in a paternalistic manner, for example, calling them patients rather than clients (Quinn & Smith, 1987). The term "clients" denotes that residents have sufficient information, can process the information, and can reach a decision. While caregivers may not agree with the residents' decisions, respect for their autonomy means the decisions will be upheld.

Autonomy is closely related to informed consent. Most people think of medical procedures, treatments, or research projects when the phrase "informed consent" is used. They tend not to associate the phrase with quality assurance monitoring; however, informed consent is an important element of any quality assurance program that systematically gathers information about residents (clients, patients), analyzes the information, and takes action based upon the analyses' findings. That is, quality assurance programs are research projects that ask questions related to the care given to persons who are in some type of health care facility. The quality assurance research questions are framed in the context of the facilities' standards of care; for example, "Patients' physiological statuses are established within 24 hours of admission."

Informed consent requires telling a person of all the human risks, any potential major problems, and the alternatives available. To give informed consent, a person should be an adult and of sound mind (Annas, Glantz, & Katz, 1981). Once the tenets of informed consent have been ascertained, then voluntary consent can be established. Voluntary consent requires that the individual has the legal capacity to give consent, free power of choice, sufficient knowledge, and comprehension of the elements of the subject matter. The two major reasons for obtaining informed consent are to promote individual autonomy and to encourage rational decision making (Annas et al., 1981).

Both reasons are especially important in long-term care facilities. Residents, because of their age and illnesses, may have their rights inadvertently violated. Seeking residents' consent for participation in quality assurance monitoring may help to maintain their trust in other areas of their care. The maintenance of trust in multiple spheres of their lives may be useful in decreasing fear of the new and unknown. More important, requesting their participation and accepting without censure their refusal gives a tangible symbol of their autonomy, which reinforces their human dignity. Furthermore, it encourages residents to actively participate in the evaluation of their care. They are able, albeit indirectly, to influence the care they receive and the environment in which it is given.

The elderly, who meet the parameters for informed consent however, may fail to act autonomously for a multitude of reasons. One reason is the power of health care professionals (Quinn & Smith, 1987). Residents of long-term care facilities are dependent on their caregivers for food, clothing, shelter, assistance with hygiene, medications, treatments, safety, recreation, and so forth. This dependency on others for basic needs may result in the elderly's thinking that they must unquestionably accept the facility's rules and regulations and all caregiver requests. They may think that their basic needs will not be adequately met if they are noncompliant. The residents' perceptions of helplessness also are reinforced by the paternalistic attitudes of caregivers. Residents have the right to take a different course of action than caregivers would take. Only the residents can determine which alternatives are more important to them (Follesdal, 1986). Benjamin and Curtis (1986) stated it most eloquently when they wrote:

Insofar as paternalistic coercion or manipulation of an adult involves a refusal to accept at face value the choices, wishes, or action of an individual who is presumed to be autonomous and self-determining, it bears an even heavier burden of justification. Paternalistic behavior, regardless of benevolent motives or the magnitude of the benefit to be secured or the harm to be avoided, overrides the right of an adult to be treated as a person. (p. 54)

When caregivers perceive the elderly more as children than adults, the elderly are denied their personhood. Ultimately this denies the elderly their trilogy of rights: the right to respect, the right to receive treatments, and the right to refuse treatment (Bandman & Bandman, 1985). The right to respect includes rights to privacy, confidentiality, dignity, regard as a rational person, and informed consent.

Respecting the autonomy of residents does involve their participation in quality assurance endeavors. Some quality assurance programs interview residents to obtain information about the care they have been given. The active participation of residents in determining their care is a right granted to them by the United States Congress (Comptroller General, 1981). That is, long-term care facilities that receive Medicare or Medicaid payments are required to maintain patients' rights in the following areas:

1. Residents are to have an active role in planning their own care.
2. Residents' privacy is to be maintained.
3. The facility is to keep records on the residents' personal property.
4. Residents are to have control over the use of chemical restraints on them.
5. Residents have the right to be informed of service changes and involuntary transfer to other facilities.

Evaluating the maintenance of these residents' rights could be a component of a quality assurance program.

When residents are interviewed about quality assurance issues, they should be fully informed about the uses of the information and all the risks and benefits to them. Unless complete information is given to the residents, they may mistakenly infer that some aspect of their care will be jeopardized. Suppose they are fully informed and know that the results of the quality assurance monitoring will be used to evaluate the caregivers employed on their units. The residents have several options: answer the questions honestly, based on their experiences, regardless of their personal feelings about the caregivers; be evasive in answering because they do not want to report anything that might lead to the caregivers' being reprimanded; or answer the questions based upon their personal opinions of the caregivers, regardless of the quality of care.

If you were in the same situation and felt vulnerable, how would you answer the questions? Brady (1986) wrote that this type of situation produces a dilemma for the individual being interviewed. Furthermore, he noted that there are few useful rules and no decision procedures that can guide people in this type of dilemma. It would seem, therefore, that prevention of the dilemma is the better option; however, this may result in the problem of how to obtain the residents' perceptions of their care without directly asking them. One solution is not to use quality assurance information in evaluating employees. Another solution is to incorporate the Resident Council in alleviating any resident misperceptions.

The question also may be asked as to whether having the residents' responses to quality assurance questions violates the ethical principle of equality and fairness. It would be difficult to defend that the residents and caregivers are equals in political, economic, and social rights, especially in situations where caregivers obviously have more power than the residents. Residents are expected to abide by a set of explicit rules and regulations. For example, they do not have the freedom to determine when, what, or where they will eat. Nor can they decide when or how to bathe, if they need assistance in bathing. Even the freedom of when to sleep or to be awake is set by rules governing rest periods and lights-out times. The impingement upon the residents' freedom of choice is justified by those in authority as being "for their own good." Residents might argue it is not for their good but rather for the caregivers' convenience.

Caregivers, however, possess the freedom of these simple basic rights. They correctly assume and behave as if decisions regarding their own basic needs belong to them. Each of us would strongly resist the curtailment of those decisions; however, nursing home residents are expected to unquestioningly defer to caregivers in these same areas. It can be asserted, therefore, that the principle of equality is not upheld universally in a health care organization. The more germane issue, however, is whether the principle of equality is upheld when collecting quality assurance information.

The principle of equality may be violated from the perspectives of both caregivers and residents. Granting the residents' position of inequality, caregivers also may be placed in positions that are neither equitable nor fair. It was noted earlier that caregivers are being evaluated on information gathered from residents who potentially may be biased. In addition to biased information, residents may have insufficient knowledge to make valid responses about their treatments, procedures, or other therapies. How can residents accurately assess the full contribution of each caregiver to the maintenance of a therapeutic milieu? Caregivers, who have specialized educational preparation and are licensed by state examining boards, are being evaluated in areas of their role performance by persons who may not have had similar training. It is questionable whether nonprofessionals can accurately assess the work of professionals. Certainly, it is not equitable for caregivers in their professional activities. To quote Luther Christman (1987), no one can use knowledge he or she does not have. However, those areas of care dealing with privacy, confidentiality of patient information, respect, and so forth can and should be assessed by residents.

Subsequently, one needs to ask, Is the principle of fairness compromised if equality does not exist between residents and caregivers? Fairness connotes actions that are impartial, unprejudiced, and just. If quality assurance results are used inappropriately, the application of those results is not necessarily impartial or unprejudiced. The denial of control over the meeting of one's basic needs is judged by society as unfair, but the placement of persons in situations that result in dilemmas may also be judged as unfair. One must ask, however, if it is fair of administrators to potentially give residents lower quality care due to failure to monitor the care residents receive.

ADMINISTRATORS' ETHICAL BEHAVIOR

The ethical conduct of health care administrators as it relates to their work environment is a concern of society. This is especially true since persons' health statuses may be affected. A trend for long-term care facilities to establish ethics committees has been noted. Since it is only an emerging trend, though, it is too early to predict if these committees will follow the pattern set by hospitals (Gibson-McIver & Kushner-Kimbrough, 1986). Historically, hospital ethics committees focused on education, policy development, and case consultation. Currently, quality patient care is an emerging area of concern to these committees (Siegler, 1986). If long-term care follows the developmental pattern of hospital committees, administrators will need to resolve the ethical issues evolving from quality assurance programs.

It is recognized that an ethics committee's functions do not transcend an administrator's responsibilities to develop and support an organizational environment that fosters ethical decision making among personnel. Trevino-Klebe (1986) developed an interaction model to describe ethical decision making in organizations. Her model incorporates situational moderators that interact with both individual moderators and decision makers' stages of cognitive moral development. The interaction of those three components results in decision making that may be labeled either ethical or unethical.

The immediate job context, the organizational culture, and the characteristics of the work comprise Trevino-Klebe's (1986) situational moderators. Through the positive manipulation of the situational moderators, administrators facilitate the ethical behavior of their staff. Positive manipulation may be accomplished by positively reinforcing staff ethical behavior, by having administrators take responsibility for the consequences of their actions, and by having administrators serve as role models. Minimizing the numbers of occurrences that lead to ethical dilemmas also is a positive manipulation of situational moderators. Administrators' decisions and behaviors need to be consistent with their professional and organizational codes of ethics. Otherwise, the staff of the facility are given contradictory messages, and support for an ethical organizational environment is undermined.

There are multiple opportunities for administrators to promote ethical decision making among their staff. Support for the preceding assertion is given in a study by Sietsema and Spradley (1987), who conducted a survey of hospital nursing administrators. The results were that 90.1 percent of the administrators reported experiencing ethical dilemmas in their work. The dilemmas most frequently encountered were in two areas: use of resources and quality of care. Logically, it would follow that administrators of long-term care facilities also would experience ethical dilemmas in their work environments. Furthermore, it follows that the areas of difficulty would be similar. It would seem that long-term care administrators might perceive quality assurance monitoring results as an appropriate method of resolving a resident-care ethical dilemma. That is, valid, reliable, and objective quality assurance results would be incorporated into the dilemma-resolution process.

There are several ways that quality assurance results might be used by administrators. Suppose, for discussion purposes, that quality assurance scores declined as the number of caregivers decreased. The data could be used appropriately to buttress an administrator's request for hiring additional caregivers. Alternatively, the data also could be used to determine the numbers of residents to be cared for, given the staffing level. In other words, the decision to open or close beds when there are a fixed number of staff could be made using the quality assurance results.

SUMMARY AND CONCLUSIONS

Administrators' responsibilities to maintain quality of care and to evaluate employees' performance may lead to ethical dilemmas. The decision of whether or not to use quality assurance data in employees' performance appraisals was examined using the ethical principles outlined by Veatch and Fry (1987). The ethical or unethical use of quality assurance information varies by which principle is examined. Administrators were encouraged to develop and maintain an organizational environment that supports ethical decision making.

It also was noted that residents of long-term care facilities may experience a moral dilemma when they are requested to give information about their caregivers. One aspect of the dilemma is the residents' lack of autonomy in the situation, a problem that is exacerbated when caregivers are paternalistic toward residents.

REFERENCES

Annas, G.I., Glantz, L.H., & Katz, B.F. (1981). *The rights of doctors, nurses and allied health professionals: A health law primer*. New York: Avon Books.

Banner, D.K., & Cooke, R.A. (1984). Ethical dilemmas in performance appraisal. *Journal of Business Ethics, 3*(4), 327–333.

Bandman, E.L., & Bandman, B. (1985). *Nursing ethics in the life span*. Norwalk, CT: Appleton-Century-Crofts.

Barhyte, D.Y. (1987). Ethical issues in automating nursing personnel data. *Computers in Nursing 5*(5), 171–174.

Benjamin, M. & Curtis, J. (1986). *Ethics in nursing* (2nd ed.). New York: Oxford University Press.

Brady, N.F. (1986). Aesthetic Components of Management Ethics. *Academy of Management Review, 11*(2), 337–344.

Christman, L.P. (1987). A view to the future. *Nursing Outlook, 35*(5), 216–218.

Comptroller General. (1981). *Analysis of proposed new standards for nursing homes participating in Medicare and Medicaid* (HRD-81-50).

Curtin, L. & Flaherty, M.J. (1982). *Nursing ethics: Theories and pragmatics*. Bowie, MD: Robert J. Brady.

Follesdal, D. (1986). Risk: Philosophical and ethical aspects. *Risk and reason: Risk assessment in relation to environmental mutagens and carcinogens* (pp. 41–52). New York: Alan R. Liss, Inc.

Ganong, J.M., & Ganong, W.L. (1984). *Performance appraisal for productivity: The nurse manager's handbook*. Rockville, MD.: Aspen.

Gibson-McIver, J. & Kushner-Kimbrough, T. (1986). Will the "conscience of an institution" become society's servant? *Hastings Center Report*.

Guralnik, D.B. (ed.) (1980). *Wester's new world dictionary of the American language*. 2nd ed. New York: Simon and Schuster.

Joint Commission on the Accreditation of Hospitals. (1986). Standard 17, Quality Assurance, Chicago: Author.

Quinn, C.A., & Smith, D. (1987). *The professional commitment: Issues and ethics in nursing*. Philadelphia: W.B. Saunders.

Robinson, W.S. (1950). Ecological correlation in the behavior of individuals. *American Sociological Review, 15*, 351–357.

Selvin, H.C. (1958). Durkheim's suicide and problems of empirical research. *American Journal of Sociology, 63*, 607–619.

Siegler, M. (1986). Ethics committees: Decisions by bureaucracy. *Hastings Center Report*.

Sietsema, M.R., & Spradley, B.W. (1987). Ethics and administrative decision making. *Journal of Nursing Administration, 17*(4), 28–32.

Simms, L.M., Price, S.A., & Pfoutz, S.K. (1985). Nurse executives: Functions and priorities. *Nursing Economics, 3*, 238–244.

Thompson, I.E., Melia, K.M., & Boyd, K. (1983). *Nursing ethics*. New York: Churchill Livingstone.

Trevino-Klebe, L. (1986). Ethical decision making in organizations: A person-situation interactionist model. *Academy of Management Review, 11*(3), 601–617.

Veatch, R.M., & Fry, S.T. (1987). *Case studies in nursing ethics*. New York: J.B. Lippincott.

Weinberg, N. (1987, December). Creating a culture of quality practice among physicians. *Quality Review Bulletin*, pp. 405–410.

Chapter 6

Directions for the Future

Joan LeSage

Key Points

- Concern about the quality of nursing home care in the future is based on several factors: demographics, a possible decrease in the functional level of future nursing homes residents, governmental fiscal constraints, an inadequate regulatory environment, and possible conflicts between quality of care and quality of life.
- External regulatory agencies will increase their focus on the evaluation of care actually provided by nursing homes.
- Recruitment and retention of registered nurses in long-term care are hindered by an inadequate supply of nurses prepared with specialized knowledge and skills to work in long-term care, as well as by salary levels and benefits that are not competitive with other sources of employment.
- Teaching nursing homes provide environments in which to implement and evaluate care innovations, to educate future long-term care health professionals, and to promote research related to nursing home care.
- Reimbursement for quality is a concept with potential to improve care.
- Research establishing linkages between the structure and processes of care and the outcomes of care will assist in producing predictable outcomes of care that reflect quality.
- There must be honest appraisal of whether quality assurance activities are really producing heightened quality in resident care programs.
- Improvement of care and commitment to quality are sources of pride for staff.

6

Self-review can become an integral part of the care that a nursing home provides for its residents. Definition of standards of care provides an important means of communicating expected performance to nursing home staff. Future quality of care, however, will not just depend on defining standards.

> Quality of care is the product of many factors, including provider willingness and capacity to provide care, consumer characteristics and behavior, the role of consumer advocates, involvement of other health professionals, third party reimbursement policies, and the state of knowledge about effective treatment and care. It is also, in no small measure, the result of government policies . . . (Office of Technology Assessment [OTA], 1987, p. 395)

CONCERN ABOUT QUALITY

Concern about quality of care in the future is based on several factors: demographics, a possible decrease in functional level of future nursing home residents, governmental fiscal constraints, an inadequate regulatory environment, and possible conflicts between quality of care and quality of life. Doty, Liu, and Wiener (1985) report that there will be a significant increase in the demand for long-term care and estimate an increase of 57 percent in the nursing home population between 1980 and 1995 (1.2 million to 1.9 million). They expect that by 2040, 4.3 million elderly will be institutionalized. Although there are more nursing home beds than hospital beds, the number of nursing home beds has been growing at only a modest rate. Approximately 23 percent of those aged 85 and over are institutionalized (Doty et al., 1985) and this is the fastest growing population group. Another group likely to need nursing home services are those with Alzheimer's disease. An estimated 1.5 million Americans currently have severe dementia. Without cures or means of preventing dementia, the number of people with severe dementia is expected to increase 60 percent by the year 2000. Five times as many people as today, 7.4 million, will be affected by the year 2040 (OTA, 1987, p. 3). Quality concerns based on demographics include the following: Will we have enough nursing home beds for these older adults? Will there be adequate numbers of trained personnel to provide care? Will effective nursing home services promoting quality of care and quality of life be developed, so that older adults of the future do not have to be fearful of living in a nursing home?

Fries (1980) has proposed that older adults of the future might have shortened periods of terminal decline before death. Schneider and Brody (1983) refute this prediction. Age-related increases in chronic disease and in functional dependency in activities of daily living could produce more demand for skilled services in nursing homes. Requirements for posthospital rehabilitative care are likely to increase. Without the involvement of more licensed professionals, such as registered nurses (RNs), physical therapists, occupational therapists, and speech therapists, it is unlikely that the public's needs and expectations for rehabilitation services in nursing homes can be met. In the 1985 National Nursing Home Survey (U.S. Department of Health and Human Services, 1987, pp. 98–99), 22.6 percent of the estimated 19,070 nursing homes reported no RN hours during the previous week; another 16.2 percent had less than 6 minutes of RN time available per patient day. Even Medicare-funded nursing homes, which are most likely to provide short-term rehabilitative services, can seek waivers from a federal requirement to have a RN at least on the day shift (8 hours) seven days a week if a full-time RN is at the facility 40 hours a week (U.S. Congress, 1987, p. 163). Early discharge of hospitalized elderly people has caused a rise in the demand for home health services and, quite positively, increased opportunities and options for noninstitutional care in the community. These supports can assist older adults to remain in their own homes longer, only seeking nursing home care when they are quite handicapped.

The provision of quality care is especially important for frail, debilitated older adults who are at higher risk for infection, malnutrition, pressure sores, adverse drug reactions, and falls. An increasing percent of the nursing home population suffering from severe dementia will add to the job stress of even the most caring staff. Segregated Alzheimer's units for older adults require special programming and additional staff. Unfortunately, the need for professional nurses is rising in a period of nursing shortages. And RNs working in nursing home settings usually receive lower salaries and benefits than hospitals offer, so these positions are less attractive. Linn, Gurel, & Linn (1977) found that facilities with more RN hours per resident had more residents alive, improved, and discharged from homes six months after transfer from a hospital. Self-review for quality assurance will be more important than ever during times of RN shortages. It could certainly be a significant factor in the identification of opportunities to improve the care of an older, more debilitated nursing home population.

Governmental fiscal constraints are another cause of concern about quality. Federal funds for Medicare and Medicaid and state budgets that provide a portion of Medicaid funding have been steadily increasing. Proposals to reform the long-term care financing system generally are designed to control government costs or to increase use of noninstitutional services. The majority of states already employ a prospective payment system for non-Medicare skilled nursing and intermediate care; it is likely that a system of prospective payment based on resource utilization rather than diagnosis will be developed for payment of Medicare skilled nursing. A common problem with the reimbursement limits of prospective payment is nonacceptance for nursing home care of severely debilitated people who require a high number of hours of nursing care per day. Another problem is the acceptance of these individuals without the resources to provide care or the intention to do so.

Although the federal government has legislated improved nursing home standards (U.S. Congress, 1987; Health Care Financing Administration, 1989), there is concern that inadequate federal and state funds will be budgeted for changes such as more registered nurse staffing, mandatory nurse aid training (minimum of 75 hours for initial training), and structured admission assessment programs. It is unlikely that future increases in the productivity of long-term care facilities will free up enough additional dollars to cover unreimbursed, new expenses. The new standards, although meant to increase quality, may only be implemented through trade-offs that delete other needed parts of established care programs.

An especially important quality concern for nursing home care is the inadequate regulatory system. State and federal agencies express dissatisfaction with the quality of care in nursing homes, yet they have opportunities to significantly influence quality through the development and monitoring of past "conditions of participation" and the standards governing nursing home operations. The Institute of Medicine report (Institute of Medicine [IOM], 1986) of government regulation of nursing homes, undertaken at the request of the Reagan administration, recommended important changes to enhance the ability of the regulatory system to assure satisfactory care for nursing home residents. It noted that more effective regulation by the federal government could substantially improve the quality of care in nursing homes. The government's interest in improving access to health care rather than enforcing minimal standards allows many nursing homes to operate with waivers of some standards. Defined "minimums," such as those set by states for staffing, may be too low to assure quality and can become the budgeted maximum in some settings. And these "minimum" care hours might be utilized to sort and deliver laundry, mop soiled floors, and empty trash, rather than to provide care to residents. State inspections for licensure and certification also demonstrate an inadequate regulatory system. Many facilities receive scheduled rather than unannounced surveys; new legislation supports unannounced surveys (HCFA, 1988a). Some states have insufficient numbers of surveyors, inadequate surveyor training, and inconsistencies in survey techniques and in the interpretation of regulations. The federal government denies that it has sufficient resources to provide direct training for approximately 3,000 long-term care surveyors (HCFA, 1988a). As nursing home personnel gain more experience with self-monitoring, they may be able to educate surveyors and state officials directing the survey process about quality appraisal in nursing homes.

The Health Care Financing Administration (HCFA) has recently implemented a resident-oriented survey process, Patient Care and Services (PaCS). Rather than focusing on structural factors or a facility's potential to provide care based on a review of paperwork, surveyors will observe care being delivered, interview residents, observe drug administration, and note outcomes of care. Doubts about the reliability of the survey methodology include concerns about protocols for resident interviews and lack of guidelines for the criteria used to make decisions about facility deficiencies (IOM, 1986, p. 131; HCFA, 1988a). Current regulations note that "deficiency citation remains primarily a matter of surveyor judgment" (HCFA, 1988a, p. 22853). There is a long-range objective to establish quantifiable standards. Even if this survey process substantially improves, many believe that inadequate enforcement would still be a roadblock to improving care. At present, many nursing homes with deficiencies are allowed to retain certification if they just have approved written plans for improvement. Decertification places a burden on the residents and state agencies during relocation from substandard facilities (OTA, 1987, p. 385). Restructuring of enforcement regulations will be necessitated by the Omnibus Budget Reconciliation Act of 1987 (OBRA '87; U.S. Congress, 1987).

The new federal rules and regulations for nursing home reform in Medicare and Medicaid funded facilities include new requirements for quality of life and resident rights. There is some overlap between the two categories. Quality of life requirements will focus on the resident's "ability to influence, and be influenced by, his or her physical and social environments and to participate fully in these environments to the full extent of his or her functional abilities" (HCFA, 1989, p. 5327). A lack of objective indicators for resident rights could lead to very subjective evaluation of nursing home compliance.

The possible conflict between quality of care and quality of life is an important concern that remains to be resolved. An example is restraining a resident to prevent falls, when the person wants to be free to walk around. Valued possessions may be considered fire hazards, and residents might be prevented from keeping or displaying them. Staff who desire to promote quality will need to proceed carefully in situations where residents' choices are severely limited because of care requirements.

PROMOTION OF QUALITY

Consumer Involvement

Concerned consumers who become involved in the development of resident care policy can have a positive impact on the quality of nursing home care. The Institute of Medicine (IOM) report (1986) notes that many decisions in nursing home settings affecting quality of life are based on individual preferences rather than on technical information. Residents and their families can be actively involved in this decision making, making their preferences known. Resident councils are an important mechanism. Exercise of personal choice meets the psychological needs of some residents (Rodin, 1986). Facility quality monitoring programs can easily include resident interviews, and, as previously noted, nursing home residents are now included in the new PaCS survey process. Family group meetings can be a forum for eliciting suggestions from residents' relatives. Increasing community participation through encouragement of visiting, making nursing home space available for community organizations needing a meeting room, initiation of foster grandparent programs, offering community college courses on site, and developing volunteer services can have a positive effect on quality of life.

Consumer advocates play a role in quality assurance. Residents who are very ill, immobile, have difficulty speaking for themselves, or have outlived family members and friends are examples of vulnerable individuals in nursing homes who require assistance to resolve difficulties they encounter in dealing with nursing home management and staff or government agencies. Most states have formal ombudsman programs, but many communities do not have active consumer advocate groups for nursing home residents and their families. The IOM (1986) has recommended that the Older Americans Act increase funding for state ombudsman programs through federal-state matching formula grants. It has also recommended that state nursing home regulatory agencies develop written agreements with state ombudsman programs covering information sharing, training, and case referral. Furthermore, the IOM report wants the Administration on Aging to provide effective national leadership for the ombudsman program by designating a full-time senior person and support staff to administer the program. A national resource for state ombudsman programs, serving as an information clearinghouse, could provide information to help state programs with training, data collection, and data analysis (IOM, 1986, pp. 180–183). Consumer advocates provide necessary assistance to residents who are unable or unwilling to tackle systems or care problems by themselves. Instead of developing adversarial relationships with consumer advocate groups, nursing homes must recognize that collaboration with these individuals may lead to opportunities to improve care.

National organizations such as the American Association of Retired Persons and the National Citizens' Coalition for Nursing Home Reform provide an important legislative lobby for nursing home reform. They attempt to keep the public informed about pending legislation and support major changes in federal regulation to improve performance standards, inspection, and enforcement in nursing homes. These organizations, along with many others, have publicized the IOM recommendations and have been active in efforts to see that they are implemented. The National Citizens' Coalition for Nursing Home Reform's (1985) study of residents' viewpoints regarding quality care has helped people to rethink definitions of quality and to give serious consideration to increasing opportunities for residents to participate more fully in decisions affecting their own care and have input into broader issues affecting their lives.

Another consumer program appealed to members of national and local organizations to become involved in a movement to make long-term care an important issue in the 1988 political campaign agenda (Long Term Care '88, 1987). The Long Term Care '88 group's national survey of a random sample of 1,000 voting-age Americans found that approximately 60 percent had already faced a long-term care problem involving their family or a close friend. Respondents, by a margin of five to two, said they were willing to pay additional taxes to provide long-term care for everyone aged 65 and older. Individuals were asked to get local organizations involved, conduct a similar survey in their communities, and share polling results with representatives of their congressional districts. If President George Bush gives funding for long-term care prominence in his legislative agenda, this could break down fiscal constraints that are likely to have an adverse effect on future quality of care in nursing homes.

Professional Involvement

Professional groups of providers and practitioners have contributed to quality assurance by developing standards that have the potential to assist in evaluation of the performance of group members. Unfortunately, the majority of administrators and nurses do not belong to these organizations. Standards of the American Nurses' Association's Council on Gerontological Nursing and of the American College of Health Care Administrators are presented in Exhibit 3-1 and Appendix B, respectively. These performance standards may, with time, provide increasing guidance to regulatory agencies and nursing homes planning quality assurance programs. Legislative lobbying related to long-term care regulation is an important function of provider and practitioner groups, allowing them to be proactive in a climate of change.

Trade associations such as the National Association of Homes for the Aging and the American Health Care Association encourage member facilities to review their own performance. The publications of these organizations can assist providers to monitor a wide variety of nursing home services. In addition, state and national meetings of these organizations furnish opportunities for members and others attending to receive up-to-date information about long-term care and to share ideas with others working in nursing homes. Large multistate nursing home corporations are likely to have internal quality review programs. A nurse who was employed by one of these organizations informed this chapter's author that managers could receive bonuses for superior performance demonstrated by the organization's quality assurance process.

Special Issues for Those with Alzheimer's Disease

The future care of those with Alzheimer's disease and related disorders will certainly benefit from current examination of quality of care issues for these individuals (OTA, 1987). Deterioration in function (although there is variability in the speed of decline among individuals) makes it difficult to specify achievable outcomes. Monitoring of positive outcomes such as protection from drug overdosage, prevention of infection, healing of pressure sores, and restoration of physical functioning, or negative outcomes such as "sentinal health events" based on New York's nursing home survey system could be useful (OTA, 1987, p. 373). Examples of negative outcomes are dehydration and malnutrition, adverse effects from medications, pressure sores, urinary incontinence, restraints, inadequate nursing care, deterioration of mental status, and poor quality of living environment (OTA, 1987, pp. 373–374). Quality of the living environment is identified as a significant factor in the residents' definition of quality. Residents with Alzheimer's disease will probably not be able to participate in interviews concerning quality issues. The Rush-Hines Veterans Administration Teaching Nursing Home Program considered how to measure quality from a resident's perspective when an individual could not answer interview items. The following criteria were developed:

- A particular name to identify resident is written on the care plan.
- A particular nurse or nurse aid is identified as the primary caretaker on care plan.
- Personal mementos are present in the resident's room.

- The resident's room and bedside are labeled with the resident's name.
- There is evidence that privacy is provided for a unit's residents.
- Staff interact with residents in a respectful manner.
- Group therapy programs are available.
- Residents have opportunities for interaction among themselves.

Long-term care insurance options have increased. Receiving assistance for costs of care that extends over long periods could have a significant positive effect on the care options for future victims of Alzheimer's disease. While benefits are limited on current policies (Wiener, Ehrenworth, & Spence, 1987), improved coverage might help pay for a variety of noninstitutional care options that could add to the quality of life of these individuals.

Information Dissemination

HCFA (1988b) has published 1987 data from state surveys of nursing homes. Each facility is profiled according to selected resident characteristics and performance indicators. Comparisons can be made with "State" and "Nation" data listed for the reported variables. The number and percent of facilities in the "State" and "Nation" who have not met the selected performance indicators are identified. Of the 16 performance indicators reported, the greatest unmet requirement nation-wide (29.8%) was a measure of basic nursing care processes: Each resident receives daily personal hygiene as needed to assure cleanliness, good skin care, good grooming, and oral hygiene taking into account individual preferences; residents are encouraged to take care of their own self-care needs. The nursing home industry and some consumer groups have criticized the report because of the current inconsistency in survey data. Resident characteristics reported (such as percent confused, with pressure sores, or confined to chair) may be due to a facility's ability to provide special services rather than inappropriate care; this fact is noted in small print. The American Nurses' Association (1988) supports sharing this data with potential users of nursing home services, but believes that the public must receive an explanation of its meaning and limitations. Review of the HCFA nursing home profiles can assist families when they are selecting the best possible facility to meet their needs. The IOM report (IOM, 1986, p. 41) recommends that HCFA should require states to have readily accessible public reports of nursing home inspection and costs. These increased sources of information can help individuals make informed choices about the quality of care provided in a specific facility.

Collection, analysis, and dissemination of information for quality assurance programs will involve more use of computers in the future. Continuing trends in cost reductions, along with ever-increasing requirements for detailed documentation of both care and eligibility for that care, are likely to make computer support for quality assurance activities cost-effective (Oatway, 1987). Special database programs, graphics, and optical scanners could reduce the everyday workload as well as provide significant assistance for monitoring and evaluation. Voice input capability, likely to be available in the future, will speed word processing. Nursing home units may be "on line" with administrative offices and have the capability to access approved records in physician offices and hospital databases. Computers will be able to present staff and managers with a great deal more information about resident care in the nursing home environment. Although it will be important for quality decisions to remain human decisions, these decisions are likely to be more effective with the availability of more information.

Regulatory agencies will also utilize computer technology to collect data on nursing home functioning; surveyors might be able to follow up deficiencies that do not require on-site inspection by using computers. Information about nursing home services and the results of past surveys could become readily available to consumers and practitioners.

The Joint Commission's "Agenda for Change"

The Joint Commission on Accreditation of Healthcare Organizations (Joint Commission) is steadily building its linkages with nursing homes. Long-term care standards are updated regularly, and regional educational sessions are held to educate nursing home personnel about these standards as well as to provide assistance in meeting them. They also sponsor national programs focusing on quality assurance in long-term care.

> The Joint Commission's "Agenda for Change" (1987) will "shift from primary reliance on the analysis of administrative process to the monitoring and evaluation of clinical and organizational performance" (p. 2).

The quality of an organization's response to undesirable indicator data is a major focus. The Joint Commission is planning now for future use of valid and reliable clinical indicators to serve as screening devices for the identification of potential problems (Joint Commission on Accreditation of Healthcare Organizations, 1987, p. 3). In the development of indicators for care in nursing homes, the Joint Commission is attempting to identify variables that are associated with normal variation in indicators, such as severity of illness and case mix, rather than change reflecting differences in the quality of care. The Joint Commission wants to minimize both false positives and false negatives arising from analysis of indicator data.

It is also expected that the Joint Commission will engage in the ongoing monitoring and evaluation of the institutions it accredits, rather than making only the current periodic visits, such as every two years. Updated information may need to be sent to the Joint Commission, possibly utilizing computer technology. Information would be processed quickly by the Joint Commission, and institutions would receive feedback between the regularly scheduled, on-site visits. The norms developed for screening with indicators will be used to evaluate nursing home data and to provide a means for the early detection of problems. This collection of information concerning indicators of high- or low-quality care in nursing homes should have a significant impact on the definition of standards of care and organizational performance in the nursing home industry.

Educating Individuals To Work in Long-Term Care

There is widespread consumer support for mandatory nurse's aide training programs, and the new federal regulations include this provision. Curricula are likely to vary among states but should become more effective as the content of educational programs is refined. Training manuals, film strips, and videotapes are currently available for orientation and inservice education. The demands of caring for a more debilitated nursing home population in the future will require better-educated bedside caregivers. The author found that nurse aide participation in inservice programs was increased when instructional materials included pictorial slides of the home's nurse aides performing desired care activities.

Schools of nursing and medicine are increasing their emphasis on geriatrics and gerontology. However, clinical experiences in nursing homes are not available for many students. The Council on Gerontological Nursing, American Nurses' Association, survey (1986) of schools of nursing in December 1985 found 83 percent of respondents (N = 461 programs; associate degree, baccalaureate, masters, and doctorate) reported student clinical experiences in extended care facilities or nursing homes. The average hours of clinical experiences per student were not identified. The American Nurses' Association (ANA) offers certification for gerontological nurses and gerontological nurse practitioners. Physicians now have subspecialty certification in geriatrics; this "specialist" status is likely to attract a larger number of talented physicians to the field of geriatrics. Certification opportunities for facility administrators are also offered by the American College of Health Care Administrators.

Nursing homes have been isolated from resources found in other parts of the health care system and from universities. In 1981 Robert Butler, former director of the National Institute on Aging, proposed linkages between universities and nursing home settings as one means to bring the education of health professionals and research into nursing home settings (Butler, 1981). He noted that as teaching hospitals had been models for community hospitals, the newly established teaching nursing homes could be models for other nursing homes. Nursing has been fortunate to have a Teaching Nursing Home Program (TNHP), co-sponsored by the Robert Wood Johnson Foundation and the American Academy of Nursing, that supported the development of 11 affiliations between university schools of nursing and nursing homes. Those involved believe that the pooling of resources will benefit both the affiliating institutions and society.

Affiliations between nursing homes and university schools of nursing can improve education and research opportunities for health professionals, as well as provide a means for changing care delivery systems and for advancing the quality of care in nursing homes. Aiken, Mezey, Lynaugh, and Buck (1985) note that

> this model is based on the premise that nursing care is the foundation on which the quality of services in nursing homes is established, and that in the absence of stable professional nursing management, it is unlikely that therapeutic and rehabilitative services can be implemented and sustained, or that physician participation will improve. (p. 198)

The Robert Wood Johnson Foundation provided $6.6 million for the five-year demonstration that ended in 1987. Within the next few years, geriatric literature will contain descriptions of the outcomes of these affiliations, plus a $1.5 million independent evaluation of the TNHP's benefits and costs (Small & Walsh, 1988). The TNHP included eight voluntary nonprofit nursing homes, two county homes, one proprietary home, and one Veterans Administration home.

As for the nursing shortage, it is likely that TNHP affiliations can

- help nursing homes compete more successfully for registered nurses in the face of a rising demand for registered nurses in hospital and community settings
- increase the number of nursing students, faculty, and nursing home staff with specialized knowledge and skills to work in long-term care
- address sources of professional dissatisfaction among nursing home nurses at a time when there is increasing emphasis on professionalism in nursing

A teaching nursing home brings sources of potential new recruits to the nursing home setting. It may provide some students, who would not ordinarily answer an advertisement to practice in a nursing home, with their first contact with a long-term care facility. A wide variety of clinical experiences can be developed in order to give students exposure to direct patient care, quality assurance, staff development, nursing administration, and research opportunities. In about four years Rush University College of Nursing brought 141 Rush nursing students to its teaching nursing home. Forty-six were master's level; two were doctoral students (D.N.Sc.). Nearly 19,000 Rush student hours have been spent at the nursing home.

Schools of nursing can bring students into long-term care settings and heighten their interest in providing care for nursing home residents, but they do not control the salary and benefit levels for nurses working in nursing homes. Salaries and benefits need to be competitive with other sources of employment. The U.S. Department of Health and Human Services (1987) has published a report of registered nurse recruitment and retention in nursing homes.

Turnover of licensed staff may be reduced by university affiliations, since the nursing home will have an influx of new people and new ideas. TNHP nursing schools are committed to encourage TNHP participation by other university programs that educate health professionals; this might provide new life for the interdisciplinary team. Nursing faculty can help bring quality assurance activities or special staff development programs into existence. Furthermore, staff get positive feedback from residents who are pleased with nursing students' care and participation in nursing home programs.

Recruitment and retention in long-term care facilities are hindered by the inadequate supply of nurses prepared with the specialized knowledge and skills to work in this setting. There is also insufficient qualified faculty to teach these courses (American Nurses' Association, 1986). TNHP affiliations increase the number of faculty prepared in geriatrics/gerontology, increase the number of students ready to work in long-term care, increase the geriatrics/ gerontology and long-term care content in the curricula of schools of nursing, and foster faculty research related to long-term care. The nursing home becomes a partner in the effort to expand the knowledge base of students and faculty. Formal and informal educational programs in geriatrics/gerontology that are developed for faculty and students can also be offered to nursing home staff. Nursing home staff appreciate the availability of continuing education and specialized degree programs in their practice field. In addition, other nurses in a teaching nursing home's geographic area benefit from these educational offerings.

The TNHP has a commitment to developing roles for professional nurses in nursing home settings. Clinical specialists with master's degrees and nurse practitioners can provide leadership for clinical care. Increased emphasis on professionalism is likely to help recruit and retain nurses in long-term care. Long-term care settings definitely offer nurses opportunities for more autonomy and control over nursing practice. The TNHP fosters this, and non-nurse managers would be wise to encourage creative nurse practice. Another source of professional satisfaction for nurses in nursing homes are the ongoing relationships they can develop with those who live there; this is in sharp contrast to current hospital nursing practice, where patients are often discharged within five to seven days. The repeated resident contacts characteristic of long-term care enhance student learning.

Reimbursement for Quality

The current regulatory system for nursing homes punishes bad behavior, rather than rewarding quality performance (IOM, 1986, p. 188). Denial of payment for substandard care may increase in the future. Some states have developed or are planning to develop systems to reward superior facilities. In Illinois there is a quality incentive program (QUIP) to encourage quality care in Medicaid-participating nursing homes. Nursing homes excelling in all designated survey areas become "6-star" homes and receive $2.00 a day for each Medicaid resident. Newspapers have published a list of these "6-star" homes, bringing recognition to the facilities and pride to their staffs. The IOM report (1986, p. 189) suggests that the certificate-of-need process can be used to reward quality. Poor providers would be denied certificate-of-need authorization to build or expand. States requiring certificates-of-need could restrict their award to only those nursing homes with superior performance.

The concept of reimbursement for quality is a good one, with great potential to improve the quality of care for future nursing home residents. The development of valid and reliable survey instruments and comprehensive training of surveyors need to be important components of quality incentive programs.

CONCLUSION

In a talk reviewing quality indicators at the 1984 annual meeting of the American Association of Homes for the Aging, Dr. Herbert Shore advised, "Take the simplest things and turn them into quality measures. Everything that happens in a facility is an opportunity" (Chapman-Cliborn, 1985, p. 68). Indeed, it is likely that many indicators of quality have not been identified yet. As more and more nursing homes become involved in self-monitoring and the talents and problem-solving ability of nursing home staff are focused on the critical issues of quality assurance, we will be able to define the structure, process, and outcome variables that are the best predictors of effective, economical care. Research establishing linkages between the structure and processes of care and outcomes of care in nursing homes will assist in producing predictable outcomes of care that reflect quality.

Many nursing homes are collecting data concerning their operations without analyzing this information for quality of care implications. A commitment to analyzing this data and developing action plans to remedy problems, if any are found, puts a facility on the road to self-review and development of a formal, comprehensive, and ongoing quality assurance program. It is the next logical step. This program itself, like clinical and organizational practices, must be appraised on a regular basis. Management support and attention to consumer and staff concerns are required to sustain staff commitment to self-monitoring. There must be honest appraisal of whether quality assurance activities are really producing heightened quality in resident care programs. It is very costly to have a quality assurance program that does not foster quality care.

Improvement of care and commitment to quality are sources of pride for staff. Residents and their families can become active participants in decision making regarding issues that affect quality of life in the nursing home, and the regulatory environment is increasingly sensitive to consumer demands. The future does hold promise for improved quality of care in nursing homes. Initiating a facility-wide quality assurance program begins that future of quality now.

REFERENCES

Aiken, L.H., Mezey, M.D., Lynaugh, J.E., & Buck, C.R. (1985). Teaching nursing homes: Prospects for improving long-term care. *Journal of the American Geriatrics Society*, *33*, 196–201.

American Nurses' Association. (1986). *Gerontological nursing currriculum*. Kansas City, MO: Author.

American Nurses' Association. (1988, January 22). HCFA plans to release consumer guide to quality care in nursing homes. *Capital Update*, 3.

Butler, R. (1981). The teaching nursing home. *Journal of the American Medical Association*, *245*, 1435–1437.

Chapman-Cliburn, G. (1985). Assuring quality in long term care. *Quality Review Bulletin*, *11*, 68.

Doty, P., Liu, K., & Wiener, J. (1985). An overview of long-term care. *Health Care Financing Review*, *6*(3), 69–78.

Fries, J. (1980). Aging, natural death and the compression of morbidity. *New England Journal of Medicine*, *303*, 130–135.

Health Care Financing Administration. (1987). Medicare and Medicaid: Conditions of participation for long term care facilities. *Federal Register*, *52*, 38582–38606.

Health Care Financing Administration. (1988a). Medicare and Medicaid; long term care survey. *Federal Register*, *53*: 22850–23101.

Health Care Financing Administration. (1988b). *Medicare/Medicaid nursing home information: Illinois* (3 Parts). Washington, DC: U. S. Government Printing Office.

Health Care Financing Administration. (1989). Medicare and Medicaid. Requirements for long term care facilities. *Federal Register*, *54*: 5316–5373.

Institute of Medicine. (1986). *Improving the quality of care in nursing homes*. Washington, DC: National Academy Press.

Joint Commission on Accreditation of Healthcare Organizations. (1987). *Overview of the Joint Commission's "Agenda for Change."* (Available from the Joint Commission, 875 North Michigan Avenue, Chicago, IL.

Linn, M., Gurel, L. and Linn, B. (1977). Patient outcome as a measure of quality of nursing home care. *American Journal of Public Health, 67*, 337–342.

Long Term Care '88. (1987). *Long term care*. Washington, DC: Author.

National Citizens' Coalition for Nursing Home Reform. (1985). *A consumer perspective on quality care: The residents' point of view*. Washington, DC: Author.

Oatway, D. (1987). The future of computer analysis for nursing quality assurance. *Journal of Nursing Quality Assurance, 1*(4), 61–71.

Office of Technology Assessment. (1987). *Losing a million minds* (OTA-BA-323). Washington, DC: U.S. Government Printing Office.

Rodin, J. (1986). Aging and health: Effects of the sense of control. *Science, 233*, 1271–1275.

Schneider, E., & Brody, J. (1983). Aging, natural death, and the compression of morbidity: Another view. *New England Journal of Medicine, 309*, 854–855.

Small, N. & Walsh, M. (1988). *Teaching nursing homes: The nursing perspective*. Owings Mills, MD: National Health Publishing.

U.S. Congress. (1987). *Omnibus budget reconciliation act of 1987. Publ. L. 100-203*. (pp. 160–221). Washington, DC: U.S. Government Printing Office.

U.S. Department of Health and Human Services. (1987). *Analysis of the environment for the recruitment and retention of registered nurses in nursing homes*. Washington, DC: U.S. Government Printing Office.

Wiencr, J.M. Ehrenworth, D.A., Spence, D.A. (1987). Private long-term care insurance: Cost, coverage, and restrictions. *The Gerontologist, 27*, 487–493.

Statement of Roles and Responsibilities for Nurse Administrators/Directors of Nursing in Long-Term Care

ASSUMPTIONS

Long-term care is where professional nursing will have a major impact.

The health care delivery system of the future will be different from the present system.

The aging population is increasing and requiring additional and different kinds of health care services.

The national movement toward self-care and personal responsibility for health has direct implications for nursing services.

Better educated, more articulate consumers have higher expectations of the quality of nursing services they will receive.

Changing family structures and relationships influence nursing services for the elderly.

The frail elderly population increasingly comprises a greater percentage of institutionalized persons and requires more complex nursing care.

The nurse administrators/directors of nursing are responsible for the management and improvement of nursing care delivery.

The compensations of nurse administrators/directors of nursing will be commensurate with their role, responsibilities, and qualifications.

The complexity of the role requires that the nurse administrators/directors of nursing place increased emphasis on administrative responsibilities.

Source: From *Professional Practice for Nurse Administrators/Directors of Nursing in Long-Term Care Facilities (Phase I)*, pp. 35-37, by M.P. Lodge, Kansas City, MO: American Nurses' Association, Inc. Copyright 1985 by American Nurses' Association, Inc. Reprinted by permission.

There is a common core of knowledge for nurse administrators/directors of nursing.

Knowledge about aging is also essential for the NA/DN:LTC.

The standards developed by nursing organizations as they relate to nursing administration are criteria for quality nursing services and education.

Increasing competition in the health care industry requires a marketing orientation by nurse administrators/directors of nursing.

Cost-containment is and will continue to be a major issue in health care.

Quality long-term care requires collaboration among individuals and professional organizations.

ROLES AND RESPONSIBILITIES

The NA/DN:LTC has four major roles with related responsibilities: organizational management (member of management team), human resources management, nursing/health services management, and professional nursing and long-term care leadership.

ROLE: ORGANIZATIONAL MANAGEMENT

As a member of the management team, the NA/DN:LTC—

- Serves as a member of the executive staff of the organization and develops effective working relationships with the chief executive officer and the medical director.
- Participates in development of institutional policies.
- Shares in development of long-range plans for the institution.
- Participates in development and administration of an evaluation plan for the institution based on institutional goals and objectives and on nursing standards.
- Works in establishing and facilitating effective employer-employee relations.
- Minimizes legal risks.
- Participates in establishing and maintaining management information systems to facilitate administration of the institution's nursing department.
- Designs and implements organizational structure for the nursing department.
- Formulates and administers policies and procedures for the nursing department.
- Implements federal, state, and local regulations pertaining to nursing service.
- Develops long-range plans for the nursing department.
- Formulates and administers the departmental budget based on nursing department goals and projected revenue.
- Participates in establishing a competitive wage, salary, and benefit plan for nursing services staff.

- Operates the department in a cost-effective manner.
- Designs and implements a quality assurance program for nursing care.
- Formulates and administers an evaluation plan for nursing services in relation to the department's established goals, objectives, and standards.
- Raises consciousness, educates, and participates in formulating policy relative to bioethical issues.
- Initiates research projects that address problems and issues specific to the nursing department.

ROLE: HUMAN RESOURCES MANAGEMENT IN NURSING

As the person responsible for nursing personnel, the NA/DN:LTC—

- Recruits, selects, and retains qualified nursing staff.
- Develops and implements a master staffing plan based on client needs and nursing service goals and standards.
- Initiates and approves position descriptions for nursing personnel.
- Promotes a scheduling system that balances employee and client needs.
- Formulates, implements, and evaluates a departmental plan for orientation and staff development.
- Assists individual staff members in development of career plans.
- Designs and implements a performance appraisal system for nursing.
- Promotes resolution of conflicts.
- Promotes and implements personnel policies.
- Creates a work climate that promotes a high-quality work life.

ROLE: NURSING/HEALTH SERVICES MANAGEMENT

As the person ultimately responsible for the quality of nursing care, the NA/DN:LTC—

- Develops philosophy, goals, and objectives for the department of nursing.
- Assesses the implementation of effective strategies and methods for delivery of nursing services.
- Implements actions to meet and maintain nursing care standards.
- Cooperates in developing and implementing a process for an interdisciplinary approach to health care services.
- Facilitates creative use of community resources.
- Ensures that clients' rights are protected.
- Encourages independence of clients through use of self-care and rehabilitation concepts.

- Initiates formal or informal testing of nursing interventions.
- Evaluates the organization of nursing care.
- Evaluates plans of nursing care.

ROLE: PROFESSIONAL NURSING AND LONG-TERM CARE LEADERSHIP

As the professional nurse and leader in long-term care, the NA/DN:LTC—

- Plans for future health and nursing care actions based on social, economic, political, and technological changes.
- Promotes changes in community health care systems based on social, economic, political, and technological changes.
- Encourages innovative methods for delivery of long-term care.
- Encourages entrepreneurial activities associated with development of nursing models for health care delivery focusing on health promotion, health education, and direct services.
- Establishes linkages with existing community resources.
- Influences public policy affecting long-term care and nursing.
- Establishes relationships with colleges and universities to promote formal educational opportunities for nursing staff, faculty practice, student learning experiences, and research.
- Promotes a positive image of long-term care, nursing in long-term care, and long-term care institutions.
- Seeks opportunities for personal and professional growth.

Standards of Practice for Long-Term Care Administrators

PREAMBLE

The long-term care administration profession is committed to providing comprehensive health, personal, and social services for persons who require various therapeutic, protective, and supervised environments and milieus. As leaders of the profession, members of the American College of Health Care Administrators are dedicated to advancing the general welfare through education, research, professional achievement, and a code of ethics. The Board of Governors of the College attests to this commitment by adopting, publishing, disseminating, and applying the following *Standards of Practice*. These *Standards of Practice* are the profession's statement of conditions and performances which are essential for quality long-term care. As an overriding principle, the long-term care administrator is expected to exercise sound judgment and decision making, assume leadership in his/her facility and community, and exemplify an administrative philosophy in congruence with the mission and goals of the organization.

I. GENERAL ADMINISTRATION

A. Develops long and short range objectives in order to assure that facility programs and resident care are maintained and improved.

B. Interprets the philosophy and goals of the facility in order to provide staff with adequate information to select appropriate objectives to attain the goals.

C. Sets an example of good resident relations and care for staff by demonstrating desired supervisory techniques and resident and family interaction.

D. Delegates responsibility and authority to appropriate staff in order to carry out the work of the facility.

E. Evaluates the quality of resident care and the efficiency of services in order to maintain care standards by reviewing the achievement or non-achievement of the facility's goals, objectives, patient care plans, and adherence to management policy and procedures.

Source: From *Journal of Long-Term Care Administration*, 15 (1), p. 11. Copyright 1987 by American College of Health Care Administrators. Reprinted by permission.

F. Coordinates departmental activities to assure departments work together toward the achievement of goals and activities by developing an information and communication system between departments which keeps them informed and allows the administrator to be informed of their activities.

G. Communicates with staff to solve problems through the selection of the appropriate communication techniques: staff meetings, department head meetings, counseling, and coordination of written information.

H. Prepares or assures the preparation of an annual budget of the facility in order to appropriately allocate resources to meet the facility's financial and program objectives and to prepare in advance potential cost control and managerial actions which may be required.

I. Ensures that the facility complies with federal, state, and local laws and regulations to meet standards of quality resident care.

J. Maintains a safe and productive working environment for staff in order to provide quality care through the use of regular inspections, allocation of resources for facility maintenance and construction, and periodic evaluations of staff morale and productivity.

K. Improves the information and administrative skills of oneself through professional development activities in order to direct effectively and efficiently the operations of the facility to assure high quality care.

Requisite knowledge and skill areas include:

- Communications
- Goal setting and implementation
- Health care system
- Long-term health care directions and state of the art practice
- Management science and practice
- Needs assessment (facility, organizational, and personal)
- Planning, implementation, evaluation strategies, and methodologies
- Problem solving/decision making
- Resource allocation/management

With expertise in:

Resident care
Personnel management
Financial management
Marketing, public/community relations
Physical resource management/ safety
Public sector/regulation

II. RESIDENT CARE

A. Ensures quality resident care through planning, implementation, and evaluation of nursing services to maintain maximum health potential; social services to meet psychological and social needs and rights; dietary services to meet nutritional requirements and needs; medical services to ensure appropriate medical care; activities to meet the social recreational and therapeutic recreational needs; medical records program to ensure continuity of care; pharmaceutical program to support appropriate medical care; and rehabilitation services that will maintain and/or maximize potential of residents; auxiliary services as necessary to enhance quality of life for residents; and environmental services to provide a pleasing environment.

B. Recruits, hires, and provides ongoing education for a health care team in order to assure quality care of the long-term care resident.

C. Obtains and coordinates consultant services as needed for total care (dental, speech and hearing, pharmacist, OT, PT, mental health, etc.) by matching needs of residents with services of consultants.

D. Coordinates the development and evaluation, with the health care team, of resident care goals and policies in order to assure that adequate resources, environments, and services are available to the residents.

E. Meets regularly with health care team to assure good care is being delivered.

F. Recruits a qualified medical director and develops a professional relationship with the medical director that ensures a well planned and implemented medical care program.

G. In cooperation with the medical director, maintains strong relationships with community medical practitioners including attending physicians and physician extenders.

H. Develops communication between facility staff and the residents in order to assure a caring environment with appropriate nursing and psychosocial services.

I. Develops facility standards for resident care by identifying those factors which affect care, as well as variables within each factor which can be adjusted and evaluated.

J. Develops program to assure staff adherence to Patient Bill of Rights.

Requisite knowledge and skill areas include:

- Communication methods for dissemination and implementation of patient care policies.
- Current literature, research, and regulations on the establishment of care standards and relevant factors (i.e., nursing, medical care, etc.)
- Family counseling/consultation
- Interpersonal relations
- Legal rights of residents including privacy, right to information, and informed consent
- Medical and psychosocial needs of the elderly and chronically ill
- Nursing, medical care, social services, activities, food services, medical records, pharmacology, and rehabilitation
- Resident care plans and goals
- Psychology of aging
- Quality assurance
- Responsibility of health care team in developing resident care plans, goals, and policies
- Roles and practices of clinicians
- Social, emotional, physical, and financial needs of residents and their families
- Staffing patterns necessary for quality care

III. PERSONNEL MANAGEMENT

A. Coordinates the development of and disseminates written personnel policies and procedures including job descriptions, employee expectations, employer benefits, and performance appraisal processes.

B. Demonstrates adherence to established personnel policies and procedures.

C. Promotes productivity and good morale among personnel to assure good resident care by providing motivation, a good working environment, and recognition of quality work.

D. Creates a positive atmosphere for communication between management and the work force through receptive management and the use of various media.

E. Establishes clear lines of authority and responsibility within the staff in order to assure understanding and production of quality work and the methods for its accomplishment.

F. Recruits and hires departmental supervisors who are qualified to meet the requirements of their position by identifying a number of qualified individuals, screening applicants, interviewing, and hiring the person who most closely meets the requirements.

G. Coordinates the development and implementation of personnel policies and procedures based on the goals of the organization in order to assure fair and efficient procedures are followed in recruitment, hiring, employment, and termination of staff.

H. Establishes wage and salary scales which attract competent staff while maintaining costs within budget.

I. Plans, implements, and evaluates a training program to facilitate adjustment of employees to the organization and the job through appropriate educational methodology.

J. Plans, implements, and evaluates a program which will provide an opportunity for the personal growth and development of employees through a performance evaluation process.

Requisite knowledge and skill areas include:

- Analysis of absenteeism and turnover rate
- Development of personnel policies, regulations, and laws including grievance procedures; job descriptions; labor, tax, minimum wage, and EEOC laws; workmen's compensation and other fringe benefit requirements and wage and benefit scales for staff and the current market value of labor in different job description categories.
- Employee recruitment, assessment, motivations, and recognition methodologies.
- Information and communication channels within the facility.
- In-service/training needs assessment, program planning, costs, implementation, and evaluation.
- organizational theory, lines of authority and responsibility, job description development and maintenance.
- Recruitment and interview techniques, job description develop-

ment, hiring practices, and wage scales for different supervisory positions.

- Staffing methodologies and patterns including job analysis techniques.
- Written and oral communication techniques for effective employee relationships.

IV. FINANCIAL MANAGEMENT

A. Plans, implements, and evaluates an integrated financial program to meet the facility's goals.

B. Coordinates the development of a budget which assures allocation of fiscal resources to meet regulatory requirements and provide quality services at a reasonable cost.

C. Evaluates the implication of budget on the quality of care.

D. Uses generally accepted accounting practices in accordance with sound financial management.

E. Establishes financial controls, checks, and balances in order to keep facility operations within budget.

F. Projects and monitors cash flow, investments, and capital expenditures to ensure financial stability.

G. Projects income and identifies revenue sources in order to meet the financial goals of the facility.

H. Transfers the financial goals of the governing body into management plans and budgets in order to achieve these goals by selecting appropriate objec-

tives such as facility size, growth, structure, level of care and service, staffing, etc. to meet these goals.

I. Plans future programs and estimates costs in order to reach decisions on growth, expansion, building, staffing, and investment by identifying objectives of the future programs and their cost.

J. Projects insurance needs of facility and secures appropriate coverage.

K. Analyzes current financial performance to ensure conformance with long-term goals and standards of quality.

Requisite knowledge and skill areas include:

- Ancillary and other revenue-producing sources
- Capital budgeting
- Cost components for service programs, expansion of facility, and new construction
- Economic trends/industry trends
- Financial analysis (i.e. resources, revenues, financial ratios)
- Generally accepted accounting practices (i.e. budgeting, cash flow, inventory, banking, auditing procedures, fixed costs, variable costs, investments, collection/billing, purchasing, etc.)
- Industry standards
- Interpreting financial results for Board and/or appropriate staff
- Insurance needs of facility
- Loan acquisition
- Materials management
- Patient financial screening, bank-

ing procedures, and account management

- Payroll procedures
- Regulatory requirements for budgeting
- Reimbursement regulations
- Tax laws and reporting
- Techniques for determining reasonable costs/pricing

V. MARKETING, PUBLIC/ COMMUNITY RELATIONS

A. Plans, implements, and evaluates a public relations program to enhance the positive image of long-term care services.

B. Establishes and maintains community relationships which enhance the image and services of the facility in the community by providing outreach services and information to the community.

C. Establishes and maintains programs which enhance relationships among residents, their families, and the facility.

D. Plans, implements, and evaluates a marketing program to advertise and provide the services of the facility.

E. Seeks to maintain occupancy of the facility at an optimum level in order to assure adequate financial resources by applying marketing and outreach techniques, knowing financial requirements of the facility, and delivering quality resident care at a reasonable cost.

Requisite knowledge and skill areas include:

- Community organizations (civic, religious, social, etc.) and importance of participation in community organizations
- Effective public speaking
- Forecasting techniques for demand for care
- Marketing of long-term care services and programs
- Media relations
- Medical/health care providers in community
- Information dissemination techniques for community awareness of services of the facility
- Outreach services, their cost and impact on referrals and community opinion
- Public relations principles

VI. PHYSICAL RESOURCE MANAGEMENT/SAFETY

A. Plans, implements, and evaluates a program for maintenance of building, grounds, and equipment.

B. Plans, implements, and evaluates a program of environmental services, which will provide a clean and attractive home for residents/patients.

C. Implements and evaluates a safety plan which will ensure the health, welfare, and safety of residents/patients, staff, and visitors.

D. Plans, implements, and evaluates employee health, safety, and educational programs which minimize the nursing home's exposure to liability.

E. Develops, implements, and evaluates a fire and disaster plan to protect the safety and welfare of residents, staff, and property.

Requisite knowledge and skill areas include:

- Architectural/environmental design for the elderly and the handicapped
- Building codes
- Community emergency resources
- Effective training and practice resources and procedures for emergencies
- Evaluation procedures for housekeeping and physical plant
- Housekeeping procedures
- Infection control
- Materials management
- Preventive maintenance
- Procedures for designating responsibility in emergency planning
- Pest control
- Safety and fire regulations in Life Safety Codes as well as local ordinances
- Sanitation procedures
- Security measures

VII. GOVERNANCE/ REGULATIONS

A. Interprets federal and state regulations as they relate to the facility in order to assure compliance and efficient integration of these regulations with the established policies and procedures of the facility.

B. Directs compliance of facility with government regulations in order to provide good resident care by knowing these regulations and how to meet their requirements.

C. Monitors medical reporting, staffing, and procedures in order to assure compliance with regulations and quality care.

D. Evaluates staff work procedures and policies to assure compliance with federal and state regulations.

E. Keeps the governing body informed by preparing management reports in order to facilitate decision making by the governing body.

F. Interprets the governing body's philosophy and goals to the staff in order to assure that the board's intent is followed and established policies and procedures reflect the governing board's philosophy.

G. Acts as liaison between the governing body and regulatory agencies.

Requisite knowledge and skill areas include:

- Affirmative Action/Equal Employment laws and regulations
- Area agencies on aging and ombudsman function
- Decision making process of the governing body
- Government regulations and guidelines (facility, life and safety, resident care, etc.)
- Governing body's philosophy and goals
- Information needs of the governing body
- Labor laws
- Legislative process
- Licensure and certification

- Long-term care survey process and procedures
- Medicare and Medicaid
- Methods for complying with government regulations and guidelines
- Preparation and format for management reports
- Procedures to monitor facility compliance with reporting, charting, review, and staffing requirements
- Professional licensing boards

- Quality assurance
- Regulations affecting reimbursement, capital expenditure, ownership, disclosure, and reports
- Regulatory agency practices
- Resident Bill of Rights
- Responsibility of administrator and governing body for compliance with regulations
- Tax laws (proprietary and nonprofit)

Nursing Care

Standard

PC.5 To assure safe and effective nursing care, a sufficient number of nursing personnel are assigned and are on duty.

Required Characteristics

PC.5.1 Nursing care is provided so that at least the following conditions are met:

PC.5.1.1 Patients/residents receive all prescribed treatments and medications.

PC.5.1.2 Patients/residents receive appropriate nursing intervention in response to physical and behavioral/emotional conditions.

PC5.1.3 Patients/residents are provided with rehabilitative/restorative and supportive nursing care, as needed.

PC.5.1.4 Patients/residents are provided with care designed to prevent the complications of immobility, such as decubitus ulcers and deformities.

PC.5.1.5 Patients/residents

PC.5.1.5.1 are kept comfortable, clean, neat, and well groomed;

PC.5.1.5.2 are protected from accident, injury, and infection; and

PC.5.1.5.3 receive assistance, as needed, with daily hygiene.

PC.5.2 Patients/residents are encouraged, assisted, and trained in self-care, as appropriate to the individual patient's/resident's status.

PC.5.2.1 The patient's/resident's family is involved in the training for patient/resident self-care, as appropriate.

PC.5.3 Patients/residents are encouraged and assisted to

PC.5.3.1 be up and about and dressed in their own clothing;

PC.5.3.2 use the dining areas if they are able, and

PC.5.3.3 participate in functional, social, and recreational activities.

PC.5.4   Patients/residents receive meals and nutritional supplements as prescribed.

PC.5.4.1 Nursing personnel monitor and respond to the nutritional needs of patients/residents and to weight loss and weight gain.

PC.5.4.1.1 Nutrition and hydration status are monitored on an ongoing basis and are documented in each patient's/resident's medical record.

PC.5.4.1.2 Assistance and instruction are provided to meet nutrition and hydration needs.

PC.5.4.1.3 Patients/residents who require help with eating receive assistance, and adaptive self-help devices are provided to assist patients/residents to eat independently.

PC.5.5   Unexpected changes in the patient's/resident's status are reported to the charge nurse and the attending physician and are noted in the medical record.

PC.5.6   The activities of nursing personnel are directed to interaction with patients/residents, rather than nonnursing activities such as administrative management, laundry, housekeeping, and dietary duties.

Standard

PC.6   A rehabilitative/restorative and supportive nursing program is an integral part of nursing care and of the interdisciplinary plan of care.

Required Characteristics

PC.6.1   Rehabilitative/restorative and supportive nursing care is directed toward measures to prevent deterioration and to achieve and maintain optimal levels of functioning and independence.

PC.6.2   Rehabilitative/restorative and supportive nursing care is performed daily and is documented.

PC.6.3   Rehabilitative/restorative and supportive nursing care includes, but is not necessarily limited to, the following:

PC.6.3.1 Proper body position and body alignment;

PC.6.3.2 Assistance to patients/residents in being up and out of their beds for reasonable periods of time, except when contraindicated by physician's order;

PC.6.3.3 Implementation of a skin integrity program;

PC.6.3.4 Bowel and bladder training;

PC.6.3.5 Ambulation, including maintenance of gait training;

PC.6.3.6 Active and passive range-of-motion exercises;

PC.6.3.7 Assistance and instruction in the activities of daily living, such as eating, dressing, grooming, oral hygiene, and toilet activities;

PC.6.3.8 Interventions (e.g., remotivation therapy, reality orientation, and sensory stimulation) in response to emotional/behavioral patterns; and

PC.6.3.9 Assistance to patients/residents and their families in adjusting both physically and emotionally to the patients'/residents' disabilities.

Criteria for Quality of Nursing Care

Source: Reprinted with permission of Rush Presbyterian-St. Luke's Medical Center, Rush University College of Nursing, Chicago, Illinois. Copyright 1982, 1983, 1986. Based upon a quality assurance instrument, funded under Public Health Service Contract NIH 72-4299, July 1972.

Directions: These criteria are to be applied to nursing home residents randomly selected for review. To be included in the sample, residents should have been in the facility at least 30 days (admission-related criteria—1.1, 1.2, 3.1) or longer than 30 days (other criteria).

Sources of information are coded as follows for all criteria:

01 Resident record
02 Observation of resident
03 Interview of resident
04 Interview of nursing personnel
05 Observation of nursing personnel
06 Observation of resident environment
07 Observer inference
08 Observation of unit management

Resident types may be described as follows: Exact "typing" based on modification of a Veterans Administration patient classification tool.

Type 1 Minimal care
Type 2 Moderate care
Type 3 Complete care
Type 4 Continuous care

A code 5 under type refers to an observation of the unit as a whole.

Responses
1 No
2 Yes incomplete, yes some (50%), yes oral
3 Yes most (75%)
4 Yes, yes complete, yes all, yes always (100%), yes written (100%)
8 Information not available (resident unable to answer, resident not in room)
9 Not applicable

Code 8, information not available, if resident is not available for interview, cannot recall information, or is unresponsive or disoriented. Use this code if observer cannot complete resident environment observations.

Code 9, not applicable, if criterion does not apply.

Source of Information	Criterion	Response		Patient Type

1.0   THE PLAN OF NURSING CARE IS FORMULATED.
1.1   THE CONDITION OF THE RESIDENT IS ASSESSED ON ADMISSION.

01*   1.102   IF THE RESIDENT DEPENDS ON PROSTHETIC DEVICES FOR ADL, IS THIS RECORDED UPON ADMISSION TO THE UNIT?

No   1
Yes   2
Incomplete
Yes   4
Complete
NA   9

Depend means that the resident uses or has prosthetic devices for ADL. "Prosthetic devices" refers to any device used for ADL, e. g., dentures, glasses, hearing aids, contact lenses, orthopedic shoes or braces, artificial limbs or eyes. May include devices such as wigs. "ADL" means minimal activities required for daily personal care, e.g., eating, toilet, dressing, ambulation. Observer must check with resident if nothing recorded.

To check, ask resident: Do you have or use any assistive items such as glasses, dentures, braces, etc.?

Code No if nothing recorded and resident has or uses prosthetic devices.

Code NA if nothing recorded and resident does not have or use prosthetic devices.

Code Yes Complete only if resident has prosthetic devices and all are recorded *within 24 hours* of admission.

01   1.103   ARE RESIDENT'S ELIMINATION PATTERNS RECORDED UPON ADMISSION TO THIS UNIT?

No   1
Yes   4

*Utility of item has not been demonstrated, and statistical analyses of the authors' dataset found that the item did not contribute to the reliability or validity of the monitoring instrument.

Source of Information	Criterion		Response		Patient Type
01*	1.104	"Patterns" refers to information about regularity/irregularity of bowel and bladder. Statement of just "constipation" or "diarrhea" is not acceptable.			
		Code Yes only if information is present and is recorded *within 3 days of* admission.			
		ARE DESCRIPTIONS INDICATIVE OF MENTAL-EMOTIONAL STATE RECORDED AT THE TIME OF ADMISSION TO THIS UNIT?	No	1	
			Yes	4	
		Applies to statements of behavior, e.g., alert, talkative, crying, laughing, or to statements of mental-emotional state, e.g., anxious, depressed, mentally retarded.			
		Code Yes only if statement recorded *within 24 hours* of admission.			
01*	1.105	IS THERE A STATEMENT WRITTEN UPON ADMISSION TO THIS UNIT ABOUT THE CONDITION OF THE SKIN?	No	1	
			Yes	4	
		Refers to dryness, turgor-hydration, absence or presence of skin lesions, localized skin color, warmth, etc. Do not accept general descriptions such as "pale."			
		Code Yes only if statement is recorded *within 24 hours* of admission.			
01*	1.111	IS THERE A STATEMENT WRITTEN ON ADMISSION INDICATING RESIDENT'S ORIENTATION TO TIME, PLACE, AND PERSON?	No	1	
			Yes	2 Incomplete	
		Code Yes only if information recorded *within 24 hours* of admission.	Yes	4 Complete	
		Code Yes Incomplete if reference is made to 1 or 2 of either (time, place, or person).			

			No	1
01	1.114	IS THERE A STATEMENT RECORDED AT THE TIME OF ADMISSION REFLECTING THE RESIDENT'S PERCEPTION OR UNDERSTANDING OF HIS ILLNESS OR CONDITION?	Yes	4
			NA	9

Refers to answers probably elicited by the questions: Can you tell me something about your illness? or What is the reason you are in the hospital? (May be recorded by any member of the health care team.)

Code NA only if resident was unresponsive or disoriented on admission.

Code Yes if statement recorded *within 1 week* of admission.

Code Yes only if quote or paraphrase is recorded.

	1.115	ON ADMISSION TO THE UNIT, IS EACH OF THE FOLLOWING RECORDED:		
01*		A. The resident's temperature?	No	1
			Yes	4
01*		B. The resident's blood pressure?	No	1
			Yes	4

Must be recorded *within 24 hours* of admission by nursing or physician.

	1.116	DOES THE HISTORY INCLUDE THE FOLLOWING INFORMATION REGARDING THE RESIDENT'S HEALTH PROBLEMS:		
01		A. When the current major health problem occurred?	No	1
			Yes	4

---

*Utility of item has not been demonstrated, and statistical analyses of the authors' dataset found that the item did not contribute to the reliability or validity of the monitoring instrument.

Source of Information	Criterion	Response		Patient Type
01	B. How the health problem occurred (i.e., mechanism of injury or situation at the onset of problem), or the progression of change from the resident's normal health state that led up to this admission?	No Yes	1 4	
01	C. Current symptoms or signs? Must be recorded *within 3 days* of admission. May be recorded by any member of health care team.	No Yes	1 4	
1.120	ON ADMISSION TO THE UNIT, IS EACH OF THE FOLLOWING RECORDED?			
01	A. The resident's heart or pulse rate and quality? Quality refers to a description such as weak, thready, regular, etc. *Both rate and quality are necessary for a Yes answer.*	No Yes	1 4	
01*	B. The resident's respiratory rate and quality? Quality refers to descriptions such as shallow, labored, Cheyne-Stokes, retracting, even, etc. *Both rate and quality are necessary for a Yes response.* Must be recorded *within 24 hours* of admission by nursing or physician.	No Yes	1 4	
1.123	01 IF THE RESIDENT HAS A SENSORY IMPAIRMENT THAT AFFECTS ADL, E.G., IMPAIRED HEARING OR VISION, IS IT RECORDED ON ADMISSION TO THE UNIT?	No Yes Incomplete	1 2	

Refers to the type of disability, not to presence of prosthetic device. If nothing recorded, observer must check with resident or see whether criterion applies.

To check, ask resident: Do you have any difficulty with your hearing or vision, or have any areas of your skin that have decreased sense of touch?

Code No if nothing recorded but resident has disabilities.

Code Yes if recorded *within 3 days* of admission.

Code NA if resident has no sensory impairment.

Yes 4
Complete
NA 9

01*   1.124   IF THE RESIDENT HAS A MOTOR IMPAIRMENT THAT AFFECTS ADL, E.G., PROBLEM WITH SPEECH, CHEWING, LOCOMOTION, IS IT RECORDED ON ADMISSION TO THE UNIT?

Refers to type of disability, not to presence of prosthetic device. If nothing recorded, observer must check with resident to see whether criterion applies.

To check, ask resident: Do you have any difficulty with walking, talking, chewing, or other muscular activity?

Code No if nothing recorded but resident has disabilities.

Code Yes if recorded *within 3 days* of admission.

Code NA if resident has no motor impairment.

No 1
Yes 2
Incomplete
Yes 4
Complete
NA 9

01   1.125   DOES THE RECORD INDICATE THE RESIDENT'S EXPECTATIONS/UNDERSTANDING OF HIS CARE?

No 1
Yes 4
NA 9

*Utility of item has <u>not</u> been demonstrated, and statistical analyses of the authors' dataset found that the item did not contribute to the reliability or validity of the monitoring instrument.

Source of Information	Criterion	Response		Patient Type

Source of Information	Criterion	Response		Patient Type
	Refers to statements about whether resident expects to get well, to go home, to die, to learn to walk, etc. If statement is recorded answer yes regardless of whether resident's expectation is realistic in your opinion. May be recorded by any member of health care team *within one week* of admission.			
	Code Yes only if quote or paraphrase is recorded.			
	1.2 DATA RELEVANT TO CARE ARE ASCERTAINED ON ADMISSION.			
01*	*IS THE GENERAL PHYSICAL APPEARANCE OF THE RESIDENT RECORDED WITHIN THE FIRST 24 HOURS OF ADMISSION TO THIS UNIT?*	*No* *Yes*	*1* *4*	
	Intent is to have a verbal physical "photograph" of resident as data base. Accept any description of physical appearance, e.g., pale, emaciated, obese, posture, dress. Applies to physical appearance rather than physiological symptom. *Do not* accept reference to age, sex, race, marital status. Does not include behavioral description. Do not accept general description, such as "in acute distress."			
	Do not code NA. Applies to all residents on unit.			
	Code Yes only if information is present and is recorded within 24 hours of admission.			
01	IS HEIGHT RECORDED UPON ADMISSION TO THIS UNIT?	No Yes NA	1 4 9	
	Code Yes if recorded *within 3 days* of admission. May be recorded by any member of health care team.			

Arm span measurement is acceptable.

Code NA if height and arm span are not obtainable.

01   1.204   IS WEIGHT RECORDED UPON ADMISSION TO THIS UNIT?

Code NA if information recorded on admission to another unit.

Code Yes only if information is present and recorded *within 3 days* of admission. May be recorded by any member of the health care team.

No	1
Yes	4
NA	9

01   1.205   IS THERE A STATEMENT WRITTEN AT THE TIME OF ADMISSION TO THIS UNIT DENOTING WHETHER THE RESIDENT HAS BEEN TAKING MEDICATIONS, AND IF YES, NAMES OR DESCRIPTIONS OF DRUGS, FREQUENCY OF ADMINISTRATION, AND LENGTH OF TIME RESIDENT HAS BEEN TAKING MEDICATIONS, INCLUDING ALCOHOL AND DRUGS?

No	1	
Yes	2	Incomplete
Yes	4	Complete
NA	9	

A clear notation of no medications or all three types of information must be present for each drug for *Yes Complete* answer. If nothing recorded, observer must find out whether resident was taking medications prior to admission. May be recorded by any member of health care team.

Code Yes if recorded within 24 hours of admission.

Code NA if resident/significant other is unable to give history.

01*   1.206   ARE EITHER THE DIET OR THE FOOD PREFERENCES OF THE RESIDENT RECORDED UPON ADMISSION TO THIS UNIT?

No	1
Yes	4

---

*Utility of item has <u>not</u> been demonstrated, and statistical analyses of the authors' dataset found that the item did not contribute to the reliability or validity of the monitoring instrument.

Source of Information		Criterion	Response		Patient Type
			NA	9	
01	1.213	Code NA if resident unable to give history on admission.			
		Code Yes only if statement is present and recorded *within one week* of admission. May be recorded by dietitian.			
		IS THERE A STATEMENT WITHIN 24 HOURS OF ADMISSION DESCRIBING THOSE ACTIVITIES OF DAILY LIVING THE RESIDENT DOES OR DOES NOT PERFORM OR NEEDS ASSISTANCE DOING?	No	1	
			Yes	2	
				Incomplete	
		Refers to activities such as bathing self, dressing, eating, ambulating, toileting.	Yes	4	
				Complete	
01	1.214	IS THERE A STATEMENT WRITTEN UPON ADMISSION INDICATING:			
		A. With whom the resident lives?	No	1	
			Yes	4	
01*		B. Whom the resident relies on in times of need or emergency. May refer to person listed as "next of kin."	No	1	
			Yes	4	
		Code Yes if recorded within one week by any member of health care team.			
01	1.215	IS THERE A STATEMENT RECORDED WITHIN ONE WEEK OF ADMISSION REGARDING THE RESIDENT'S LIFESTYLE PRIOR TO ADMISSION, I.E., DAILY ROUTINE, ACTIVITIES, OR STRESSES?	No	1	
			Yes	4	
		May be recorded by any member of health care team.			
01	1.216	IS THERE A STATEMENT ABOUT ALLERGIES WRITTEN AT THE TIME OF ADMISSION TO THIS UNIT?	No	1	
			Yes	4	
			NA	9	

Refers to statement of the presence or absence of allergies.

Code Yes only if statement is present and recorded within first 24 hours of admission.

1.221 DOES THE RESIDENT'S RECORD INCLUDE THE FOLLOWING DATA?

01*	A. Time of admission?	No 1 / Yes 4
01*	B. Date of admission?	No 1 / Yes 4
01*	C. Identification number?	No 1 / Yes 4
01*	D. Mode of arrival, e.g., ambulatory, wheelchair, cart?	No 1 / Yes 4
01*	E. By whom or with whom resident brought to facility or that resident came alone?	No 1 / Yes 4

Must be recorded *within 24 hours* of admission.

01	1.222 IS THERE A WRITTEN STATEMENT WITH REGARD TO THE FAMILY'S LEVEL OF UNDERSTANDING, CONCERNS, OR VIEW OF THE RESI-DENT'S CONDITION?	No 1 / Yes 4 / NA 9

*Utility of item has not been demonstrated, and statistical analyses of the authors' dataset found that the item did not contribute to the reliability or validity of the monitoring instrument.

Source of Information	Criterion	Response		Patient Type
01	May be recorded by any member of health care team *within 3 days* of admission. Look for documentation in the care record or Kardex.			
	Code NA if the resident has no family or significant other.			
1.223	IS THERE A STATEMENT WRITTEN ON ADMISSION INDICATING A TENTATIVE DISCHARGE ARRANGEMENT?	No	1	
		Yes	4	
		NA	9	
	Code Yes if information is recorded *within 2 weeks* of admission to the unit.			
	Code NA if there is a note that this nursing home placement is considered permanent.			
01	1.224 IS THERE EVIDENCE OF A COLLABORATIVE APPROACH AMONG HEALTH CARE PROFESSIONALS IN ESTABLISHING THE RESIDENT'S PLAN OF CARE?	No	1	
		Yes	4	
		NA	9	
	Collaborative approach refers to a team meeting or conference for which the objective is to communicate about resident care goals.			
	Code Yes only if this occurs *within 2 weeks* of admission. Check record for documentation of such conference or check with charge nurse to see if a conference was held.			
	1.3 THE CURRENT CONDITION OF THE RESIDENT IS ASSESSED.			
01	1.301 IS THERE A WRITTEN STATEMENT ABOUT THE CONDITION OF THE SKIN?	No	1	3–4
		Yes	4	

Related to dryness, turgor-hydration, absence or presence of skin lesions, localized skin color, warmth, etc. *Do not accept* general description such as "pale." Should apply to present status or *within past month*.

Code NA if skin condition is not an active or potential problem.

NA   9

01   1.303   ARE DESCRIPTIONS INDICATIVE OF THE CURRENT EMOTIONAL STATE RECORDED?

No   1
Yes   4

1-2-3-4

Applies to statements of behavior, e.g., alert, talkative, crying, laughing, becoming more restless; or to statements of mental-emotional state, e.g., anxious, depressed, mentally retarded, presence of hallucinations, delusional, etc. Accept statement recorded *within past month*. May be recorded by any member of health care team.

01   1.325   DOES THE RECORD CONTAIN A RECENT REASSESSMENT OF THE RESIDENT'S HEALTH STATUS AND OVERALL PROGRESS TOWARD GOALS?

No   1
Yes   2   Incomplete
Yes   4   Complete

1-2-3-4

Applies to statements recorded *within the past month* about level of function or level of independence or dependence. Does not apply to admission assessment. May be recorded by any member of health care team.

1.4   *THE WRITTEN PLAN OF NURSING CARE IS FORMULATED.*

---

*Utility of item has not been demonstrated, and statistical analyses of the authors' dataset found that the item did not contribute to the reliability or validity of the monitoring instrument.

Source of Information	Criterion	Response		Patient Type
				1–2–3–4
01	1.401 A. ARE GOALS OF CARE WRITTEN?	No	1	
		Yes	4	
	Note: If no for A, code no for B and C.			
01	B. ARE THE GOALS CURRENT?	No	1	
	To nurse in charge of resident: In your opinion, are the goals of care written on Mr. _____'s care plan current?	Yes	2	
		Some		
		Yes	4	
		All		
01*	C. ARE THE GOALS MEASURABLE?	No	1	
		Yes	2	
		Some		
		Yes	4	
		All		
01*	1.402 A. ARE THERE WRITTEN NURSING *INTERVENTIONS* APPROPRIATE TO THE RESIDENT'S CONDITION OR SYMPTOMS?	No	1	1–2–3–4
		Yes	2	
	Does not apply to medical orders.		Incomplete	
	Observer must identify appropriate nursing interventions/orders, e.g., elevation of head for shortness of breath, measures for decubitus care, exercises for immobile residents, etc., that should be specified for this resident, then check nursing plan, e.g., Kardex, care plan, progress notes, treatment plan, etc. to see if interventions/orders are listed.	Yes	4	
			Complete	
		NA	9	
	Code as Incomplete if any significant intervention/order is not written, even though others are listed.			

01

B. DO SPECIFIC TIMES AND METHODS ACCOMPANY NURSING INTERVENTIONS/ORDERS?

No	1
Yes	2
	Incomplete
Yes	4
	Complete
NA	9

Code NA if no therapeutic measure required. May Code NA if specific activities are continuous and cannot be scheduled, e.g., limit setting program for aggressive or acting out behavior. For *Complete*, each order should indicate specific time activity to be done, and method of performing activity. For diagnostic procedure, acceptable if reference is made to file or Rolodex. Does not refer to the instruction of resident.

Statements such as BID, TID, etc., are not acceptable as times unless specific hours stated in facility policy.

01

1.403 IN THE PLAN OF CARE IS THERE A STATEMENT ABOUT ACTIVITIES THE RESIDENT IS EXPECTED TO DO FOR HIMSELF AND ACTIVITIES THE NURSING STAFF SHOULD PERFORM FOR THAT RESIDENT?

1-2-3-4

No	1
Yes	2
	Incomplete
Yes	4
	Complete

Check lists acceptable: Refers to basic ADL, e.g., eating, toilet, dressing, bathing, walking, and other types of participation in care (wound dressing, etc.)

01

1.407 IS THE PLAN FOR TURNING AND POSITIONING THE RESIDENT STATED IN WRITING IN THE NURSING CARE PLAN?

3-4

No	1
Yes	4
NA	9

If not stated in writing, to see if applicable, may ask nurse: Is Mr. _____ able to turn and position himself?

Code NA only if resident does not need to be turned or positioned. Accept only written plan.

---

*Utility of item has not been demonstrated, and statistical analyses of the authors' dataset found that the item did not contribute to the reliability or validity of the monitoring instrument.

Source of Information	Criterion	Response		Patient Type
01*	1.409 IS THERE A NURSING PLAN FOR SYSTEMATICALLY INCREASING THE RESIDENT'S INDEPENDENCE OR RESTORING HIM TO A HIGHER LEVEL OF FUNCTION, I.E., INCREASING SELF-HELP OR INCREASING ACTIVITY IN AN ORGANIZED MANNER? Applies only if resident needs attention to such care. Applies to care not included in medical regimen.	No Yes NA	1 4 9	2–3
01*	1.415 IS THERE A PLAN FOR MAINTENANCE AND COMFORT OF THE RESIDENT WHO WILL NOT ACHIEVE A HIGHER LEVEL OF FUNCTIONING? Applies only if promoting self-help is unrealistic, i.e., if in semi-conscious, unconscious state or care plan defines goals of care as maintenance level only.	No Yes NA	1 4 9	3–4
01*	1.416 IS THERE A SPECIFIC PLAN FOR ASSISTING THE RESIDENT IN DEVELOPING INTERACTIONAL OR COMMUNICATION SKILLS (SPEECH) IF THIS IS A PROBLEM? Includes those with behavioral problems. Plan may be recorded by any member of health care team.	No Yes NA	1 4 9	1–2–3–4
04	1.417 IS DISCHARGE PLANNING CARRIED OUT? To nurse: Are any of your residents expected for discharge from this unit within the next 2 weeks? If yes, ask: What is being done to plan or coordinate the discharge? Code Yes if resident seen by social service or resident/family conference held to discuss arrangements or referral made.	No Yes NA	1 4 9	5

Code *NA* if no discharges from the unit are expected within the next 2 weeks.

1.5 THE PLAN OF NURSING CARE IS COORDINATED WITH THE MEDICAL PLAN OF CARE.

01* 1.501 ARE MEDICALLY PRESCRIBED TREATMENTS INCLUDED IN THE NURSING PLAN OF CARE (KARDEX, CARE PLANS, TREATMENT SHEET, ETC.)?

Check nursing record of treatments with active medical orders for this resident.

No	1	1-2-3-4
Yes	2	
Incomplete		
Yes	4	
Complete		
NA	9	

01* 1.502 IS THERE A NURSING PLAN FOR MAKING OBSERVATIONS OF SIGNS OR SYMPTOMS IN REGARD TO MEDICAL TREATMENT, MEDICATIONS, DISEASE PROCESS, POSSIBLE COMPLICATIONS OR FUNCTIONAL STATUS?

Refers to major signs and symptoms in regard to this resident's present condition. Does not apply to observations indicated in physician's orders. Observer must determine if resident's condition indicates need for specific observation.

No	1	1-2-3-4
Yes	2	
Incomplete		
Yes	4	
Complete		
NA	9	

04 1.503 HAS THE NURSE DISCUSSED OR REVIEWED PLANS OF CARE FOR THE RESIDENT WITH THE PHYSICIAN?

No	1	3-4
Yes	4	

---

*Utility of item has <u>not</u> been demonstrated, and statistical analyses of the authors' dataset found that the item did not contribute to the reliability or validity of the monitoring instrument.

Source of Information	Criterion	Response	Patient Type
	To nurse in charge of resident: Have a nurse and the doctor or nurse practitioner responsible for _____ reviewed or discussed the resident's orders or plans *in the last month?* "Nurse in charge of the resident" can refer to primary nurse, team leader, charge nurse, or equivalent. *Code Yes* if nurse indicates monthly.		
04	1.504 HAS THE NURSE DISCUSSED PLANS FOR THE RESIDENT WITH HEALTH CARE WORKERS OTHER THAN THE PHYSICIAN WHO ARE ALSO WORKING WITH THE RESIDENT? Determine whether other personnel are working with the resident. If so: To nurse: In the past month, have you had a chance to discuss _____'s care with personnel other than physicians or nursing staff who are working with him? Also *Code Yes* if written documentation by any member of health care team that there was discussion with the nurse.	No 1 Yes 4	1-2-3-4
01*	1.505 DO NURSING ORDERS SPECIFY TIMES AND METHODS FOR MEDICAL THERAPEUTICS OR DIAGNOSTIC MEASURES ORDERED BY A PHYSICIAN OR NURSE PRACTITIONER AS APPROPRIATE? *Code NA* only if there are no medical or relevant nursing orders. *Code Yes Complete* only if each nursing order indicates specific time activity is to be done and method of performing activity. For diagnostic procedure, acceptable if reference made to use of file or Rolodex. Does not refer to instruction of resident. Statements such as BID, etc., are not acceptable as times unless specific hours stated in facility policy.	No 1 Yes 2 Incomplete Yes 4 Complete NA 9	1-2-3-4

01* 1.507 HAS THE NURSE NOTIFIED THE APPROPRIATE PERSON OR SERVICE (E.G., PHYSICIAN, NURSE PRACTITIONER, ETC.) OF SIGNIFICANT CHANGES IN THE RESIDENT'S CONDITION?

No	1
Yes	4
NA	9

1-2-3-4

Applies to any significant changes that occurred *in past month*. Check nursing records to determine whether significant changes occurred, then check to see whether physician was notified (progress note stating such, or new MD/GNP order related to condition change). *Code NA* if no significant changes occurred.

2.0 *THE PHYSICAL NEEDS OF THE RESIDENT ARE ATTENDED.*
2.1 *THE RESIDENT IS PROTECTED FROM ACCIDENT AND INJURY.*

02 2.101 IS THE RESIDENT WEARING AN ACCEPTABLE MEANS OF IDENTIFICATION?

No	1
Yes	4
Information Not Available	8

1-2-3-4

Type 2-4 residents must have some form of identification on their person such as bracelet, tag, or photo. Type 1 may be identified by picture ID stored on chart or Kardex. *Do not answer NA.*

02 2.102 IS THE RESIDENT IN A POSITION OF OPTIMAL BODY ALIGNMENT?

No	1
Yes	4
Information Not Available	8
NA	9

3-4

Observe position of feet, legs, knees, trunk, shoulders, arms, and head.

Code No if any part of body not properly aligned, or if the resident's extremities are restricted by dressings. *Code NA* for residents who are not confined to bed or wheelchair, or are able to position themselves.

*Utility of item has <u>not</u> been demonstrated, and statistical analyses of the authors' dataset found that the item did not contribute to the reliability or validity of the monitoring instrument.

Source of Information	Criterion	Response		Patient Type
04*	2.105 ARE ASSIGNED NURSING STAFF INFORMED OF THE RESIDENT'S PRESENT STATUS? To nurse: What is Mr. _____'s condition today, or his/her present status? Observer must know resident's present status. Ask for specifics. Do not accept general responses such as "fair" or "improved." If nurse answers incorrectly record No.	No Yes	1 4	1-2-3-4
06*	2.107 IS THE BEDSIDE TABLE AND OTHER SELF-CARE EQUIPMENT POSITIONED WITHIN THE RESIDENT'S REACH? If resident is not in room, ask resident, "when you are in bed are personal items within your reach?" Code NA only if resident is unable to use equipment, e.g., residents who are comatose.	No Yes Information Not Available NA	1 4 8 9	3-4
06*	2.109 ARE SIDE RAILS UP IF THE CONDITION OF THE RESIDENT WARRANTS? Observer must determine if resident's condition warrants having side rails, e.g., residents who are restless, immobile, on seizure precautions, have received narcotics or sedatives, etc., or as indicated in policy.	No Yes Information Not Available NA	1 4 8 9	3-4
07	2.115 ARE PROTECTIVE OR SUPPORTIVE DEVICES (E.G., RESTRAINTS, MATTRESSES, HEEL GUARDS, FOOTBOARDS, SANDBAGS, PILLOWS, ETC.) BEING USED PROPERLY TO PROVIDE SUPPORT OR PREVENT INJURY?	No Yes Information Not Available	1 4 8	3-4

01*   NA   9

Check position of protective or supportive device in relation to body area. Proper use includes meeting any special requirements, such as documentation and position change, release and exercise of extremities if restraints are used.

2.116   No   1   1-2-3-4
Yes   4
NA   9

IS THERE A LIST OF RESIDENT'S ALLERGIES IN A PLACE ADEQUATELY VISIBLE TO PREVENT ADMINISTRATION OF CONTRAINDICATED SUBSTANCES?

List may appear on front of chart, or on each physician order sheet. Not acceptable if allergies recorded only in history and physical, progress notes, or medication record.

01*   2.123   No   1   2-3-4
Yes   4
NA   9

IF RESIDENT REQUIRES SPECIAL PRECAUTIONS OR OBSERVATIONS, IS THERE DOCUMENTATION THAT APPROPRIATE NURSING ACTIONS ARE BEING TAKEN?

Refers to any situation in which resident needs special assistance or observation, e.g., assistance in ambulating when tubes, dressings, equipment, or weakness present; proper use of protective or supportive devices such as footboards, restraints, etc.; monitoring of resident on MAO inhibitors; resident on special precautions such as suicide, smoking, escape, or seizure precautions.

Observer must identify existence of need for special precautions or observation, and determine whether appropriate nursing action was taken. *Code NA* only if resident does not need precautions or observation.

---

*Utility of item has <u>not</u> been demonstrated, and statistical analyses of the authors' dataset found that the item did not contribute to the reliability or validity of the monitoring instrument.

Source of Information	Criterion	Response		Patient Type
06*	2.127 ARE MEDICATIONS AND OTHER CHEMICAL SUBSTANCES STORED AND LOCKED SO THAT THEY ARE NOT ACCESSIBLE TO CONFUSED OR WANDERING RESIDENTS? (E.G., CLINITEST TABS, H_2O_2)	No Yes NA	1 4 9	1–2–3–4
	For residents on self-medication program, drugs may be properly stored but not locked for a yes answer.			
	Applies to individual's items only.			
	Code NA if resident does not use any such substances.			
06*	2.128 ARE THERE SAFETY RAILS ADJACENT TO THE TOILET AS REQUIRED?	No Yes NA	1 4 9	2–3–4
	Code NA if resident does not use toilet or does not require safety rails.			
	2.2 THE NEED FOR PHYSICAL COMFORT AND REST IS ATTENDED.			
02	2.202 WAS THE RESIDENT'S HAIR COMBED TODAY?	No Yes Information Not Available	1 4 8	3–4
	Ask only if not determinable by observation.			
	To resident: Was your hair combed today?			
02	2.205 IS THE CALL LIGHT WITHIN THE RESIDENT'S REACH?	No Yes	1 4	3–4

03		Observe whether light is within resident's reach. *If resident is not in room, ask resident*, "When you are in bed is the call bell positioned within your reach?"	Information Not Available 8	
03	2.209	**DOES THE RESIDENT HAVE UNINTERRUPTED PERIODS OF SLEEP AND REST?** To resident: For the *past two nights* have you been able to sleep or rest for at least several hours without being awakened by someone else? *Code NA* if resident's condition requires interruption, i.e., for turning, meds, etc.	No 1 Yes 4 Information Not Available 8 NA 9	1-2-3-4
03*	2.212	**IS THE RESIDENT'S CALL FOR ASSISTANCE ANSWERED PROMPTLY?** To resident: In the *past week*, when you called for assistance, did someone come to the room/to you within a reasonable amount of time? *May be NA* only if resident has not called for nurse in past week.	No 1 Yes 2 Some of the time 3 Yes 3 Most of the time Yes 4 All of the time Information Not Available 8 NA 9	3-4
03	2.213	**IS THE MALE RESIDENT SHAVED AS NEEDED?**	No 1 Yes 4	3-4

*Utility of item has not been demonstrated, and statistical analyses of the authors' dataset found that the item did not contribute to the reliability or validity of the monitoring instrument.

Source of Information	Criterion	Response	Patient Type
	To resident: Are you shaved or are you helped to shave yourself as often as you would like?	Information Not Available 8 NA 9	

2.3   THE NEED FOR PHYSICAL HYGIENE IS ATTENDED.

Source of Information	Criterion	Response	Patient Type
02*	ARE THE RESIDENT'S FINGERNAILS BOTH CLEAN AND TRIMMED?	No 1 Yes 4 Information Not Available 8	3–4
03	ARE THE RESIDENT'S HANDS WASHED AFTER USING THE BATHROOM OR BED PAN? To resident: In the *past two days*, did someone help you wash your hands after using the bathroom or bed pan if you could not do it yourself? *Code NA* if no assistance is required.	No 1 Yes 2 Some of the time Yes 3 Most of the time Yes 4 All of the time Information Not Available 8 NA 9	3–4
06	IS EQUIPMENT AVAILABLE FOR BATHING? Observer may observe for equipment, or may interview resident. Check to see that towels, washcloth, and soap are in the resident's room.	No 1 Yes 4 Information Not Available 8	1–2–3–4

To resident: In the past two days, have you had the necessary things you needed for your bath like towels, washcloths, basin, and soap when you wanted them?

Code No if any necessary item not available when resident desired them.

06

2.304   IS ADEQUATE EQUIPMENT FOR ORAL HYGIENE AVAILABLE?

No 1
Yes 4
Information Not Available 8

1-2-3-4

Check to see that all necessary equipment is present: toothbrush, toothpaste, and mouthwash or swab, solution, denture cup if indicated. Observer may observe for equipment or may interview resident.

To resident: In the past two days, when you wanted to brush your teeth (or care for your dentures), have you had the necessary things you needed like toothpaste, gargle, etc.?

Code No if necessary item not available when resident desired them.

06

2.305   IS THE BED PAN AND/OR URINAL, IF REQUIRED, CLEAN AND STORED?

No 1
Yes 4
NA 9

3-4

Code No if placed on overbed table, on floor, or on window sill, etc.

Acceptable if positioned within resident's reach for convenience or stored according to facility norm.

03*

2.312   WAS THE RESIDENT'S HAIR WASHED IN THE PAST WEEK?

No 1
Yes 4

1-2-3-4

To resident: Could you tell me when your hair was washed the last time?

*Utility of item has not been demonstrated, and statistical analyses of the authors' dataset found that the item did not contribute to the reliability or validity of the monitoring instrument.

Source of Information	Criterion	Response	Patient Type
	Code Yes only if hair was washed in past week. Code NA only if hair washing was contraindicated.	Information Not Available 8 NA 9	
07	2.313 IS THE RESIDENT WEARING APPROPRIATE CLOTHES THAT ARE CLEAN AND FIT WELL? Applies to those for whom street clothes are appropriate.	No 1 Yes 4 Information Not Available 8 NA 9	1-2-3

2.4   THE NEED FOR A SUPPLY OF OXYGEN IS ATTENDED.

Source of Information	Criterion	Response	Patient Type
02	2.401 IS THE RESIDENT IN A POSITION FOR MAXIMAL LUNG EXPANSION? Observe elevation of bed, use of pillows, and position of head, neck, and chest. Code Yes only if all indicators good.	No 1 Yes 4 Information Not Available 8	3-4
02	2.407 ARE RESIDENT'S EXTREMITIES POSITIONED FOR PROPER CIRCULATION? Applies to any resident who has current or potential problem with circulation to extremities, e.g., resident with peripheral vascular disease, diabetes mellitus, stroke, pedal edema, injury to extremity, etc. Check for elevation of extremities as indicated and for no tight fitting clothing, proper placement of pillow or other supports.	No 1 Yes 4 Information Not Available 8 NA 9	2-3-4

01* 2.408 ARE COLOR AND WARMTH OF EXTREMITIES RECORDED?

No 1 3–4
Yes 4
Information Not
Available 8
NA 9

Applies to any resident who has *current problems* with circulation to extremities, e.g., resident with peripheral vascular disease, diabetes mellitus, stroke, injury to extremity. If resident should be observed, both color and warmth should be noted *within past week* for yes answer.

2.5 *THE NEED FOR ACTIVITY IS ATTENDED.*

03* 2.502 IS THE RESIDENT ASSISTED WITH ADL (EATING, TOILET, DRESSING, WALKING, ETC.) AS NEEDED?

No 1 2–3–4
Yes 4
Information Not
Available 8
NA 9

To resident: In the past couple of days did you need some help with your bath or doing things for yourself?

If no, *Code NA*
If yes, ask: Did someone help you soon after you asked them to?

"Needed", "reasonable amount of time," and "soon after you asked them" are defined by resident.

04 2.509 UNLESS CONTRAINDICATED, IS THE RESIDENT OUT OF BED FOR SEVERAL HOURS EVERY DAY?

No 1 3–4
Yes 4
NA 9

Applies to any resident for whom exercise and a change of immediate environ-

*Utility of item has not been demonstrated, and statistical analyses of the authors' dataset found that the item did not contribute to the reliability or validity of the monitoring instrument.

Source of Information	Criterion	Response	Patient Type
	ment may be beneficial. May *Code NA* if resident is unconscious or if his physical status contraindicates movement. *Code No* if resident could be out of bed but is not.		
	Ask nursing staff member: In the past two days, has Mr. _____ been out of bed for several hours every day?		
01	2.510 IF RESIDENT IS CONFINED TO BED OR CHAIR, DO NURSING STAFF ASSIST OR ENCOURAGE THE RESIDENT TO PERFORM EXERCISES OF THE EXTREMITIES EVERY DAY?	No 1 Yes 4 NA 9	3-4
	Applies to any confined resident, even if resident is also seen by physical therapist, unless exercises are contraindicated. If nursing record does not indicate performance of exercises, ask the nurse: In the past two days has Mr. _____ had daily exercises to his arms and legs? If resident should have such exercises and not done, or if done only by physical therapist, *Code No*.		
03	2.512 DO THE NURSING STAFF ENCOURAGE ACTIVITY, WITH CONSIDERATION OF PERIODS OF REST?	No 1 Yes 4 Information Not Available 8 NA 9	1-2
	To resident: Do the nurses encourage you to be up and about, and have plenty of exercise?		
	If no, answer no. Answer NA only if resident should not be encouraged to exercise. If yes, ask resident: Do they also let you rest or tell you how to plan your activities to avoid getting tired or out of breath?		

2.6   *THE NEED FOR NUTRITION AND FLUID BALANCE IS ATTENDED.*

03* 2.601 ARE NURSING PERSONNEL ACCESSIBLE TO RESIDENT DURING MEALS?

To resident: In the past two days, have you needed or requested some help with your meal tray?

If no, *Code NA.*
If yes, ask: When you needed some help, did someone from the nursing staff assist you within a reasonable amount of time?

No 1   3–4
Yes 2
   Some of the time
Yes 3
   Most of the time
Yes 4
   All of the time
Information Not
   Available 8
NA 9

01* 2.603 IS THE AMOUNT OF FLUID INTAKE AND OUTPUT RECORDED?

Applies to resident for whom intake and/or output record is needed. May apply to output only if so designated in record. Complete if recordings made each shift in past week for applicable residents.

No 1   4
Yes 2
   Incomplete
Yes 4
   Complete
NA 9

01 2.608 IS THERE A WRITTEN STATEMENT REGARDING THE RESIDENT'S IN-TAKE OF FOOD AND FLUIDS OR NUTRITIONAL STATUS?

Applies to resident who does not require I and O recording.

May be recorded by dietary personnel.

Code Yes if documentation in the past *week* for those with identified nutritional problems.

No 1   2–3–4
Yes 4
NA 9

---

*Utility of item has not been demonstrated, and statistical analyses of the authors' dataset found that the item did not contribute to the reliability or validity of the monitoring instrument.

Source of Information	Criterion	Response		Patient Type
	Code *Yes* if documentation in the past month for others.			
01*	2.610 IS THE RESIDENT'S WEIGHT RECORDED WITHIN THE PAST MONTH?	No	1	1-2-3-4
		Yes	4	
	May be recorded by dietary personnel.			
	Check for documentation on chart or flow sheet.			
	Cannot code NA.			
	2.7 *THE NEED FOR ELIMINATION IS ATTENDED.*			
01*	2.703 ARE UNUSUAL BOWEL OR URINARY PROBLEMS NOTED (E.G., PASS-ING BLOOD, BURNING, FREQUENCY, ETC.)?	No	1	1-2-3-4
		Yes	4	
		NA	9	
	To determine if applicable, ask resident: In the *past week*, have you had any problems with your bowels or on urination?			
	Does not refer to routine daily recording (such as graphic) of bowel movement or urinary output, unless records clearly state a problem exists.			
	"Unusual problems" are those defined as such by the observer or the resident. Refers to all residents including those with a urinary catheter or colostomy.			
03*	2.704 DOES THE NURSING STAFF ASSIST THE RESIDENT TO THE BATHROOM OR WITH BEDPAN/URINAL WITHIN A REASONABLE AMOUNT OF TIME WHEN REQUESTED?	No	1	3-4
		Yes	4	
		Information Not Available	8	

01   To resident: In the *past week*, have you asked for help in going to the bathroom (or with the bedpan or urinal)?   NA   9

If no, *Code NA*.
If yes, ask: Did the nurses give you enough help in a reasonable amount of time?

"Assistance needed," "reasonable amount of time," and "soon after you asked them" are defined by the resident.

2.711   IF RESIDENT IS INCONTINENT OF BOWEL OR BLADDER, IS THERE EVIDENCE OF AN ACTIVE RETRAINING PROGRAM OR PLAN TO MANAGE INCONTINENCE?

No	1	3–4
Yes	2	Incomplete
Yes	4	Complete
NA	9	

Code Yes Complete only if there is a plan for bowel and bladder when resident is incontinent of both.

2.8   *THE NEED FOR SKIN CARE IS ATTENDED.*

2.801   IS THERE A WRITTEN STATEMENT OF THE CARE GIVEN TO PRESSURE AREAS ON THE SKIN?

No	1	3–4
Yes	4	
NA	9	

01   Refers to direct care of skin provided to prevent skin breakdown, such as massage. Does not refer to specific care given for decubitus.

Code NA only if resident does not require such care.

*Utility of item has not been demonstrated, and statistical analyses of the authors' dataset found that the item did not contribute to the reliability or validity of the monitoring instrument.

Source of Information		Criterion	Response		Patient Type
06	2.803	ARE THE UNDERSHEETS CLEAN, DRY, AND SMOOTH?	No	1	3–4
			Yes	4	
		Applies to residents who spend at *least 12 hours per day* in bed.	NA	9	
		Code *NA* for use of high humidity.			
01	2.804	IS CARE GIVEN TO AREAS OF SKIN BREAKDOWN AS OFTEN AS REQUIRED?	No	1	3–4
			Yes	2	
				Incomplete	
		Applicable to any areas of breakdown, such as decubitus, laceration, or sheet burn. Includes care of skin around ostomies, damage due to tape, IV fluid burns, and bruising due to capillary fragility. Check resident or ask nurse if special care is needed and how often care is required.	Yes	4	
				Complete	
			NA	9	
		Code *No* if care should be given and is not.			
		Code *Yes Incomplete* if care is given, but not as often as required.			
		Code *Yes Complete* if care is given as often as it should be.			
06	2.807	ARE SUPPLIES AVAILABLE FOR SELF-CARE OF SKIN?	No	1	1–2
			Yes	4	
		Applies to resident with current or potential skin problem. Supplies include lotion and other supplies as needed.	Information Not Available	8	
			NA	9	

2.9   THE RESIDENT IS PROTECTED FROM INFECTION.

04 2.905 IS THE RESIDENT TURNED/POSITIONED AS OFTEN AS HE SHOULD BE?

No 1   3–4
Yes   2
       Incomplete
Yes   4
       Complete
NA   9

Check records to determine if resident should be turned and when. If no plan for turning/positioning observer should determine whether resident should be turned, e.g., if resident is bedfast, cannot turn self, etc.

To nurse: How often is Mr. _____ turned?

Code *No* if resident should be turned and is not.

Code *Yes Incomplete* if resident is turned, but not as frequently as required.

Code *Yes Complete* if resident is turned as frequently as required.

2.907 IF THE RESIDENT HAS A TRACHEOSTOMY, ENDOTRACHEAL TUBE, NASOTRACHEAL OR FEEDING TUBE:

02 A. ARE THE TUBES CLEAN?

No   1
Yes   4
Information Not
  Available   8
NA   9

Observe for presence of mucus or blood on or around tubes.

02* B. ARE MATERIALS AROUND THE TUBES CLEAN AND PROPERLY IN PLACE?

No   1
Yes   4
Information Not
  Available   8
NA   9

E.g., no accumulated mucus or blood on skin or surrounding materials; neck strip and gauze securely attached for trach tubes; and tape adhering to skin without pulling for endotrach and nasotrach tubes.

---

*Utility of item has not been demonstrated, and statistical analyses of the authors' dataset found that the item did not contribute to the reliability or validity of the monitoring instrument.

Source of Information	Criterion	Response	Patient Type
2.911	FOR THE RESIDENT WITH AN INDWELLING OR EXTERNAL URINARY CATHETER:		3-4
02*	A. ARE THE DRAINAGE TUBING AND BAG PATENT, PROPERLY CONNECTED, AND POSITIONED FOR MAXIMAL DRAINAGE AND PREVENTION OF STASIS? Applies to urinary or other tubes. Acceptable only if all catheter and tubing placed for continuous drainage. Not acceptable if catheter or tubing looped or slanted upward at any point. All parts must be right for yes answer. *May be NA* in unusual cases, such as TUR or bladder gravity when medical or nursing orders specify other than straight gravity drainage.	No 1 Yes 4 Information Not Available 8 NA 9	
02*	B. IS IT NOTED ON THE RESIDENT RECORD WHEN THE CATHETER AND/OR DRAINAGE BAG WAS LAST CHANGED OR CLEANED?	No 1 Yes 4 NA 9	
02*	2.914 IF RESIDENT REQUIRES SPECIAL ATTENTION FOR PREVENTION/SPREAD OF INFECTION, ARE APPROPRIATE MEASURES TAKEN? Applies to residents with infections, with wounds to be cleaned/covered, clean and patent tubes, proper connection of drainage tubing, etc. *Code NA* only if resident has no need for such care.	No 1 Yes 4 NA 9	2-3-4
06	2.918 DO ALL PERSONAL ITEMS BEAR THE RESIDENT'S NAME OR BED NUMBER? Applies to items such as bedpan, urinal, denture cup. May ask resident if items not in clear view.	No 1 Yes 4 Information Not Available 8	1-2-3-4

03* 2.919 ARE TISSUES/TOILET PAPER AVAILABLE FOR THE RESIDENT TO USE AS NECESSARY?

To resident: Do you have tissues/toilet paper when you need them?

No 1 1-2-3-4
Yes 4
Information Not
   Available 8

03* 2.920 IS THERE A PROBLEM WITH PESTS IN THE RESIDENT'S ROOM?

To resident: Do you ever have a problem with bugs or mice in your room? *REVERSE SCORE.*

No 1 1-2-3
Yes 4
Information Not
   Available 8

03* 2.921 DOES THE RESIDENT HAVE ADEQUATE FOOT COVERING?

To resident: Do you have shoes or slippers to wear when out of bed?

No 1 1-2-3-4
Yes 4
Information Not
   Available 8
NA 9

04 2.922 ARE SPECIAL PRECAUTIONS TAKEN TO PREVENT THE SPREAD OF RESPIRATORY INFECTIONS CARRIED BY STAFF?

To nurse: Are there any special precautions you take when you are sick with a cold?

Code Yes if nurse replies she wears a mask or does not care for suscepti-ble/debilitated residents.

No 1 5
Yes 4

*Utility of item has <u>not</u> been demonstrated, and statistical analyses of the authors' dataset found that the item did not contribute to the reliability or validity of the monitoring instrument.

Source of Information	Criterion	Response		Patient Type
	3.0　THE NONPHYSICAL NEEDS (PSYCHOLOGICAL, EMOTIONAL, MENTAL, SOCIAL, SPIRITUAL) OF THE RESIDENT ARE ATTENDED. *3.1　THE RESIDENT IS ORIENTED TO THE FACILITIES ON ADMISSION.*			
03	3.101　IS THE RESIDENT CONTACTED BY THE NURSING STAFF IMMEDIATELY AFTER ARRIVAL ON UNIT? To resident: When you first arrived on this unit, how long was it before someone on the nursing staff came to see you? Code *Yes* if resident contacted immediately after arrival; maximum delay—15 minutes. Code *NA* if resident cannot recall.	No Yes Information Not Available NA	1 4 8 9	8
03	3.102　ON ADMISSION TO THIS UNIT, IS RESIDENT INFORMED HOW TO CALL/CONTACT THE NURSE? To resident: Did someone tell you how to call the nurse or ask if you already knew how to call? If the answer is yes, ask: When did you find out how to call someone. Code *No* if resident was not informed within first 24 hours of admission.	No Yes Information Not Available	1 4 8	8
03*	3.103　DO THE STAFF INFORM THE FAMILY OF THE FACILITY'S ROUTINE ON ADMISSION OR FIRST VISIT? Ask resident or family member: When you/your family member was admitted to this unit or when you first visited, did the nursing staff talk to you about visiting routines, etc.? If family member given information guide or booklet, ask: Did someone tell you what is included in the booklet?	No Yes Information Not Available	1 4 8	8

Acceptable if brochure or written guide is given to inform family, and nursing staff or other member of the health care team informs family that this information is in this guide.

Code NA if no family.

03   3.104   IS THE RESIDENT INFORMED OF VISITING HOURS ON ADMISSION TO THE UNIT?

         No   1
         Yes   4
         NA   9

To resident: Did someone tell you what the visiting hours are for this unit or did they refer you to a resident guide for information about the visiting hours?

If yes, ask: When did they tell you?

Code Yes only if resident was told visiting hours within first 24 hours of admission.

03   3.105   IS THE RESIDENT INFORMED OF AVAILABILITY OF RELIGIOUS COUNSELORS AND FACILITIES ON ADMISSION TO THE FACILITY?

         No   1
         Yes   4
         NA   9

Ask resident: Most facilities have a chapel or clergymen for residents and families. Did someone tell you how to make use of these services?

If answer is yes, ask: When did you find out about that?

Code Yes only if resident was told whether a chapel or clergyman was available within the first 24 hours of admission. Acceptable if resident informed by clergy or facility brochure.

---

*Utility of item has <u>not</u> been demonstrated, and statistical analyses of the authors' dataset found that the item did not contribute to the reliability or validity of the monitoring instrument.

Source of Information	Criterion	Response	Patient Type
03	3.106 IS RESIDENT TOLD THE LOCATION OF THE TELEPHONE AND HOW TO USE IT ON ADMISSION? *Code NA* if resident initially admitted to another unit or disoriented/unresponsive on admission. To resident: When you were first admitted to this unit, did someone tell you how to use the facility telephone, such as how to get an outside line? *Code Yes* only if resident was told within 24 hours after admission. Acceptable if volunteer or other non-nursing personnel informed resident.	No 1 Yes 4 Information Not 　Available 8 NA 9	8
03	3.107 IS THE RESIDENT INFORMED OF NECESSARY PERSONAL FACILITIES SUCH AS THE LAVATORY AND BATHROOM ON ADMISSION? *Code NA* if resident initially admitted to another unit or if resident was not up to bathroom on admission. To resident: When you came to this room, did someone tell you where the bathroom or shower is located? *Code Yes* only if resident was informed within the first 24 hours of admission.	No 1 Yes 4 Information Not 　Available 8 NA 9	8
03*	3.108 ARE SMOKING REGULATIONS EXPLAINED ON ADMISSION TO THE UNIT? To resident: When you arrived on this unit, were you told about or referred to an information booklet for smoking regulations? Acceptable if safety measures included in resident brochure and resident was referred to brochure for information.	No 1 Yes 4 Information Not 　Available 8 NA 9	8

03   3.109   IS THE RESIDENT INFORMED UPON ADMISSION OF THE EMERGENCY CALL SYSTEM IN THE BATHROOM?

Ask resident: When you first came to the room, did someone tell you how to call for a nurse if you are in the bathroom and need help.

Code Yes only if resident was informed within *first 24 hours* of admission.

Code NA if resident is confined to bed.

No   1
Yes   4
Information Not Available   8
NA   9

---

03   3.110   IS THE RESIDENT INFORMED OF UNIT FACILITIES ON ADMISSION?

Includes TV, dining, craft, and other general facilities.

To resident: When you came to this unit, did someone tell you about general facilities such as a TV area, dining room, craft room, or other places for group activities and mingling with other residents?

Code Yes only if resident was informed *within 24 hours* of admission by any member of health care team.

No   1
Yes   4
Information Not Available   8

---

03   3.111   IS THE RESIDENT INFORMED ON ADMISSION OF FIRE PROCEDURES, INCLUDING A DESCRIPTION OF THE FIRE ALARM AND WHERE EXITS ARE LOCATED?

Code NA only if resident's condition on admission prohibited this instruction.

No   1
Yes   4
Information Not Available   8
NA   9

---

*Utility of item has <u>not</u> been demonstrated, and statistical analyses of the authors' dataset found that the item did not contribute to the reliability or validity of the monitoring instrument.

Source of Information	Criterion		Response		Patient Type
03	3.112	ARE SAFETY MEASURES RELATED TO MOBILITY/TRANSFER EXPLAINED ON ADMISSION TO THIS UNIT?	No	1	
			Yes	4	
		To resident: When you arrived on this unit, were you told about safety in moving around, such as getting in and out of bed or in transferring from bed to chair?	Information Not Available	8	
			NA	9	
03*	3.113	IS THE POLICY ON CARE OF VALUABLES EXPLAINED TO RESIDENT ON ADMISSION?	No	1	
			Yes	4	
		To resident: When you arrived, were you told about the policy on care of your valuables, i.e., money and jewelry?	Information Not Available	8	
			NA	9	
03	3.114	IS THE RESIDENT INFORMED ABOUT THE NURSING HOME ADMISSION PRIOR TO ENTRY?	No	1	
			Yes	4	
		To resident: Did you receive any information about this nursing home before you were admitted? If yes, ask resident: What were you told about the home?	Information Not Available	8	
			NA	9	
		Code *Yes* if resident was informed about facilities, services, or activities.			
		Code *NA* if resident is confused or unresponsive.			
	3.2	*THE RESIDENT IS EXTENDED SOCIAL COURTESY BY THE NURSING STAFF.*			
03	3.201	DO THE NURSING STAFF CALL RESIDENT BY DESIRED NAME?	No	1	1-2-3-4
			Yes	2	

To resident: When speaking to you, have the nursing staff called you by the name you prefer?

Some of the time	
Yes	3
Most of the time	
Yes	4
All of the time	
Information Not Available	8

03* 3.202 DO NURSING STAFF MEMBERS AND THERAPISTS INTRODUCE THEMSELVES TO THE RESIDENTS?

To resident: Do new members of the nursing and therapy staffs introduce themselves to you?

No	1	1-2-3-4
Yes	2	
Some of the time		
Yes	3	
Most of the time		
Yes	4	
All of the time		
Information Not Available	8	

03 3.203 ARE PERSONNEL COURTEOUS TO RESIDENT AND HIS FAMILY?

To resident: In the past couple of weeks, have staff been friendly to you and your family?

Code Yes, all of the time only if always courteous to both resident and family. If family has not been present code for resident only.

No	1	1-2-3-4
Yes	2	
Some of the time		
Yes	4	
All of the time		
Information Not Available	8	

---

*Utility of item has not been demonstrated, and statistical analyses of the authors' dataset found that the item did not contribute to the reliability or validity of the monitoring instrument.

Source of Information	Criterion	Response		Patient Type
	3.3 *THE RESIDENT'S PRIVACY AND CIVIL RIGHTS ARE HONORED.*			
03*	3.303 ARE SPECIAL PROCEDURES AND STUDIES EXPLAINED TO THE RESIDENT?	No	1	2-3-4
		Yes	2	
	To resident: Have you had any special tests or blood samples taken within the *past month?*	Sometimes		
		Yes	4	
	If yes, ask: Did someone tell you about the procedure or reason for test? May be explained by any health professional.	Always		
		Information Not		
		Available	8	
	Code NA if resident had no test or special procedures.	NA	9	
03	3.304 ARE CURTAINS DRAWN, AREA SCREENED, OR DOOR CLOSED FOR EXAMINATION, TREATMENT, OR PRIVACY?	No	1	2-3-4
		Yes	4	
	To resident: When you have had an examination or treatment or when you just wanted to be alone, were the curtains drawn around your bed or the door closed?	Information Not		
		Available	8	
	Code NA if resident never had examination or treatment, or did not desire privacy.			
03*	3.305 DO PERSONNEL KNOCK BEFORE ENTERING A RESIDENT'S ROOM?	No	1	1-2-3
		Yes	2	
	To resident: Do staff knock or announce themselves before entering your room?	Some of the time		
		Yes	4	
		All of the time		
		Information Not		
		Available	8	

03 | 3.308 | IS OPPORTUNITY PROVIDED FOR RESIDENT'S PRIVACY AND SOLITUDE?

To resident: When you want to be alone or perhaps want to be alone with another person, can you do so here?

Code NA only if resident reports no desire for privacy or solitude.

No 1 — Yes 4 — Information Not Available 8 — NA 9 — 1-2-3

03 | 3.309 | HAS THE RESIDENT BEEN INFORMED OF HIS RIGHTS AS A RESIDENT IN THE FACILITY?

To resident: There is a list of rights that all residents are entitled to. It includes things like your right to privacy, respect, and information about your care. Did someone tell you about these rights?

No 1 — Yes 4 — Information Not Available 8 — NA 9 — 1-2-3

03 | 3.310 | IS THERE READY ACCESSIBILITY TO A PHONE FOR INCOMING AND OUTGOING CALLS?

To resident: Can you easily or with assistance make outgoing phone calls and receive incoming calls?

No 1 — Yes 4 — Information Not Available 8 — NA 9 — 1-2-3-4

03 | 3.311 | IS THERE A SYSTEM FOR PICKING UP AND DELIVERING RESIDENT'S MAIL?

A. Ask resident: Are you able to obtain stamps and mail letters if you wish?

No 1 — Yes 4 — Information Not Available 8 — NA 9 — 1-2-3

---

*Utility of item has not been demonstrated, and statistical analyses of the authors' dataset found that the item did not contribute to the reliability or validity of the monitoring instrument.

Source of Information	Criterion	Response		Patient Type
03*	B. Do you receive your mail in a timely way?	No	1	
		Yes	4	
		Information Not Available	8	
		NA	9	
03*	3.312 ARE RESIDENT BELONGINGS SECURE?	No	1	1-2-3-4
	Ask resident: Do you feel your personal belongings are secure here?	Yes	4	
		Information Not Available	8	
		NA	9	
03	3.313 IS THE RESIDENT ADVISED OF FINANCIAL/BILLING STATUS?	No	1	
	Ask resident: If you have any concerns about financial or money matters, your bill, or your account here, is there someone at the home you could discuss it with?	Yes	4	
		Information Not Available	8	
		NA	9	
03	3.314 IS THE RESIDENT INFORMED OF THE FUNCTIONS OF THE RESIDENT COUNCIL?	No	1	
	To resident: What is the purpose of the resident council?	Yes	4	
	Code No if home does not have an elected council or if resident is not aware of existence of a council or cannot state any purpose.	Information Not Available	8	
	Code Yes if answer includes that it is a forum for having a voice in home matters, expressing concerns or grievances, or receiving information from home administration.	NA	9	

Code NA if resident is disoriented, unresponsive.

3.4 THE NEED FOR PSYCHOLOGICAL-EMOTIONAL WELL-BEING IS ATTENDED.

03	3.401 IS OPPORTUNITY PROVIDED FOR RESIDENT TO DISCUSS FEAR AND ANXIETIES?	No 1 1-2-3-4 Yes 4 Information Not Available 8 NA 9
	To resident: In the past week was there anything that concerned or worried you?	
	If no, *Code NA.*	
	If yes, ask: Did you feel you had a chance to talk with any of the nurses about it?	
03	3.402 DO THE NURSING STAFF DISCUSS THE PHYSICAL DEPENDENCE-INDEPENDENCE OF THE RESIDENT WITH HIM/HER?	No 1 1-2-3-4 Yes 4 Information Not Available 8 NA 9
	To resident: Has your illness had any effect on what you can do for yourself such as daily hygiene, eating, getting around or taking care of yourself in general?	
	If no, *Code NA.*	
	If yes, ask: Has anyone from the nursing staff talked in detail with you about how much you should do for yourself or how to increase what you can do?	

*Utility of item has not been demonstrated, and statistical analyses of the authors' daraset found that the item did not contribute to the reliability or validity of the monitoring instrument.

Source of Information	Criterion	Response	Patient Type
03*	3.409 DO STAFF LISTEN TO THE RESIDENT?	No 1	1-2-3-4
	Code No if resident merely informed of activities but not engaged in discussion about the level of his/her involvement in care.	Yes 2	
	To resident: When you talk to the staff (nursing, therapists, doctors) or ask questions, do you feel that they listen to you and show an interest in what you say?	Some of the staff 3	
	Applies to all care providers.	Most of the staff	
	Code NA if resident is unresponsive.	Yes 4	
		All of the staff	
		Information Not Available 8	
		NA 9	
03	3.411 CAN THE RESIDENT IDENTIFY A PARTICULAR NURSE AS "HIS NURSE?"	No 1	1-2-3-4
	To resident: Is there one particular nurse that is "your nurse" or one specific nurse you could discuss your special concerns with?	Yes 4	
	Acceptable if resident indicates 1–3 nursing personnel.	Information Not Available 8	
	Code No if resident indicates several nurses.		
03	3.412 IS SUPPORT GIVEN TO THE RESIDENT IN DISTRESS, I.E., CRYING, BEING HIGHLY ANXIOUS, FEARFUL?	No 1	1-2-3-4
	Ask resident: During the past month, have you had times when you have been very upset, worried, or felt very nervous?	Yes 4	
		Information Not Available 8	
		NA 9	

Code NA if resident is confused, disoriented, does not respond, if responds negatively, or that concealed distress from staff.

If resident responds positively, ask: Did the nursing staff/special counselors spend time with you?

3.418	IS THERE APPROPRIATE VERBAL AND NONVERBAL COMMUNICA-TION WITH THE RESIDENT?	No 1 1-2-3-4 Yes 2 Some Yes 4 A great deal Information Not Available 8

05*

Observe staff with resident to see whether they talk to resident and use touch in a comforting way, aside from providing technical care

3.419	IS THERE EVIDENCE OF STAFF CREATING A PLEASING ENVIRON-MENT IN THE RESIDENT'S ROOM (I.E., PLANTS, PICTURES, CALENDARS)?	No 1 1-2-3-4 Yes 4

06*

Refers to resident's preference.

3.5   THE RESIDENT IS TAUGHT MEASURES OF HEALTH MAINTENANCE AND ILLNESS PREVENTION.

---

*Utility of item has <u>not</u> been demonstrated, and statistical analyses of the authors' dataset found that the item did not contribute to the reliability or validity of the monitoring instrument.

Source of Information	Criterion	Response	Patient Type
06*	3.501 DO THE NURSING STAFF INFORM THE RESIDENT TO REPORT SIGNS AND SYMPTOMS RELATED TO HIS ILLNESS (E.G., RASH, DIZZINESS, PAIN) TO THE NURSING STAFF? Applicable if there are any signs and symptoms which resident should be aware of to report. To resident: Did the nurses tell you if there are any signs or symptoms related to your illness that you should report to them?	No 1 Yes 4 Information Not Available 8 NA 9	3–4
04	3.502 HAVE INSTRUCTIONS TO BE GIVEN TO THE RESIDENT BEEN OUTLINED EITHER VERBALLY OR IN WRITING? To determine if applicable, ask nurse: Are there any special instructions to be given to Mr. _____? If yes, ask: Are they in writing? Applicable if any special instructions are indicated, such as pre-diagnostic testing, teaching residents to do own treatments, medications, working machinery, driving, etc. Does not refer to orientation on admission. Code Yes Written if instructions are both verbal and written or if teaching team is instructing resident.	No 1 Yes 2 Oral only Yes 4 Written NA 9	1–2–3–4
03	3.509 IS THE RESIDENT INSTRUCTED ABOUT SPECIAL PREVENTIVE OR THERAPEUTIC MEASURES IN SELF-CARE? Applies to resident for whom any special measures are indicated, e.g., foot care of diabetic, caution in transferring in and out of wheel chair, taking medications. To resident: Have you been instructed in any special measures for managing your own health, i.e., taking your own meds, taking your pulse, getting around safely?	No 1 Yes 4 Information Not Available 8 NA 9	1–2–3

03	3.510	ARE HEALTH PROMOTION PROGRAMS AVAILABLE TO THE RESIDENT?	No 1 Yes 4	1-2
		To resident: Have you had the opportunity to attend any special programs or group discussions about keeping healthy, *in the past month*, e.g., nutrition, exercise, A.A.	Information Not Available 8 NA 9	
		Code No if there are no programs offered by the home.		

3.6 THE RESIDENT'S FAMILY IS INCLUDED IN THE NURSING CARE PROCESS.

03*	3.602	DO THE NURSE, RESIDENT, AND FAMILY DISCUSS THE FAMILY'S PARTICIPATION IN THE CARE OF THE RESIDENT?	No 1 Yes 4	1-2-3-4
		To resident: Does your family come to visit you?	Information Not Available 8 NA 9	
		If yes, ask: In the past month have any of the nurses talked with you and your family about what things they might help you do?		
04*	3.603	IS OPPORTUNITY PROVIDED FOR FAMILY TO DISCUSS FEARS AND ANXIETIES?	No 1 Yes 4 NA 9	1-2-3-4
		To nurse: Has Mr. _____'s family been in to visit him in the past month?		
		If no, *Code NA*.		

*Utility of item has <u>not</u> been demonstrated, and statistical analyses of the authors' dataset found that the item did not contribute to the reliability or validity of the monitoring instrument.

Source of Information	Criterion	Response		Patient Type
01	If yes, ask nurse: Have you or other professionals spent some time with them to see if they have any particular fears or problems related to Mr. _____'s condition?			
	3.604 IS A DESCRIPTION OF CARE GIVEN BY THE FAMILY RECORDED?	No Yes NA	1 4 9	2–3–4
	To determine if applicable, ask resident: Have your family and/or friends visited you here *in the past month?*			
	If no, *Code NA.*			
	If yes, ask: Are there any specific things they do for you related to your care while they are here?			
01*	3.605 IS THE FAMILY NOTIFIED WHEN THERE ARE CHANGES IN THE RESIDENT'S CONDITION?	No Yes NA	1 4 9	3–4
	Applies to previous month. Check progress notes to determine if there were significant changes in the resident's condition, i.e., transfer to ER, injury from incident, or fall. If there were, check records or ask nurse about family notification.			
	To nurse: Mr. _____ seems to have had a change in his condition or fall in the last month. Would you know if his family was notified?			
01	3.620 IS A DESCRIPTION PLACED IN THE RESIDENT'S RECORD OF THE RESIDENT/FAMILY INTERACTION DURING VISITS WITH THE FAMILY?	No Yes NA	1 4 9	1–2–3–4
	Ask resident to determine if applicable: Within the *past month,* have you visited with family here or at home?			

Observer should check chart for general patterns of interaction, e.g., hostile, tense, warm, or supportive or effect on resident's mood.

May be recorded by any member of health care team.

Code NA if there have not been any visits in past month.

3.7 *THE NEED FOR PSYCHO-EMOTIONAL WELL-BEING IS ATTENDED BY A THERAPEUTIC MILIEU.*

03

3.703 ARE RESIDENTS ENCOURAGED TO ASSUME UNIT RESPONSIBILITIES?

Ask resident: Have you been encouraged to assume unit responsibilities, such as welcoming new residents, planning activities, watering plants, making your bed, assisting other residents, etc.?

Code NA if resident's condition precludes unit responsibilities.

No	1	1-2
Yes	4	
Information Not Available	8	
NA	9	

08*

3.704 IS THERE EVIDENCE OF STAFF ATTENTION TO CREATING A PLEASING UNIT ENVIRONMENT FOR RESIDENTS (E.G., PLANTS, COLORFUL ARRANGEMENTS, SEASONAL OR HOLIDAY DISPLAYS, ETC.)?

No	1	1-2-3
Yes	4	

05

3.705 DO NURSING STAFF INTERACT WITH RESIDENTS IN ADDITION TO ANSWERING REQUESTS AND PROVIDING SPECIFIC THERAPEUTIC MEASURES?

No	1	1-2-3-4
Yes	4	

---

*Utility of item has not been demonstrated, and statistical analyses of the authors' dataset found that the item did not contribute to the reliability or validity of the monitoring instrument.

Source of Information	Criterion	Response	Patient Type
03	3.706 DOES THE RESIDENT FEEL THAT THE ATMOSPHERE OF THE UNIT IS ONE OF CONCERN AND SUPPORT FOR HIS TOTAL WELL-BEING? To resident: Do people here make you feel welcome and feel that they have a genuine interest in you?	No 1 Yes 2 Some of the time Yes 4 All of the time Information Not Available 8	1-2-3-4
03	3.707 IS THE RESIDENT ENCOURAGED TO INTERACT WITH OTHER RESIDENTS ON THE UNIT? To resident: Do the nurses encourage you to participate in activities with other residents here?	No 1 Yes 4 Information Not Available 8 NA 9	1-2-3
03*	3.708 IS THERE ADEQUATE STAFFING TO ASSIST RESIDENT TO ATTEND RT/SOCIAL ACTIVITIES OF THEIR CHOICE? To resident: When you want to attend an activity or visit another resident, is someone available to take you? Code NA if resident does not require this assistance.	No 1 Yes 4 Information Not Available 8 NA 9	2-3
	4.0 ACHIEVEMENT OF NURSING CARE OBJECTIVES IS EVALUATED. *4.1 RECORDS DOCUMENT THE CARE PROVIDED FOR THE RESIDENT.*		
01	4.101 IF TREATMENTS ARE ORDERED IN EITHER MEDICAL OR NURSING ORDERS, DO RECORDS DOCUMENT THEIR PERFORMANCE OR REASON FOR OMISSION?	No 1 Yes 2 Incomplete	1-2-3-4

01   E.g., dressings, irrigations, compresses, group therapy.

Applies to *past month*.

Yes   4
Complete
NA   9

1–2–3–4

4.102   DO RECORDS DOCUMENT THE VITAL SIGNS AND BLOOD PRESSURE AS INDICATED IN MEDICAL OR NURSING ORDERS?

Applies to *past month*.

01   No   1
Yes   2
Incomplete
Yes   4
Complete
NA   9

1–2–3–4

Note: A minimum of a week and a maximum of a month of data should be reviewed for criteria 4.103–4.106.

4.103   DO RECORDS DOCUMENT THE REASONS FOR OMISSION OF MEDICATIONS?

Code Yes if record contains statement, "out on pass."

01   No   1
Yes   2
Some of the time
Yes   3
Most of the time
Yes   4
All of the time
NA   9

1–2–3–4

4.104

01*   No   1
Yes   2
Some of the time

1–2–3–4

---

*Utility of item has <u>not</u> been demonstrated, and statistical analyses of the authors' dataset found that the item did not contribute to the reliability or validity of the monitoring instrument.

Source of Information	Criterion	Response	Patient Type
01	DO RECORDS DOCUMENT THE REASONS FOR ADMINISTRATION OF PRN MEDICATIONS?	Yes 3 Most of the time Yes 4 All of the time NA 9	
4.105	DO RECORDS DOCUMENT THE EFFECT OF PRN MEDICATIONS?	No 1 Yes 2 Some of the time Yes 3 Most of the time Yes 4 All of the time NA 9	1–2–3–4
4.106	DO RECORDS DOCUMENT THE ADMINISTRATION OF MEDICATION ON THIS UNIT INCLUDING:		1–2–3–4
01	A. Time given?	No 1 Yes 4 NA 9	
01*	B. Route of administration (PO, SC, IM, IV, PR, vaginal, skin, OU, OS, OD must be specified)?	No 1 Yes 4 NA 9	
01	C. Name and title of person who gave medication? Initials of resident acceptable for those recording own self-meds.	No 1 Yes 4 NA 9	
01	D. Dosage?	No 1 Yes 4 NA 9	

4.2 THE RESIDENT'S RESPONSE TO THERAPY IS EVALUATED.

01	4.201	ARE OBSERVATIONS RELATED TO MEDICAL TREATMENT, MEDICATIONS, DISEASE PROCESS, OR POSSIBLE COMPLICATIONS NOTED, E.G., CHANGES IN CONDITION, OBSERVATIONS TO DETECT ONSET OF COMPLICATIONS, ETC.?

No 1
Yes 2
Incomplete
Yes 4
Complete
NA 9

1-2-3-4

Statement of observations may refer to either presence or absence of problems. Includes any nursing observations not included in medical orders. Includes side or untoward effects of current therapy. Consider condition of resident and determine whether specific observations should be made. If not recorded, *Code No.*

Applies to *past month.*

01	4.202	DO RECORDS DOCUMENT THE RESIDENT'S RESPONSE TO EXPLANATION OF HIS CARE OR GENERAL UNDERSTANDING OF HIS CURRENT TREATMENT PLAN?

No 1
Yes 4
NA 9

1-2-3-4

If nothing written, ask nurse: In the *past month* has Mr. ———— been given any explanation about his condition or care?

May include response to any type of formal or informal explanation or instruction given by nurse or other health personnel.

Code NA if nursing answer is negative. Answer *Code Yes* must refer to written statement about resident's response or apparent comprehension. Answer *Code No*

---

*Utility of item has not been demonstrated, and statistical analyses of the authors' dataset found that the item did not contribute to the reliability or validity of the monitoring instrument.

Source of Information		Criterion	Response		Patient Type
		means record did not document the resident's response to an explanation actually provided.			
01	4.203	DO RECORDS DOCUMENT THE NEED FOR ADDITIONAL INSTRUCTIONS?	No	1	1-2-3-4
			Yes	4	
		If nothing written, ask nurse: Have any kind of explanations been given to Mr. _____ in regard to his condition or care? Are any additional explanations needed in regard to Mr. _____'s condition or care?	NA	9	
		Answer *Code Yes* refers to written statement about what additional explanations are needed.			
		Applies to *past month*.			
01	4.204	IS THE RESIDENT'S PERFORMANCE OF SELF-CARE ACTIVITIES (E.G., EATING, TOILET, WALKING, BATHING, DRESSING, DOING OWN TREATMENTS, ETC.) RECORDED ON RESIDENT CARE RECORD, KARDEX, OR CARE PLAN?	No	1	1-2-3-4
			Yes	2 Incomplete	
		Must reflect current ability.	Yes	4 Complete	
01	4.207	DO RECORDS DOCUMENT THE ACCOMPLISHMENT OF GOALS OR PROGRESS TOWARD GOALS LISTED IN THE CARE PLAN?	No	1	1-2-3-4
			Yes	2 Incomplete	
		Applies to *past month*. Observer must check to see what goals are listed in care plan. Look in resident's chart in the past month to determine if there is documentation that goals are accomplished or progress is being made toward accomplishing goals.	Yes	4 Complete	
		May be recorded by any member of health care team.			

5.0 *UNIT PROCEDURES ARE FOLLOWED FOR THE PROTECTION OF ALL RESIDENTS.*

5.1 *ISOLATION AND DECONTAMINATION PROCEDURES ARE FOLLOWED.*

05	5.102	IS THE PROCEDURE FOR DISPOSAL OF DIRTY/USED LINEN, SUPPLIES, AND EQUIPMENT FOLLOWED? Check procedure used by home. Does not refer to isolation procedure.	No 1 Yes 4 5
04	5.103	ARE PRECAUTIONS TAKEN BY NURSING STAFF TO PROTECT RESIDENTS FROM KNOWN INFECTIONS AND OTHER COMMUNICABLE DISEASES? To nurse in charge: In the past two weeks, have there been any respiratory infections, diarrhea, draining wounds, or other communicable diseases on this unit? *If yes:* What was done? Code *Yes* only if nurse can state specific precautions that were taken.	No 1 Yes 4 NA 9 5
05	5.104	DO THE STAFF WASH THEIR HANDS BETWEEN RESIDENTS? Should be done after any direct contact with body or linens of resident.	No 1 Yes 4 NA 9 5

---

*Utility of item has not been demonstrated, and statistical analyses of the authors' dataset found that the item did not contribute to the reliability or validity of the monitoring instrument.

Source of Information	Criterion		Response		Patient Type
		5.2 THE UNIT IS PREPARED FOR EMERGENCY SITUATIONS.			
04	5.201	ARE PLANS FOR INTERVENTION DURING A CARDIAC OR RESPIRATORY ARREST KNOWN BY THE NURSING STAFF?	No	1	5
			Yes	2	
		To nurse: What would you do if there were a cardiac or respiratory arrest on this unit?	Incomplete		
			Yes	4	
		Probe if necessary: Is there anything else you can think of?	Complete		
		Code Yes Complete if answer includes cardiopulmonary resuscitation and notification of the appropriate personnel.			
		May Code NA if the nurse being interviewed has been asked this question within the past month.			
04*	5.202	ARE EMERGENCY SUPPLIES CHECKED AS PER POLICY?	No	1	5
			Yes	4	
		Code No if there is no policy.			
04	5.204	ARE ACTIONS TO BE TAKEN IN CASE OF FIRE KNOWN BY THE NURS-ING STAFF?	No	1	5
			Yes	2	
		To nurse: What would you do if a fire were discovered on the unit? Probe if necessary: Is there anything else you could do?	Incomplete		
			Yes	4	
		Code Yes Complete if answer includes, at least, notifying appropriate persons, protecting residents from smoke and fire, e.g., closing doors, removing residents from fire area, etc.	Complete		
			NA	9	

May Code NA if nurse being interviewed has been asked this question within the past month.

04   5.205   ARE PLANS FOR INTERVENING IN RESIDENT VIOLENCE OR THREATENING BEHAVIOR KNOWN TO NURSING STAFF?

No	1
Yes	2
	Incomplete
Yes	4
	Complete

5

Ask nurse: What do you do if a resident becomes violent or threatens to harm others?

Code Yes Complete if nurse responds with all of the following:
1. Be calm and firm, distract resident while help is sought.
2. Protect self from potential injury.
3. Call for help, other people in unit, additional males, security.
4. Assist resident into non-stimulation/protective environment.

Code Yes Incomplete if nurse responds with three of the above four.

5.3   *MEDICAL-LEGAL PROCEDURES ARE FOLLOWED.*

04   5.301   FOR EACH RESIDENT WHO IS TRANSFERRED TO ANOTHER INSTITUTION, HAS A COMPLETED RECORD BEEN SENT WITH THE RESIDENT?

No	1
Yes	2
	Some of the time
Yes	4
	All of the time

5

To nurse: In the past two weeks have any residents been transferred to other institutions?

---

*Utility of item has not been demonstrated, and statistical analyses of the authors' dataset found that the item did not contribute to the reliability or validity of the monitoring instrument.

Source of Information	Criterion	Response	Patient Type
	If no, *Code NA.* If yes, ask: Was a completed record sent with each resident?	Information Not Available 8 NA 9	
04*	5.304 ARE THE APPROPRIATE CIVIC OR PUBLIC HEALTH AGENCIES NOTIFIED WHEN REQUIRED?	No 1 Yes 4	8
	To nurse: In the past week, have you had any residents whose conditions or their causes were reportable to the police department or local health authorities? If no, *Code NA.* If yes, ask: Who was notified in each case?	Information Not Available 8 NA 9	8
	5.4 UNIT SAFETY AND PROTECTION PROCEDURES ARE FOLLOWED.		
06	5.402 IS THE MEDICATION ROOM/CART LOCKED?	No 1 Yes 4	5
07	5.405 ARE ALL FIRE EXITS FROM THE UNIT CLEAR AND UNOBSTRUCTED?	No 1 Yes 4	5
04	5.406 IS THE POLICY AND PROCEDURE FOR USE OF RESTRAINTS KNOWN BY STAFF? To nurse: What is the policy and procedure for using restraints here?	No 1 Yes 4	5

6.0   THE DELIVERY OF NURSING CARE IS FACILITATED BY
ADMINISTRATIVE AND MANAGERIAL SERVICES.
6.1 NURSING REPORTING FOLLOWS PRESCRIBED STANDARDS.

01	6.101	ARE NURSING NOTES WRITTEN AS OFTEN AS REQUIRED BY POLICY?	No — 1 Yes — 4	1-2-3-4
01*	6.102	ARE ALL NURSING NOTES LEGIBLE?	No — 1 Yes — 4	1-2-3-4
01*	6.103	ARE NURSING NOTES PROPERLY SIGNED AS REQUIRED BY POLICY?	No — 1 Yes — 4	1-2-3-4
01*	6.104	IF ABBREVIATIONS ARE USED IN THE NURSING RECORDS, ARE THEY ACCEPTABLE ACCORDING TO POLICY?	No — 1 Yes — 4	1-2-3-4
04*	6.105	DO NURSING STAFF REPORT TO THE NURSE IN CHARGE AT THE END OF THE SHIFT?	No — 1 Yes — 4 NA — 9	5

To nurse in charge: using yesterday, or the last day you worked as an example, did you get a summary report from each aide or LPN working with you at the end of the shift?

"Nurse in charge" refers to the team leader, primary nurse, charge nurse, or equivalent.

*Utility of item has <u>not</u> been demonstrated, and statistical analyses of the authors' dataset found that the item did not contribute to the reliability or validity of the monitoring instrument.

Source of Information	Criterion	Response		Patient Type
04*	*May Code NA if nurse works alone and reports directly to the oncoming nurse as, for example, a primary nurse.*			
6.107	DO ALL NURSING PERSONNEL ON THE ONCOMING SHIFT RECEIVE A REPORT ON RESIDENTS TO WHOM THEY WILL GIVE NURSING CARE THAT SHIFT?	No Yes	1 4	5
	To nurse in charge: Using this shift as an example, did all nursing personnel receive a report on residents to whom they are now giving care?			
	6.2 NURSING MANAGEMENT IS PROVIDED.			
07	6.201 WAS A REGISTERED NURSE IN CHARGE AND PRESENT ON THE UNIT EVERY SHIFT FOR THE LAST TWO DAYS?	No Yes	1 4	5
	This means an RN on the unit. It is not acceptable to have the same RN cover more than one unit. Check the staffing roster.			
04	6.202 ARE RESIDENT CARE ASSIGNMENTS DELEGATED ACCORDING TO BOTH RESIDENT NEEDS AND LEVEL OF SKILL OF THE PERSONNEL?	No Yes NA	1 4 9	5
	Locate nurse on that shift who assigns residents or tasks to personnel.			
	Ask nurse: Using today as an example, how did you determine resident care assignments?			
	Code No if assignment made according to numbers of personnel.			

Code *Yes* if assignment made considering both resident severity and personnel skill level.

Code *NA* if no appropriate nurse available to respond. *May be NA* in primary or modular setting in which nurse works alone.

04*	6.203	DOES THE NURSE IN CHARGE OF THE RESIDENT SEE HIM AT LEAST TWICE DURING THE SHIFT?	No 1 Yes 4 NA 9	1-2-3-4

"Nurse in charge" in team nursing refers to head nurse, or equivalent charge nurse or team leader. "Nurse in charge" in primary or modular nursing refers to primary nurse.

To nurse in charge: How many times would you say you were able to see Mr. ___ during the shift, using yesterday (or the last day you worked) as an example?

Code *NA* if resident is away from unit most of the shift.

04*	6.204	DOES THE NURSE IN CHARGE CHECK TO SEE THAT WORK ASSIGNED TO OTHER PERSONNEL HAS BEEN PERFORMED?	No 1 Yes 4	1-2-3-4

"Nurse in charge" in team nursing refers to head nurse, or equivalent charge nurse or team leader. "Nurse in charge" in primary nursing refers to primary nurse.

To nurse in charge: Using yesterday as an example, how did you find out whether the work you had assigned to other personnel had been carried out?

---

*Utility of item has <u>not</u> been demonstrated, and statistical analyses of the authors' dataset found that the item did not contribute to the reliability or validity of the monitoring instrument.

Source of Information	Criterion	Response		Patient Type
04	6.205 ARE RESIDENT CONFERENCES CONDUCTED TO PLAN AND COORDINATE A SPECIFIC RESIDENT'S CARE?	No	1	5
		Yes	2	
	To nurse in charge: In the past two weeks, have you had any resident care conferences?	1–3 times		
		Yes	4	
		More than 3 times		
	"Resident care conferences" refers to any conferences held about a specific resident for the purpose of planning and coordinating his care. *Not Acceptable* if the only conferences in the past two weeks were routine, in-service programs, or other meetings not related to a specific resident's care or to his family's needs.			
04	6.206 FOR CONTINUITY OF CARE, HAVE, AT MOST, TWO NURSING STAFF BEEN ASSIGNED TO THE RESIDENT FOR THE OBSERVED SHIFT FOR THE PREVIOUS SEVEN DAYS?	No	1	1–2–3–4
		Yes	4	
	Check assignment sheets if available, or ask nurse in charge: How many nurses have cared for Mr. _____ on this shift in the last seven days?			
	If more than two nurses assigned to give care, *Code No.*			
04*	6.207 DOES THE ONCOMING NURSE IN CHARGE, EARLY IN THE SHIFT, CONFIRM THE REPORT GIVEN HER OF ALL THE RESIDENTS IN HER CHARGE BY SUCH METHODS AS ROUNDS, WALKING ROUNDS, OR VERBAL REPORTS FROM HER TEAM MEMBERS?	No	1	5
		Yes	2	
		Incomplete		
		Yes	4	
		Complete		
	"Nurse in charge" refers to head nurse, charge nurse, team leader, or in primary nursing or modular nursing, any randomly chosen primary nurse.			
	Ask nurse in charge: How do you make sure that the report given you by the outgoing shift is correct or up to date? When do you do this?			

Code Yes Complete if the answer indicates both a confirmation (or inspection) and its early timing.

Code Yes Incomplete if the answer indicates a confirmation, but not timeliness.

03* 6.208 IS AN OPPORTUNITY PROVIDED FOR THE RESIDENT OR THE FAMILY TO EVALUATE THE CARE GIVEN BY THE NURSING STAFF?

No	1	1-2-3-4
Yes	4	

To resident: At any time in the past month has anyone from the nursing staff asked you or your family what you think about the nursing care you have received?

Information Not Available	8	
NA	9	

Code NA if resident disoriented, nonresponsive.

05* 6.210 IS THERE A LIST OF NURSING STAFF ON DUTY FOR THIS SHIFT KEPT AT THE DESK, OR IN A READILY ACCESSIBLE PLACE ON THE UNIT?

No	1	5
Yes	4	

6.3 CLERICAL SERVICES ARE PROVIDED.

01 6.301 IS THE CHART ASSEMBLED IN THE CORRECT ORDER AS SPECIFIED BY PROCEDURE?

No	1	1-2-3-4
Yes	4	

01 6.302 ARE TRANSCRIBED MEDICATION AND TREATMENT ORDERS DATED?

No	1	1-2-3-4
Yes	2	

*Utility of item has not been demonstrated, and statistical analyses of the authors' dataset found that the item did not contribute to the reliability or validity of the monitoring instrument.

Source of Information	Criterion	Response	Patient Type
	From Kardex and/or Med cards. *May Code Yes Complete for dated and timed computer generated orders.*	Yes Complete Incomplete 4	
08	**6.305 DOES SOMEONE OTHER THAN LICENSED NURSES ANSWER THE UNIT TELEPHONE?** To nurse: For the past two days or last two you worked, have you had to answer the phone? If nurses have answered the phone, *Code No*	No 1 Yes 4	5
04*	**6.306 DOES SOMEONE OTHER THAN LICENSED NURSES HANDLE COMMUNICATIONS WITH OTHER DEPARTMENTS OR AGENCIES UNLESS DIRECT COMMUNICATION BY A NURSE IS REQUIRED?** To nurse: In the past two days, has someone other than a licensed nurse taken care of all communications with other departments unless direct communication by a nurse is required? If nurse took care of any routine requisitions *Code NA only* if nurse is required, i.e, if specific nursing knowledge is needed. Does not refer to answering telephone. *May Code Yes if communications are handled by a computerized MIS system.*	No 1 Yes 2 Some Yes 4 All	5
01	**6.307 ARE ALL PAGES OF THE CHART IDENTIFIED WITH RESIDENT'S NAME AND NUMBER?**	No 1 Yes 4	1-2-3-4

For Yes answer all pages must be marked (stamped, written, typed) with resident's name and number.

6.308	IS THE NAME AND/OR PHONE NUMBER OF FAMILY OR FRIEND TO CONTACT IN CASE OF EMERGENCY LISTED ON THE KARDEX OR OTHER APPROPRIATE RECORD?	No 1 Yes 4

01*

Applies to records that can be located on unit.

Code Yes if there is a written statement that there is no one to be contacted.

6.311	DOES SOMEONE OTHER THAN THE LICENSED NURSE PREASSEMBLE FORMS FOR CHARTS OF NEW ADMISSIONS?	No 1 Yes 2 Some of the time Yes 4 All of the time

04

6.312	DOES SOMEONE OTHER THAN THE LICENSED NURSE INSERT NEW/BLANK FORMS INTO THE CHART AS NEEDED?	No 1 Yes 2 Some of the time Yes 4 All of the time

04*

1-2-3-4

5

5

6.4 ENVIRONMENT AND SUPPORT SERVICES ARE PROVIDED.

---

*Utility of item has not been demonstrated, and statistical analyses of the authors' dataset found that the item did not contribute to the reliability or validity of the monitoring instrument.

Source of Information	Criterion	Response		Patient Type
06	**6.401 IS THE RESIDENT'S ROOM CLEAN?** Refers to cleanliness of floor, bed aside from linens, walls, major pieces of equipment, and tables. All must be clean for *Yes answer.* Does not refer to trash cans.	No Yes	1 4	1–2–3–4
06	**6.402 IS THE SINK IN THE RESIDENT'S ROOM OR ADJACENT BATHROOM USED BY THE RESIDENT CLEAN?** If unit has communal bathroom, examine all sinks. Unsatisfactory cleanliness refers to dust, dirt, foreign substances, long-standing water stains, soap or cleanser residue, fungus, or mildew.	No Yes	1 4	1–2–3–4
06*	**6.403 HAS WASTE BEEN REMOVED FROM THE RESIDENT'S ROOM?** Check for emptied trash cans and for clutter in room. Does not apply to items left in resident's bed. Trash cans should be sufficiently empty to allow for likely accumulation of trash until next tour by housekeeping personnel.	No Yes	1 4	1–2–3–4
06	**6.404 IS ALL OF THE RESIDENT'S EQUIPMENT IN THE ROOM:** A. Being used or on a stand-by basis?	No Yes NA	1 4 9	1–2–3–4
06*	B. Stored properly or as best able?	No Yes NA	1 4 9	1–2–3–4

Refers to any type of equipment currently used in treating residents, e.g., oxygen equipment, IPPB machine, suction equipment, wheelchairs etc., or equipment anticipated for immediate use because of resident's condition.

06* 6.405 IS THE AIR IN THE RESIDENT'S ROOM FREE FROM SMOKE, DUST, AND FOUL ODORS?

No   1   1-2-3-4
Yes   4

03   6.406 IS THE ROOM TEMPERATURE COMFORTABLE FOR THE RESIDENT?

To resident: Is the temperature in your room comfortable for you now?

No   1   1-2-3-4
Yes   4
Information Not Available   8

06* 6.407 IS THE CORRIDOR CLEAR OF ALL EQUIPMENT?

Observe for stretchers and machines or any other equipment currently in corridor. If isolation or dietary equipment present, code as various kinds of equipment.

No   1   5
Various kinds of equipment
No   2
Emergency equipment present
Yes   4
None present

06* 6.408 AT THE SINK USED BY STAFF AND RESIDENTS ARE THERE HAND-WASHING SUPPLIES, E.G., SOAP AND TOWELS?

No   1   1-2-3-4
Yes   4

04* 6.410 DOES SOMEONE OTHER THAN THE LICENSED NURSE DELIVER ALL MEAL TRAYS?

No   1   5
Yes   4

---

*Utility of item has not been demonstrated, and statistical analyses of the authors' dataset found that the item did not contribute to the reliability or validity of the monitoring instrument.

Source of Information	Criterion	Response		Patient Type
	To nurse: In the past two days, has someone other than licensed nurses delivered all trays to non-isolated residents' bedsides? This includes late trays. Code *No* if any trays are delivered by nurses. Code *NA* if residents go to cafeteria or do not have meal trays delivered.			
04*	6.411 DOES SOMEONE OTHER THAN A LICENSED NURSE REMOVE MEAL TRAYS FROM RESIDENTS' ROOMS? To nurse: In the past two days has someone other than licensed nurses removed all trays from non-isolated residents' rooms including late trays? Code *No* if any meal trays removed by nurses. Code *NA* if no trays in residents' rooms.	No	1	5
		Yes	4	
		NA	9	
06	6.412 IS THERE ADEQUATE SEATING FOR RESIDENTS AND THEIR VISITORS IN THE ROOM? Code *Yes* if there is at least one chair per resident.	No	1	5
		Yes	4	
06*	6.415 IS THE LIGHTING IN THE RESIDENT'S ROOM ADEQUATE FOR READING OR CLOSE WORK?	No	1	5
		Yes	4	
04*	6.416 ARE HOUSEKEEPING SUPPLIES/EQUIPMENT AVAILABLE TO CLEAN UP SPILLS, ETC. PROPERLY, AS NEEDED?	No	1	5
		Yes	4	
07	6.417 ARE DRINKING FOUNTAINS ON THE UNIT CLEAN?	No	1	5
		Yes	4	
		NA	9	

| 04* | 6.418 | ARE MAJOR HOUSEKEEPING TASKS PERFORMED BY THAT SERVICE? | No | 1 | 5 |
| | | | Yes | 4 | |

To nurse: In the *past week*, have you had to do any major housekeeping tasks, i.e., mopping the floor, washing beds or furniture?

Note: *REVERSE SCORE*

6.5 *PROFESSIONAL AND ADMINISTRATIVE SERVICES ARE PROVIDED.*

| 04 | 6.501 | IS THERE AN ADEQUATE SUPPLY OF LINEN INCLUDING BLANKETS PROVIDED? | No | 1 | 5 |
| | | | Yes | 4 | |

To nurse: In the past two weeks, have you had enough linen for all of your residents?

Code No if unit had to borrow from other units or if nurses left unit to secure supplies.

| 04 | 6.502 | ARE ADEQUATE SUPPLIES FOR ROUTINE TREATMENTS PRESENT ON THE UNIT? | No | 1 | 5 |
| | | | Yes | 4 | |

To nurse: In the *past two weeks* have you had adequate supplies other than linen on the unit for routine care and treatments?

Probe: Did nurses leave the unit to get any supplies?

Code No if unit had to borrow from other units or if nurses left unit to secure supplies.

*Utility of item has <u>not</u> been demonstrated, and statistical analyses of the authors' dataset found that the item did not contribute to the reliability or validity of the monitoring instrument.

Source of Information	Criterion		Response		Patient Type
04	6.503	ARE MEDICATIONS AND PHARMACEUTICAL SUPPLIES AVAILABLE WHEN NEEDED?	No	1	5
			Yes	4	
		To nurse in charge: In the *past two weeks*, have all routine and stat medications and supplies been available when needed or delivered to the unit within a reasonable time?			
		Applies to all shifts.			
04	6.504	ARE SUPPLIES FROM CENTRAL SUPPLY AVAILABLE WHEN NEEDED?	No	1	5
			Yes	4	
		To nurse in charge: During the *past two weeks*, have you been able to obtain needed items from central supply within a reasonable time?			
		Applies to all shifts.			
04	6.509	ARE LABORATORY SERVICES AND DIAGNOSTIC REPORTS PROVIDED WITHIN A REASONABLE AMOUNT OF TIME?	No	1	5
			Yes	4	
			NA	9	
		To nurse: In the *past two weeks*, when laboratory services have been requested, has the test been done and the results received within a reasonable amount of time?			
		Code NA if no laboratory services are requested.			
04	6.513	IS THERE SUFFICIENT NUMBER OF CARTS AND WHEELCHAIRS FOR CARE OF RESIDENTS?	No	1	5
			Yes	4	
		To nurse: In the *past two weeks*, have you had a sufficient number of carts and wheelchairs for the care of residents?			

06*	6.515	ARE THERE LISTS OF MEDICAL STAFF MEMBERS WHO ARE ON CALL AND AVAILABLE KEPT AT THE DESK OR IN A READILY ACCESSIBLE PLACE ON THE UNIT?	No	1
			Yes	4
				5
		Code Yes only if both lists are present and readily accessible.		
06*	6.517	ARE COPIES OF A STAFFING SCHEDULE POSTED ON THE UNIT (OR EASILY AVAILABLE TO NURSING PERSONNEL AT ALL TIMES)?	No	1
			Yes	4
				5
04	6.518	ARE SUPPLIES, I.E., COMMODES, SHOWER CHAIRS, PRIVACY SCREENS, PILLOWS, AVAILABLE WHEN NEEDED?	No	1
			Yes	4
				5
		Ask nurse: In the past two weeks have you had sufficient commodes, shower chairs, privacy screens, and pillows available when you needed them?		
04	6.519	DOES THE NURSE ADMINISTRATOR OR DIRECTOR OF NURSING MAKE ROUNDS AT LEAST WEEKLY, INTERACTING WITH RESIDENTS ON THE UNIT?	No	1
			Yes	4
				5
04	6.520	DOES THE NURSE ADMINISTRATOR/DIRECTOR OF NURSING COMMUNICATE WITH STAFF IN STAFF MEETINGS OR CONFERENCES AT LEAST MONTHLY?	No	1
			Yes	4
				5
	6.521	WHEN A RESIDENT'S PERSONAL CLOTHING IS SENT TO THE LAUNDRY:		

---

*Utility of item has <u>not</u> been demonstrated, and statistical analyses of the authors' dataset found that the item did not contribute to the reliability or validity of the monitoring instrument.

Source of Information	Criterion	Response		Patient Type
04*	A. IS IT RETURNED WITHIN A WEEK?	No	1	5
		Yes	2	
		Sometimes		
		Yes	4	
		Always		
04*	B. ARE ALL ITEMS RETURNED (NOT LOST)?	No	1	5
		Yes	2	
		Sometimes		
		Yes	4	
		Always		

---

*Utility of item has not been demonstrated, and statistical analyses of the authors' dataset found that the item did not contribute to the reliability or validity of the monitoring instrument.

Family Interview
Questionnaire

	Criterion	Response
1	**2.605 IS THE FAMILY AWARE OF PRESCRIBED DIET?** To significant other: Is _____'s diet restricted in any way? If yes, how?	No 1/ Yes 4/ Information Not Available 8/ NA 9/
2	**3.305 DO STAFF DISCUSS THEIR OWN PERSONAL PROBLEMS WITH FAMILY?** To significant other: Have any of the staff discussed their personal problems with you? Reverse score.	No 1/ Yes 4/
3	**3.202 DO NEW NURSING STAFF MEMBERS INTRODUCE THEMSELVES TO FAMILY?** To significant other: During the past month have new members of the nursing staff you saw providing care to _____ introduced themselves to you?	No 1/ Yes Sometimes 2/ All of the time 4/ NA 9/
4	**3.203 ARE NURSING HOME EMPLOYEES COURTEOUS TO THE FAMILY?** To significant other: During the past month have employees of the nursing home been courteous to you?	No 1/ Yes Some of the time 2/ Yes All of the time 4/ NA 9/
5	**3.402 DO THE NURSING STAFF DISCUSS THE PHYSICAL DEPENDENCE/ INDEPENDENCE OF THE RESIDENT WITH THE FAMILY?** To significant other: Has _____'s illness had much effect on what he can do for himself, such as bathing, dressing, eating, or taking care of himself in general?	No 1/ Yes 4/ NA 9/

If no, *Code NA*.

If yes: Has anyone told you in detail what you can do to help him?

3.403 **IS THE USE OF SPECIAL EQUIPMENT (E.G., TUBES, O$_2$) EXPLAINED TO THE FAMILY?**

        To significant other: If _____ has some special equipment, has anyone told you how it works or why he needs it?

    No 1/
    Yes 4/
    NA 9/

3.409 **DO STAFF LISTEN TO THE FAMILY AND RESIDENT?**

    A. To significant other: When you talk to the staff or ask questions, do you feel that they listen to you and show an interest in what you say?

    No 1/
    Yes
    Some of the time 2/
    Yes
    All of the time 4/

    B. When _____ talks to staff or asks questions, do you feel that they listen to him and show an interest?

    No 1/
    Yes
    Some of the time 2/
    Yes
    All of the time 4/

3.411 **HAS FAMILY BEEN TOLD WHOM TO CONTACT IF THEY HAVE ANY CONCERNS ABOUT RESIDENT'S CARE?**

    To significant other: Who would you call at the nursing home if you had any concerns about _____'s care?

    No 1/
    Yes 4/

	Criterion	Response
10	**IS THE FAMILY GIVEN FOLLOW-UP CARE INSTRUCTIONS BY NURSING?**	No 1/ Yes 4/
	To significant other: Has anyone from the nursing staff talked to you about care at home or about further medical care in the nursing home for your relative related to his injury/illness?	
11	**IS OPPORTUNITY PROVIDED FOR FAMILY TO DISCUSS FEARS AND ANXIETIES?**	No 1/ Yes 4/
	To significant other: During the past month have any of the staff nurses spent some time with you to see if you have any particular fears or problems related to _____'s illness?	
12	**ARE FAMILY ENCOURAGED TO VISIT?**	No 1/ Yes 4/
	To significant other: Do the staff encourage you to visit _____?	
13	**IS THE FAMILY AWARE OF SERVICES AVAILABLE TO RESIDENT?**	No 1/ Yes 4/
	To significant other: You may be aware of services the home offers to residents, e.g., barber/beautician, shopping for personal items. Do you/your _____ know how to arrange for those services?	
14	**IS THE FAMILY AWARE OF SPECIAL PROGRAMS OR GROUPS OFFERED FOR THEM?**	No 1/ Yes 4/ Information Not Available 8/
	To significant other: Have you been told or read about the family support group that meets on Tuesdays?	
15	**IS AN OPPORTUNITY PROVIDED FOR THE FAMILY TO EVALUATE THE CARE GIVEN BY THE NURSING STAFF?**	No 1/ Yes 4/

16

To significant other: At any time in the past month, has anyone from the nursing staff asked you what you think about the nursing care _____ has received?

6.506 IS FAMILY ADVISED OF THE CARE OF PERSONAL BELONGINGS OR VALUABLES?

To significant other: When _____ entered the unit, did someone tell you what to do with personal belongings such as clothes or valuables, i.e., jewelry or money?

No 1/
Yes 4/
Information
    Not Available 8/

Glossary

Criteria standards, rules, tests, or measurable elements of care by which a judgment about actual practice occurrences can be made

Dilemma the choice between two equally desirable or undesirable alternatives

Ethics the study of morals

Indicator a defined, measurable dimension of the quality or appropriateness of an important aspect of patient care (Joint Commission on Accreditation of Healthcare Organizations, 1987, p. 4)

Justice the ethical principle that persons are given merit according to their individual efforts

Minimal score the institutionally determined lowest acceptable score for each subobjective and each major objective

Mission statement the general purpose of an organization that guides members in their achievement of organizational goals or objectives

Morals the standards of behavior actually held or followed by individuals and groups (Thompson, Melia, & Boyd, 1983, p. 3)

Outcome approach the monitoring of measurable changes in the residents' states of health and their satisfaction with the care they have received

Perceptual elements the residents' subjective thoughts and feelings about the care they receive

Performance appraisal the evaluation by an administrator of employees' behaviors and accomplishments for a finite period of time

Process approach a method of evaluating both the interactions between health care providers and residents (patients, clients) and the nature and sequence of events or activities in the delivery of health care

Quality assurance a phrase describing a broad range of activities, which has the overall purpose of evaluating the care provided to residents, including efforts to maintain or modify materials and services based on the evaluation of the actual services provided

Quality of care comparison of the actual level of care with the defined, targeted level of care (Chambers, 1985)

Score the percentage of "yes" responses to all valid responses excluding all "not applicable" and "information not available" responses. Mathematically, a score is represented as f(yes Y)/f(Y)

Structure approach an evaluation method focusing on the characteristics of an organization, such as size, ownership, fiscal resources, physical facilities, equipment, and the types of personnel and their qualifications

REFERENCES

Chambers, L.W. (1985). *Quality assurance in long-term care: Policy, research and measurement.* Paris: International Center of Social Gerontology.

Joint Commission on Accreditation of Healthcare Organizations. (1987). *Overview of the Joint Commission's "Agenda for Change."* (Available from Joint Commission on Accreditation of Healthcare Organizations, 875 North Michigan Avenue, Chicago, IL.)

Thompson, I.E., Melia, K.M., & Boyd, K. (1983). *Nursing ethics.* New York: Churchill Livingstone.

Index

A

Accountability, program development, 43-44

Accreditation, nursing homes, 13

Activity Program Form, monitoring, 75-76

Administration
  roles
    board of directors, 15
    care evaluation committee, 16-17
    chief administrative officer, 15
    department/service head, 15-16
    interdisciplinary quality assurance committee, 16, 17

Administrators
  ethical behavior, 153-154
  standards of practice (Appendix B), 179-186

Alzheimer's disease, long-term care issues, 165-166

American Association of Retired Persons (AARP), 164

American College of Health Care Administrators (ACHCA), standards of care, 45, 47

Approach-time frame matrix, 32-34

B

Board of directors, role of, 15

Budgeting, manager's role, 116-117

C

Care evaluation committee, 77
  committees, 16-17
  role of, 16-17

Certification
  gerontological nurses, 168
  nursing homes, 12-13

Chief administrative officer, role of, 15

Committees
  interdisciplinary, 9-10
  unit committee, 106
  See also specific committees

Concurrent process monitoring
  nursing care, 134-141
  results of, 139-141

Concurrent time frame, 29

Consent
  for quality monitoring information, 85-88
  protocols for family telephone interviews, 87-88

Consumer influences, 14
  quality of life issues, 55